THE POWER OF DELIBERATION

The Power of Deliberation

INTERNATIONAL LAW, POLITICS AND ORGANIZATIONS

Ian Johnstone

OXFORD
UNIVERSITY PRESS

Oxford University Press, Inc., publishes works that further Oxford University's objective of excellence in research, scholarship, and education.

Oxford   New York
Auckland   Cape Town   Dar es Salaam   Hong Kong   Karachi   Kuala Lumpur   Madrid   Melbourne
Mexico City   Nairobi   New Delhi   Shanghai   Taipei   Toronto

With offices in
Argentina   Austria   Brazil   Chile   Czech Republic   France   Greece   Guatemala   Hungary   Italy
Japan   Poland   Portugal   Singapore   South Korea   Switzerland   Thailand   Turkey   Ukraine
Vietnam

Copyright © 2011 by Oxford University Press, Inc.

Published by Oxford University Press, Inc.
198 Madison Avenue, New York, New York 10016

Oxford is a registered trademark of Oxford University Press
Oxford University Press is a registered trademark of Oxford University Press, Inc.

All rights reserved. No part of this publication may be reproduced, stored in a retrieval system, or transmitted, in any form or by any means, electronic, mechanical, photocopying, recording, or otherwise, without the prior permission of Oxford University Press, Inc.

Library of Congress Cataloging-in-Publication Data
Johnstone, Ian, 1960-
The power of deliberation : international law, politics, and organizations / Ian Johnstone.
   p. cm.
Includes bibliographical references and index.
ISBN 978-0-19-539493-1 (hardback : alk. paper)
1. International law. 2. International relations. 3. Discourse analysis. I. Title.
KZ3410.J64 2011
341—dc22
                                                                            2010043997

1 2 3 4 5 6 7 8 9
Printed in the United States of America on acid-free paper

Note to Readers
This publication is designed to provide accurate and authoritative information in regard to the subject matter covered. It is based upon sources believed to be accurate and reliable and is intended to be current as of the time it was written. It is sold with the understanding that the publisher is not engaged in rendering legal, accounting, or other professional services. If legal advice or other expert assistance is required, the services of a competent professional person should be sought. Also, to confirm that the information has not been affected or changed by recent developments, traditional legal research techniques should be used, including checking primary sources where appropriate.

(Based on the Declaration of Principles jointly adopted by a Committee of the American Bar Association and a Committee of Publishers and Associations.)

You may order this or any other Oxford University Press publication by visiting the Oxford University Press website at www.oup.com

To Maia and Matthew
for their spirit

Contents

Acknowledgments ix

1. *Introduction* 3

PART ONE | THE POWER OF DELIBERATION
2. *Deliberation* 13
3. *Interpretive Communities* 33

PART TWO | THE PRACTICE OF DELIBERATION
4. *Responsibility to Protect* 55
5. *Counter-Terrorism* 81
6. *Nuclear Non-Proliferation* 114
7. *Peace Operations* 136
8. *Operational Activities* 160
9. *Trade* 183

10. *Conclusion* 203

Index 213

Acknowledgments

This book is the culmination of research I have been engaged in for several years. Along the way, I have benefited from the advice and assistance of many people.

I am grateful for comments on parts of the text, either directly or in workshops, seminars and lectures, by Emanuel Adler, Salman Ahmed, Philip Alston, José Alvarez, Sarjoh Bah, Michael Barnett, Corneliu Bjiola, Kristen Boon, Jutta Brunée, Simon Chesterman, Jean-Marc Coicaud, Neta Crawford, Bruce Cronin, Michael Doyle, Raymond Duvall, Martha Finnemore, Lori Fisler Damrosch, Richard Gardner, Michael Glennon, Richard Gowan, Andrew Grene, Michael Griesdorf, David Haeri, Antonia Handler Chayes, David Harland, Alan Henrikson, Ian Hurd, Bruce Jones, David Kennedy, Paul Keating, David Malone, Jennifer Mitzen, Bernard Oxman, Michael Pugh, Steven Ratner, Adam Roberts, Anthea Roberts, Alfred Rubin, John Ruggie, Beth Simmons, Duncan Snidal, Fiona Simpson, Nishkala Suntharalingam, Ayaka Suzuki, Alex Thompson, Joel Trachtman, Cora True-Frost, Tom Weiss, and Alexander Wendt.

Many students provided research assistance, comments on drafts, and a steady stream of ideas and insight. I cannot name all who influenced my thinking, but those who had a direct impact on this book include Ulrik Ahnfeldt-Mollerup, Caroline Andresen, Mauricio Artinano, Emma Belcher, Tania Belisle-Leclerc, Rahul Chandran, Gillian Cull, Adam Day, Karoun Demirjian, Sajid Khan, Huria Ogbamichael, Courtney Richardson, Cornelia Schneider, Garth Schofield, Philip Shetler-Jones, Laura Sitea and Jason Yeager.

In addition to the individuals listed above, I have benefitted from wonderful collaborators at the Fletcher School of Law and Diplomacy, Tufts University and the Center on International Cooperation, New York University.

Research for some of the chapters involved interviews. I am grateful to the many United Nations official, diplomats and other experts who gave their time. Most are identified by name in the footnotes. Some preferred to remain anonymous.

I owe deep intellectual debts to two mentors, Oscar Schachter and Thomas Franck. They were an inspiration to me and to the countless other international lawyers they taught and befriended.

Finally, Gabriela Artavia and Robert Johnstone were instrumental in the final stages of the book. Thank you both, with all my heart.

Parts of this book draw on material published elsewhere. "Managing Consent in Contemporary Peacekeeping Operations", 18 *International Peacekeeping* 160 (2011) "Legal Argumentation in International Decision-making", in *The Faultlines of Legitimacy* (Hilary Charlesworth and Jean-Marc Coicaud eds., Cambridge University Press, 2009); "Normative evolution at the United Nations," in *Cooperating for Peace and Security* (Bruce Jones and Shepard Forman eds., Cambridge University Press, 2009); "Lawmaking through the operational activities of international organizations", 40 *George Washington International Law Review* (2008); "Legislation and Adjudication in the United Nations Security Council: Bringing Down the Deliberative Deficit", 102 *American Journal of International Law* 275 (April 2008); "The Secretary-General as Norm Entrepreneur", in *Secretary or General? The Role of the UN Secretary-General in World Politics* (S. Chesterman ed., Cambridge University Press, 2007); "Consolidating Peace: Priorities and Deliberative Processes", in *Annual Review of Global Peace Operations 2007* (I. Johnstone ed., Lynne Rienner Publishers, 2007); "The plea of necessity in international legal discourse: counter-terrorism and humanitarian intervention" 43 *Columbia Journal of Transnational Law* 100 (2005); "The Power of Interpretive Communities", in *Power in Global Governance*, (M. Barnett and R. Duvall eds., Cambridge University Press, 2005); "US-UN relations after Iraq: the end of the world (order) as we know it?", 15 *European Journal of International Law* 813 (2004); "Security Council deliberations: the power of the better argument", 14 *European Journal of International Law* 437 (2003). I am grateful to the publishers for permission to reprint the relevant sections.

THE POWER OF DELIBERATION

1

INTRODUCTION

I. INTRODUCTION

ARGUING ABOUT MATTERS of public policy is pervasive in democracies. Indeed, the ability to resolve conflicts through peaceful contestation is a measure of any well-ordered society. Arguing is almost as pervasive in international affairs, yet it is not viewed as an important element of world order or as having significant impact on the behavior of states. In this book, I challenge that assumption. I claim that argumentation influences world politics through a diffuse but consequential discursive process. To understand how and why, I focus on legal discourse as a distinctly powerful form of argumentation. Yet the book is not about international law or international organizations per se. It is about the way in which all discursive interaction among states and non-state actors affects the behavior of those actors and shapes the international order. The discursive interaction is deeply affected by power, but to understand the dynamics of power in the international system, one must understand the dynamics of deliberation.

The book is prompted by a simple question: why, if the rhetoric of law is inconsequential, do governments and other international actors bother engaging in it? The United States worked hard to to make the best legal case it could for military action in Iraq in 2003. Advocates for intervention in Darfur and Myanmar invoke an emerging "responsibility to protect." Trade relations are rife with disputes about how to balance trade law with other values. Some of this disputation occurs in judicial and quasi-judicial bodies. More often, it occurs in diplomatic interaction between states, deliberation in international organizations (IOs), and justificatory discourse in public fora. Existing explanations of why the language of law looms large in this discursive interaction are inadequate.

Legal discourse is just one species of argumentation. To understand why it matters requires looking beyond the field of international law. International relations scholars and democracy theorists have begun to consider why any argumentation occurs beyond the level of the nation-state. This book joins that effort by focusing on deliberation in and around IOs. I draw on various strands of legal, political, and international relations theory to identify common features of legal argumentation and deliberative politics. My central claim is that IOs are places where "interpretive communities" coalesce, and the quality of the deliberations that these communities provoke is a measure of the legitimacy of the organization. This introductory chapter begins by summarizing the theoretical argument developed more fully in Chapters 2 and 3, which is then used as a framework for analyzing a number of cases. Those cases cover six areas of practice engaged in by IOs, described briefly below and then presented in Chapters 4 to 9.

II. THEORY: ARGUMENTATION, DELIBERATION, AND INTERPRETIVE COMMUNITIES

That argumentation matters in politics is the logic of communicative action as developed by German philosopher Jürgen Habermas. The theory has been tested and elaborated by deliberative democrats and is now being extended to the transnational level by a critical mass of social constructivists and theorists of global governance. Drawing on Habermas, Thomas Risse contrasts the logic of arguing with the "logic of consequentialism" and the "logic of appropriateness"—two poles of the debate between rational choice and social constructivism that has dominated U.S. international relations theory for decades.[1] The former treats interests as fixed and assumes that states interact with other states to maximize those interests. The latter is driven by norms and assumes that states act in accordance with collective expectations of what constitutes appropriate behavior for actors with a given identity. Communicative action is connected to the logic of appropriateness, but it assumes that what constitutes appropriate behavior in a particular situation is not self-evident. It is determined discursively, through deliberation or reasoned exchange.

The theory of deliberative democracy rests on the principle that voting is not all that matters in a well-functioning democracy. The quality of deliberations—the exchange of good arguments—that precede and follow votes is a measure of legitimacy. What counts

---

[1] Thomas Risse, "'Let's Argue': Communicative Action in World Politics," 54 *International Organization* 1, 2–7 (2000). On the two logics, see James March and Johan Olsen, *Rediscovering Institutions* (1989); James March and Johan Olsen, "The Institutional Dynamics of International Political Orders", 52 *International Organizations* 943 (1998).

as a "good" argument varies from setting to setting, depending on the normative framework and purpose of the enterprise in which the deliberative exchange occurs. The style of reasoning in courts is not the same as in religious institutions, science journals, or the Security Council of the United Nations. But, as a general matter, good arguments in any public setting are impartial and are cast in terms that all who are affected understand as being relevant to the nature of the enterprise. Purely self-serving arguments, or those seen as arbitrary or beside the point, are simply not persuasive. For that reason, they are rarely heard when public policy choices are being debated.

A good deal of democratic theory and practice at the national level is built on that simple but deceptively powerful proposition. A central question that this book considers is whether it extends to the transnational level. Can meaningful deliberation involving the exchange of "good" arguments take place beyond the nation-state? Many observers see evidence of it, and they claim it is consequential, that the argumentation is not meaningless rhetoric. It may not be sincere—the arguments may be put forward for strategic reasons in order to gain some advantage—but it has an impact on how decisions are made and how the international order is shaped. Deliberative democrats not only see evidence of meaningful deliberation at the transnational level; they also make claims about the conditions for that deliberation and the type of reasoning that is persuasive in particular settings. I elaborate on those conditions in Chapter 2 and argue that IOs are conducive to principled, impartial deliberation. This is especially true of the European Union (EU) but also global institutions like the United Nations (UN). In the language of deliberative democracy, international organizations (IOs) serve as "public spheres" where states and, increasingly, nonstate actors discuss, debate, and generate shared understandings about the terms of international life.[2] As James Bohman puts it, international institutions open political space for "informal networks of association and communication at the transnational level" and, as such, function "as a forum and audience for democratization".[3]

---

[2] A good introduction to Habermas's definition of the public sphere is James Gordon Finlayson, *Habermas: A Very Short Introduction* 8–15 and 109–13 (2005). For a sophisticated consideration of whether international public spheres exists, see Jennifer Mitzen "Reading Habermas in Anarchy: Multilateral Diplomacy and Global Public Spheres," 99 *American Political Science Review* 401 (2005). A good application of public sphere theory to international relations is in Patricia Nanz and Jens Steffeck, "Global Governance, Participation and the Public Sphere," in *Global Governance and Public Accountability* 190, 196–200 (D. Held and M. Koenig-Archibugi eds., 2005). Joshua Cohen suggest that "global public reason" is emerging in IOs, comprised of "norms, values and forms of argumentation suited to justification in global politics." Joshua Cohen, "Democracy's Reason, Global Reason", Tanner Lecture on Human Values II, University of California at Berkeley, April 11, 2007 (on file with author). See generally Joshua Cohen, *Philosophy, Politics, Democracy: Selected Essays* (2009).

[3] James Bohman, "International Regimes and Democratic Governance", 75 *International Affairs* 499, 500 and 505 (1999). In public sphere terms, Bohman states: "As various international institutions emerge, they can become the focus of a critical public sphere as actors in transnational civil society expand and maintain their public interaction across various political, cultural and functional boundaries" at 507.

The attention that deliberative democrats are devoting to transnational relations corresponds to the growing interest of international relations scholars in the influence of nonstate actors: nongovernmental organizations, epistemic communities, international lawyers, transgovernmental networks, and the like.[4] In this book, I do not enter the debate over the power of these actors in relation to states, but I do consider the source of whatever power and influence they have. The notion of "interpretive communities" is introduced to help identify that source. Related to but a narrower concept than epistemic community, interpretive communities are involved in the creation, implementation, and application of norms. They have room to operate, and their influence is felt because the international legal system is decentralized, global governance is "without government," and the line between public and private power is blurred. Interpretive communities not only fill governance gaps,[5] they are part of the governance machinery. They exercise power not through coercion or the deployment of material resources but through advocacy, persuasion, and disputation. The machinery—in the form of international regimes and organizations—is increasing the space for them to exercise that power.

Before expanding on the role of interpretive communities, the distinctive nature of legal argumentation must be introduced. Legal argumentation is a specialized and recognizable form of deliberation: lawyers, policy makers, diplomats, and attentive publics know a legal argument when they hear one. It is also an especially powerful mode of argumentation because the international legal system is built on state consent. By its very nature, international law embodies shared understandings about appropriate standards of behavior. Unlike other modes of argumentation (moral, for example), it is not easily brushed off as culturally specific or beside the point. Few governments dismiss the relevance of international law out of hand, and if they do, it is rarely in public. The "stickiness" of international law is something governments must deal with, like it or not.[6] There is a long tradition in international diplomacy and politics of "speaking law to power," in which legal norms are invoked to challenge brute assertions of material power.[7] This does not mean that law is divorced from power, but that it is a mode of argumentation whose

---

[4] See, for example, the collection of essays in *Civil Society Participation in European and Global Governance: A Cure for the Democratic Deficit?* (J. Steffek, C. Kissling and P. Nanz eds., 2008).

[5] Tanja Bruhl and Volker Rittberger, "From international to global governance: actors, collective decision-making and the United Nations in the world of the 21st century," in *Global Governance and the UN System* 1–47 (V. Rittberger ed., 2001).

[6] The term 'stickiness' is used by Harold Koh in his influential writing on transnational legal process. See for example, Harold Koh, "The 1998 Frankel Lecture: Bringing International Law Back Home" 35 *Houston International Law Journal* 623 (1998); Harold Koh, "Why Do Nations Obey International Law?", 106 *Yale Law Journal* 2599 (1997).

[7] Paul Khan, "Speaking Law to Power: Popular Sovereignty, Human Rights and the New International Order," 1 *Chicago Journal of International Law* 1,13 (2000). See also Kal Raustiala, "Form and Substance in International Agreements," 99 *American Journal of International Law* 581, 606 (2005).

influence depends on something other than the power that comes with superior military and economic resources.

As I argue in Chapter 2, international law operates in large part through a process of justificatory discourse. Claims are made and criticized, actions approved and condemned, actors persuaded and dissuaded in an often cacophonous discursive interaction where legal norms loom large.[8] The legal discipline is characterized by argumentative practices that shape and give content to the rules of international life. In that sense, law serves a communicative function. The justificatory discourse is consequential in that it generates pressure on states to behave in accordance with the law, for both instrumental and constructivist reasons. As I elaborate in Chapter 3, states have an interest in maintaining a reputation for good faith compliance with the law, and that interest becomes internalized in bureaucratic, legal, and political routines. Yet that assumes there is some way of distinguishing good legal claims from bad. In a decentralized legal system, where most disputes are not settled in courts, who makes that distinction? The question is important because, without knowing what counts as a good legal claim, a state's reputation for law abidingness cannot be affected. If no one can say with authority what the law is, how can reputation be affected one way or the other? Indeed, what would be the point of making legal arguments at all? Yet, there is ample evidence of states doing precisely that, of seeking to justify their actions in legal terms, not only in courts and quasi-judicial committees but also in inter-governmental political bodies, diplomatic exchanges, and in domestic political debates. ("Iran's right to enrich uranium is (not) guaranteed by the Nuclear Non-Proliferation Treaty"; "Kosovo's unilateral declaration of independence is (not) contrary to general international law or Security Council resolutions"; "waterboarding does (not) violate the Torture Convention.") Those making the arguments must assume some purpose is served by it. Logically, therefore, they must assume there is some mechanism for assessing the validity of legal claims. That mechanism, I argue, is the interpretive community.

The existence of an interpretive community can be inferred from the ubiquity of legal discourse in nonlegal settings; if it did not exist, attempts at legal justification would rarely be heard. While it is an abstraction whose composition cannot be specified with precision, I describe it as three concentric circles: an inner circle of those directly involved in making and implementing a particular legal norm, a middle circle comprised of those with expertise in the area of law and practice regulated by the norm, and an amorphous outer circle of all whose interests are affected by the action taken (or not taken) on the basis of the norm. It includes not only judges and lawyers but also diplomats, government

---

[8] Abram Chayes and Antonia Handler Chayes, *The New Sovereignty: Compliance with International Regulatory Agreements*, 25-26 and 119-34 (1995). See also, Jutta Brunnée and Stephen Toope, *Legitimacy and Legality in International Law: An Interactional Account* (2010), who build on the work of the Chayes' and Koh among others to develop an interactional theory of legal obligation and compliance.

officials, international civil servants, academics, representatives of nongovernmental organizations, and engaged citizenry. The first two circles inter-penetrate one another and tend to coalesce around IOs. The extent to which the third penetrates the first two is an open question and has important normative implications: is the interpretive community a device that silences dissenting voices, or is it a more pluralistic entity that disciplines the conduct of international affairs without excluding interests and points of view that fall outside the mainstream?

To understand what interpretive communities are, one must consider what they do. First, they set the parameters of legal discourse and pass judgment on legal claims, thereby impacting compliance with law. They do this mainly by extracting reputational costs for noncompliance. Second, they define, interpret, and extend the rules of international behavior, thereby impacting evolution of the law. They do this mainly by giving content to the normative climate in which incremental extensions of the law occur. These two functions are interconnected because the line between interpreting and making the law is blurry. The power of interpretive communities is felt in bilateral and multilateral diplomatic interaction but tends to be felt most strongly in and around IOs. That is where a good deal of international law is made and where expectations of behavior that conform to the law are expressed most vigorously. The process is self-reinforcing: to the extent that interpretive communities coalesce in IOs, the justificatory discourse there becomes more demanding. The parameters of acceptable argumentation are more apparent, deviation from those standards is easier to spot, and the cost of straying beyond accepted argumentative practices is felt more acutely.

The power of an interpretive community on any given issue depends on how cohesive its judgments are. If international legal opinion is evenly divided on a question, then the interpretive community's impact will be limited. In those circumstances, it is probably not useful to speak of a 'community' at all. There could be multiple groupings of experts and practitioners who see the issue in quite different terms. My point is not that a single global legal community exists, but rather that if one can discern a relatively cohesive judgment on a legal claim, then something like an interpretive community must be at work.

On its face, that would seem to enhance the legitimacy of IOs. After all, the more demanding the legal discourse—the more one can "speak law to power"—the more legitimate the decision-making process would seem to be. Critiques of the legitimacy of IOs tend to get framed in terms of the democratic deficit, and proposals for reform tend to center on representation and voting arrangements, latching onto only one dimension of democracy. This book shifts attention to the quality of deliberations in and around the IO. If interpretive communities set the parameters for deliberation, then the legitimacy of IOs depends on the legitimacy of the interpretive communities associated with them. Whose values and interests do they express? At the end of Chapter 3, I consider two possible challenges to the legitimacy of interpretive communities: that they are dominated by a hegemon, and that they are overly technocratic. While there is truth in both claims, neither fully accounts for the *inter-subjective* nature of interpretation and argumentation: a deliberative process that seeks to ascertain what a norm means to the participants collectively rather than to each individually or in the abstract. Deliberation does not eliminate the influence of power, but to the extent that political struggle takes place discursively, through the exchange of arguments, it reduces inequalities in power—it diminishes the tilt in the playing field, even if it does not level it. Similarly, the disciplining force of legal argumentation depends on expertise, but it is not so technocratic that outside voices are silenced. Though far from perfectly equal, interpretive communities are nascent forms of democratic deliberation: open, inclusive, and penetrable by perspectives other than those of the hegemon or technocrats. This suggests an agenda for institutional reform that preserves the disciplinary constraints on discursive interaction while opening up that interaction to new voices and perspectives.

III. PRACTICE: LAW AND POLITICS IN INTERNATIONAL ORGANIZATIONS

In Chapters 2 and 3, I expand on the theoretical propositions summarized above. The remaining chapters test and elaborate those propositions through various case studies. Each covers a particular area of IO practice and the argumentation that surrounds that practice. Chapters 4 to 6 are about three high-profile security issues: humanitarian intervention, counter-terrorism, and nuclear non-proliferation. I start with these because they are the hard cases; if legal argumentation, deliberative politics, and interpretive communities have any traction there, presumably they will have even more in areas where material power and zero-sum interests count for less. The Security Council (SC) of the UN figures prominently in all three chapters. The Council is portrayed not as an autonomous body (or shell) perched atop a hierarchical order, but as a deliberative setting and influential actor in a diffuse system of global security governance. Chapters 7 to 9 look beyond the SC to other institutions and areas of practice: peacekeeping, operational activities like electoral assistance, and trade. These are areas where, like hard security, states are the primary actors, but nonstate actors (IO officials, experts, and nongovernmental organizations (NGOs)) also play an influential role. As such, they add nuance and depth to the explanation of how and why legal argumentation, democratic deliberation, and interpretive communities matter.

Chapter 4 is about humanitarian intervention and the emerging "responsibility to protect." Focused on Kosovo, the central argument is that discourse about the legality of NATO's intervention in Kosovo had a significant impact on how the crisis played out and set the stage for the Secretary-General of the UN and other "norm entrepreneurs" to push the law in a direction it might not otherwise have gone. The chapter begins with an examination of the UN Security Council as a forum for justificatory discourse. I argue that, while far from Habermas's ideal, the minimal preconditions for reasoned argumentation exist even in that quintessentially political body. I describe it as a four-tier deliberative setting, with the five permanent members comprising the top tier;

the nonpermanent members the second tier; the rest of the UN membership the third; and the constellation of engaged representatives of nongovernmental organizations, organs of international public opinion and other citizens who have a stake in what goes on in the Council, the fourth. I summarize the debates on the legality of the Kosovo intervention in making the case that the positions taken by governments in those debates can only be explained by the notion of discourse within an interpretive community. I also consider the impact of the episode on the law of humanitarian intervention. The endorsement of the "responsibility to protect" (R2P) at the World Summit of 2005 was a significant moment, but events since then suggest that the norm has failed to crystallize. I examine the debates on the norm itself, its application and (misapplication) in a range of situations—from Iraq and Darfur, to Myanmar and Georgia—and what this says about how the law evolves through discursive interaction. While the norm is still "emerging" at best, the story of R2P illuminates the power of deliberation within an interpretive community.

Chapter 5 addresses counter-terrorism, another security issue that has risen on the agenda of IOs, states, and nonstate actors. The chapter is divided into three parts. The first assesses the significance of the contrasting reactions to self-defense claims made to justify military action in Afghanistan and Iraq in the aftermath of 9/11, as well as United States drone strikes in Pakistan that began under the George W. Bush administration and increased under the Obama administration. The second part looks at the legitimacy of quasi-legislative action by the UN Security Council in adopting resolutions 1373 and 1540, aimed at suppressing support for terrorism. The third section is about the quasi-judicial nature of the targeted sanctions regime imposed on individuals suspected of association with Al-Qaeda and the Taliban. Together, the three parts of the chapter illustrate that the lines between making, interpreting and implementing international law are not sharp and that interpretive communities play a role in all three.

Chapter 6 is about nuclear non-proliferation, a field in ferment. This chapter considers three sets of issues that have contributed to the ferment: interpretative disputes over the Nuclear Non-Proliferation Treaty; action to rid Iraq of its weapons of mass destruction; and the interdiction of ships suspected of carrying material related to weapons of mass destruction. These issues highlight the multiple roles of the SC, not only as an enforcement agency and deliberative setting but also as a manager of regimes and a pulpit from which threatening and reassuring signals are sent. It also situates the Council in a network of actors and institutions engaged in a fluid process that is struggling to meet new proliferation challenges without destroying the integrity of the existing non-proliferation regime. Legal considerations, even if not central to deliberations on proliferation, are an important part of the context in which those deliberations occur. They shape the political dynamics and, as the Iraq invasion shows, affect the calculations of costs and benefits even by the world's most powerful states.

Chapter 7, on peace operations, bridges the divide between hard security issues covered in Chapters 4 to 6 and nonsecurity issues in Chapters 8 and 9. It also bridges the divide between areas of international practice that are centered on the UN Security

Council and areas where other organizations and actors are central. In it, I consider two dominant features of contemporary peace operations: liberal peacebuilding and the protection of civilians. The central argument is that peacekeeping shapes and is shaped by the normative climate in which it operates. In other words, the activities of peace operations, like liberal peace building and the protection of civilians, are a product of a normative environment that values democratic principles and human rights; to the extent the promotion of democratic values and human rights are demonstrably successful in helping to secure peace, the norms are reinforced. Conversely, if those activities are unsuccessful, the norms are undermined.

That point is elaborated in Chapter 8, which is about other operational activities. The chapter demonstrates how international law can harden through the programmatic work of IOs and the argumentation that surrounds them. It looks at three areas of practice: the impact of electoral assistance on the right to political participation, the impact of conflict prevention activities on ethnic minority rights, and the impact of humanitarian action on the rights of internally displaced persons. The chapter argues that a more fluid, less state-centric form of law making is underway and that discursive interaction between IO officials, governments, and nonstate actors is central to that law-making process. Interpretive communities set the parameters of that discourse in each case, providing a degree of cohesiveness that makes incremental hardening of the norms possible though far from inevitable.

Chapter 9 is about international trade. It considers whether trade institutions (GATT and the World Trade Organization) are dominated by a technocratic group of "insiders," one of the democratic deficit critiques leveled at this and other IOs. I explore this issue through the lens of trade-environment disputes, focusing on the *Shrimp-Turtle* case. The critique is important because it stands as a direct challenge to the claim that interpretive communities enhance deliberative legitimacy. If the interpretive community is a homogenous, technocratic body that silences alternative points of view, can it be called legitimate? Trade is also a good field for studying the *power* of interpretive communities, because it is an area of law where a relatively reliable and authoritative dispute settlement system exists. There would seem to be less room or need for an interpretive community to function in this area. Yet, the WTO is the locus of a lively interpretive community that has been wrestling with "trade and... ." issues for more than a decade.

The concluding chapter synthesizes the findings from the case studies to substantiate the claim that argumentation influences international politics through a diffuse discursive process. I elaborate on the convergence between legal argumentation and deliberative politics. I recap my thesis that the discursive process can only be understood by considering the role of interpretive communities, whose power comes from the reputational costs they can extract, while also setting the parameters for constructive dialogue about incremental extensions of existing legal regimes. The judgment and dialogue occurs in many settings, but it is most concentrated in IOs. A theme highlighted in the conclusion is that the operational and discursive practices of IOs are a new source of international law.

I also return to the argument that one measure (though not the only measure) of the legitimacy of IOs is how well they serve as venues for and participants in reasoned, inclusive deliberation. I describe the logic of arguing as an accountability mechanism and consider whether international organizations are nascent public spheres, defined as "sites of public deliberation between policy-makers and stakeholders."[9] Complete transparency and universal participation is neither practical nor desirable of course; the question is whether IOs are capable of striking the right balance between closed decision making and deliberative inclusiveness. Asking the same question of interpretive communities, are they exclusive bodies, immune to outside voices or nascent sites for more inclusive, democratic deliberation? This is of both theoretical and policy interest because, if the practices of IOs are a source of international law, then better deliberation within and around them is a way of "democratizing" the international legal system. It is a way improving the prospects for implementation of decisions taken at the international level, while pointing the way to reform of international institutions in a manner that respects the diversity of values and interests in the global order.

---

[9] Nanz and Steffeck, *supra* note 2, at 197.

ONE

The Power of Deliberation

2

DELIBERATION

I. INTRODUCTION

MOST LAWYERS TEND to have faith in the power of arguments. Reasoned exchange—in courts, in negotiations, and in legislative processes—is their stock in trade. In a decentralized international legal system, where single authoritative interpretations of the law are hard to come by, argumentation seems especially important. The law is determined in large measure by claims and counterclaims made by interested parties in response to international incidents.[1] The claims and reactions to those claims often take the form of arguments: explanation, approval, critique, and condemnation.[2] International lawyers who employ rational choice theory tend to be more skeptical. To them, argumentation is "cheap talk," rationalizations for actions taken out of narrow self-interest that change as often as interests change and therefore have no independent impact on behavior.[3]

---

[1] I use the term "incident" here in the sense conveyed by Michael Reisman and A. Willard eds. *International Incidents: the Law that Counts in World Politics*, (1988), i.e., an international event that provokes reactions of decision makers and legal authorities which, taken as a whole, contribute to our understanding of the relevant law.

[2] Abram Chayes and Antonia Handler Chayes, *The New Sovereignty: Compliance with International Regulatory Agreements* 119 (1995).

[3] Jack Goldsmith and Eric Posner, *The Limits of International Law* 167–84 (2005). For a critique of Goldsmith and Posner from the perspective of rational theory itself, see Oona Hathaway and Ariel Lavinbuk, "Rationalism and Revisionism in International Law", 19 *Harvard Law Review* 1404, 1406 (2006). For a more nuanced

Increasingly, however, social constructivists are taking seriously the proposition that argumentation matters to world politics, and these theorists are doing empirical work to demonstrate its impact.[4] In this chapter, I link this strand of international relations theory to the work of deliberative democrats, who see the possibility of reasoned exchange beyond the level of the nation-state. I then turn to legal argumentation as a distinctive and uniquely powerful form of deliberation in international affairs. The chapter concludes with the claim that legal argumentation and democratic deliberation are a measure of the legitimacy of decision making in IOs.

II. DELIBERATION IN WORLD POLITICS

Much of international politics is an exercise in communication: to signal intentions, express interests, negotiate agreements, or accomplish myriad other goals. Arguing is a particular form of communication, whose purpose is to offer reasons for acting or not acting in a certain manner. Habermas's theory of communicative action holds that there are at least three kinds of communicative behavior: bargaining based on fixed preferences; strategic argumentation, in which arguments are used to justify positions and persuade others to change their minds; and "true reasoning," in which actors seek a reasoned consensus on the basis of shared understandings, where each actor not only tries to persuade but is also open to persuasion.[5] The last is Habermas's ideal of communicative action. He imagines an "ideal speech situation," within which discourse occurs unaffected by relationships of power and coercion or any other factors extraneous to "the force of the better argument."[6] Whenever people use language to coordinate their actions, they enter into a commitment to justify their words and actions on the basis of good reasons.[7]

---

application of rational choice theory to international law, but one that is no less skeptical about the power of words as opposed to deeds, see Michael Glennon, *The Fog of Law: Pragmatism, Security and International Law*, 44-50 (2010).

[4] See, for example, Neta Crawford, *Argument and Change in World Politics: Ethics, Decolonization and Humanitarian Intervention*, (2002); Corneliu Bjiola and Markus Kornprobst eds., *Arguing Global Governance: Agency, Lifeworld and Shared Reasoning* (2010); Thomas Risse, "Global Governance and Communicative Action," in *Global Governance and Public Accountability* 164–89 (D. Held and M. Koenig-Archibugi eds., 2005); Harald Muller, "Arguing, Bargaining and All That: Communicative Action, Rationalist Theory and the Logic of Appropriateness in International Relations," 10 *European Journal of International Relations* 395 (2004); Corneliu Bjiola, "Legitimatizing the Use of Force in International Politics: A Communicative Action Perspective," 11 *European Journal of International Relations* 266 (2005).

[5] Thomas Risse, "'Let's Argue': Communicative Action in World Politics," 54 *International Organization* 7–9 (2000). This is Risse's summary of Jurgen Habermas's *Theory of Communicative Action, Vol 2* (1981).

[6] Jürgen Habermas, *The Theory of Communicative Action* 2 Volumes (Trans. Thomas McCarthy, 1985); Jurgen Habermas, *Legitimation Crisis* (Trans. Thomas McCarthy, 1975); Jurgen Habermas, "Why Europe needs a Constitution," 11 *New Left Review* (September–October 2001).

[7] James Gordon Finlayson, *Habermas: A Very Short Introduction* 26 and 36 (2005).

Like John Rawls, Habermas stresses the importance of "public reason," though he offers a more inclusive and pluralistic conception of what counts as a good reason, and he insists that those reasons are uncovered discursively, through argumentation.[8] The discursive interaction is not a communicative free-for-all, in which any argument is as good as any other. As an *inter-subjective* practice, it is constrained by the felt need to make arguments that the intended audience sees as relevant, rather than arbitrary or beside the point: arguments that they can understand and accept in principle, even if they disagree with the ultimate outcome of the debate. This ideal is not meant to describe an actual state of affairs, but its basic principles are presupposed in any linguistic communication.[9] If we assumed people lied all the time, or that they were wrong most of the time, or that they were irrational, then the whole idea of speech would be meaningless and the effort to communicate pointless.[10] That does not mean people never lie or that power relations never have an impact on the argumentative exchanges. The ideal speech situation does not describe the real world but rather is a construct against which the quality of actual deliberations can be measured.

The field in which Habermas has been most influential is deliberative democracy. As an element of public policy decision making, deliberation operates alongside voting, defined as the aggregation of fixed preferences; and bargaining, which involves the making of offers and counteroffers by actors seeking to achieve fixed interests.[11] Deliberative democrats hold that voting alone cannot legitimate collective decisions; the decisions must be *justified* in terms those who are subject to them can accept.[12] They do not present their theory as an alternative to representative democracy; rather, they stress that deliberation is an important and undervalued feature of all democratic societies.

---

[8] Stephen Macedo, "Introduction," in *Deliberative Politics: Essays on Democracy and Disagreement* 4 (Stephen Macedo ed., 1999). See also Seyla Benhabib ed., "Towards a Deliberative Model of Democratic Legitimacy" in *Democracy Indifference: Contesting the Boundaries of the Political* 67, 73–75 (1996); Joshua Cohen, *Philosophy, Politics, Democracy: Selected Essays* (2009); James Bohman "Citizenship and norms of Publicity: Wide Public Reason in Cosmopolitan Societies," 27 *Political Theory* 180 (1999); Iris Marion Young, "Difference as a Resource for Democratic Communication," in *Deliberative Democracy: Essays on Reason and Politics* 383 (J. Bohman and W. Rehg eds., 1997).

[9] Habermas argues that the ideal speech situation is embedded in the very nature of the discourse. "Insofar as participants understand themselves to be engaged in a cooperative search for common ground solely on the basis of good reasons, then they must—as a condition of the intelligibility of their activity—assume that the conditions of the ideal speech situation are satisfied." See Lars Lose, "Communicative Action and the World of Diplomacy," in *Constructing International Relations: The Next Generation* (K. Fierke and K.E. Jorgensen, eds., 2001). See also Frank Cunningham, *Theories of Democracy: A Critical Introduction* 176 (2002).

[10] As Willian Van Reijin puts it, "if we had to assume that most people generally lie... and that everybody always behaves in a cynical way, then language would lose its mission and understanding would be impossible." William Van Reijen "The Erosion of Western Culture: Habermas' Magum Opus," in *Habermas, An Introduction*, 59, 64 (Detlef Horster translator, 1992).

[11] Jon Elster, "Introduction," in *Deliberative Democracy* 6 (J. Elster ed., 1998).

[12] This subsection builds on Ian Johnstone, "Legal Deliberation and Argumentation in International Decision-Making," in *Fault Lines of International Legitimacy* 175-203 (H. Charlesworth and J.M. Coicaud eds, 2010).

The legitimacy of democratic institutions depends in part on the extent to which they permit "free and unconstrained public deliberation of all about matters of common concern."[13] As Jon Elster and others claim, "pre-suppositions of rational discourse" steer (or ought to steer) the course of public debates in any democratic society.[14] Rational discourse, at a minimum, entails appeals to "impartial values." These are values that reach beyond narrow self-interest; appeals based on them are not entirely self-serving.[15] Public policy disagreements are settled through the exchange of what Amy Gutmann and Dennis Thompson call reciprocal reasons: "you make your claims on terms that I can accept in principle. . . I make my claims on terms that you can accept in principle."[16] In other words, good arguments are based on values and reasons that are shared or could be shared by all who are affected by the decision taken. Obviously, consensus is not always possible in a pluralistic society; that is why legislatures vote. Those votes are often traded in a bargaining process where power and self-interest matter, but the bargains struck and outcome of votes are shaped by engagement in public debate and reason-giving.

This is not to say that all argumentation is "true reasoning" in the Habermasian sense. Indeed, distinguishing sincere communicative action from strategic argumentation may be impossible.[17] How does one know whether a stated reason for acting is sincere or genuinely oriented toward reaching consensus? Fortunately, it is not necessary to make that distinction in order to support the case that argumentation matters in public affairs. As Elster asserts, in public settings, impartial arguments and appeals to collective interest always fare better than self-serving arguments, regardless of whether the speaker really means it.[18]

---

[13] Benhabib, "Toward a Deliberative Model of Democratic Legitimacy," *supra* note 8 at 68; Joshua Cohen, "Deliberation and Democratic Legitimacy," in Bohman and Rehg eds., *supra* note 8 at 67. See generally, Bohman and Rehg eds, *supra note* 8; Frank Cunningham, *Theories of Democracy: A Critical Introduction* (2002).

[14] Elster, "Introduction," *supra* note 11 at 12, quoting Jurgen Habermas, *Between Facts and Norms: Contributions to a Discourse Theory of Law and Democracy* 540 (William Rehg translator, 1996).

[15] Jon Elster uses the term "impartial values," *id* at 12. See also Jon Elster, "The Market and the Forum: Three Varieties of Political Theory," in Bohman and Rehg, eds., *supra* note 8 at 12. For a discussion of the role of different kinds of arguments in world politics, see Crawford, *supra* note 4.

[16] Amy Gutmann and Dennis Thompson, *Democracy and Disagreement* 55 (1996). See also, Amy Gutmann and Dennis Thompson, *Why Deliberative Democracy?* 98–102 (2004); Amy Gutmann, "Deliberative Democracy and Majority Rule: Reply to Waldron," in *Deliberative Democracy and Human Rights* 234 (H. Koh and R. Slye, eds. 1999).

[17] For an argument that Habermas does not adequately defend the distinction between true and strategic communicative action, see James Johnson, "Arguing for Deliberation: Some Skeptical Considerations," in *Deliberative Democracy* 161, 173 (John Elster ed., 1998).

[18] Jon Elster, "The Strategic Uses of Argument" in *Barriers to Conflict Resolution* at 236 (K. Arrow, R. Mnookin, L. Ross, A. Tversky and R. Wilson eds, 1995). See also the chapters by Jon Elster, "Introduction", "Deliberation and Constitution-Making," and James Fearon, "Deliberation as Discussion" in *Deliberative Democracy* (Jon Elster ed. 1998). According to Danilo Turk, President of Slovenia and former Permanent Representative of Slovenia to the United Nations when Slovenia was a member of the Security Council during the Kosovo debates, arguments based on national interest are often couched in quasi-judicial terms because the legitimizing role of the Council is valued. Interview with the author, August 21, 2001.

For various reasons, what matters is that the speaker *appears* to be genuine.[19] Elster refers to the "civilizing force of hypocrisy": even if impartial arguments are used hypocritically, they often lead to concessions and more equitable outcomes.[20] This is because the argument or justification cannot correspond perfectly with self-interest, or it will be discounted by the listener. Nor can the speaker change position the moment it is in his or her interest to do so because that will be seen as opportunistic. If the rhetoric changes with every shift in short-term interests, then it will be dismissed as "cheap talk," and the entire purpose of making impartial arguments is lost.[21] Since reasoned argumentation is a prominent feature of democratic politics, presumably those who engage in it believe it does serve a purpose and therefore will seek to avoid acting and speaking in a manner that is transparently hypocritical.

Thomas Risse, Harald Mueller, and others have sought to apply Habermas's theory to international affairs. To do so, they must overcome the objection that global politics lacks any of the preconditions for communicative action identified by Habermas and others. The ideal of deliberation requires that participants have equal standing and equal voice in public debates.[22] The rules of discourse presuppose that "no speaker may be prevented, by internal or external coercion," from joining the debate.[23] Moreover, if the speakers are to speak to rather than at or past one another, they must share a "common lifeworld": the repository of experiences, assumptions, and understandings that makes communicative action possible, "a supply of collective interpretations [actors have] of the world and of themselves, as provided by language, a common history or culture."[24] Do these exist beyond the level of the nation-state? At least some deliberative democrats see the possibility of meaningful deliberation or reason-giving at the transnational level. While a common language, history, and culture do not exist—a degree of homogeneity that often does not exist on the national level either—there is a weaker sort of bond, at least at the European level, that makes it possible for people to speak to rather than past each other. This bond is the foundation for, and strengthens as the result of, transnational

---

[19] According to Elster, the reasons are: others are more willing to back down if they believe one is arguing from principle; public-regarding language can be used as a subterfuge for a deal among special interests; impartial arguments may actually persuade others; there is a social norm against taking positions that cannot be justified in terms of benefits to the collectivity; and arguments based on principle rather than bargaining power may help an opponent save face. Elster, "Strategic Uses of Argument" *id.* at 246–7. See also, Elster "Deliberation and Constitution-Making" *id.* at 101.

[20] Elster, "Strategic Uses of Argument," *supra* n. 18 at 249. See also Diego Gambetta, "Claro!: An Essay on Discursive Machismo" in *Deliberative Democracy* 19, 23 (J. Elster ed., 1998).

[21] Cf. Jack Goldsmith and Eric Posner, "Moral and Legal Rhetoric in International Relations: A Rational Choice Perspective" 31 *Journal of Legal Studies* 115 (2002); Goldsmith and Posner, *supra* note 3 at 167-84.

[22] Cohen, *supra* note 13, at 74.

[23] Habermas, cited in Cunningham, *supra* note 9, at 176.

[24] Risse, "Let's Argue," *supra* note 5 at 10–11, citing Habermas's, *Theory of Communicative Action, Vol 2* 209 (1981). Neta Crawford describes Habermas's lifeworld as the "background of shared interpretations (unconsciously held inter-subjective beliefs) and practices. . . that allow meaningful conversations and arguments to occur among individuals and groups." Crawford, *supra* note 4 at 59.

political deliberation. Following Habermas, deliberative democrats speak of multiple public spheres in which a range of opinions is developed and exchanged on matters of common concern: "a highly complex network that branches out into a multitude of overlapping international, national, regional, local and sub-cultural arenas."[25] Public reasoning and justification occurs in the institutions of government and intergovernmental bodies, as well as political parties, nongovernmental organizations, social movements, and other elements of civil society, whose activities are not confined by national borders.[26] Corneliu Bjiola has coined the term "institutional lifeworld" to describe the collective understandings, rules, and diplomatic norms that underpin IOs that engage in security functions, like the UN, NATO, EU, and OSCE.[27]

Transnational democracy theorists, not surprisingly, have tended to focus on Europe. They challenge the "no-demos" thesis of the German Constitutional Court enunciated in a famous decision on the Maastricht Treaty:

> A democratic polity depends on a sense of social cohesion, shared destiny and collective self-identity. . . [which in turn] is conditioned on some though not necessarily all of the following elements: common language, common history, common cultural habits and sensibilities, common ethnic origin, common religion.[28]

These elements, the Court held, are lacking at the European level, and therefore the chances of a Europe-wide democratic polity ever emerging are slim. Habermas, Michael Zurn, Joseph Weiler, and others reject the no-demos thesis and posit a notion of European citizenship that rests on a civic conception of "the nation" or peoplehood.[29] People can be political and civic members of a society without all being from the same national/ethnic background, as long as they are committed to a shared set of values. Various developments in the EU are cited to support the proposition that a European "public sphere" is

---

[25] Habermas quoted in Schlesinger, Philip and Kevin, Deirdre "Can the European Union become a Sphere of Publics?" in *Democracy in the European Union: Integration through Deliberation?* 211 (Eriksen and Fossum eds., 2000). On global public sphere theory generally, see Jennifer Mitzen, "Reading Habermas in Anarchy: Multilateral Diplomacy and Global Public Spheres," 99 *American Political Science Review* 401-417 (2005); Dana Villa, "Postmodernism and the Public Sphere," 86 *American Political Science Review* 712 (1992).

[26] Benhabib, *supra* note 8 at 74.

[27] Bjiola, *supra* note 4 at 279.

[28] Quoted in Daniel Bodansky, "The Legitimacy of International Governance: A Coming Challenge for International Environmental Law," 93 *American Journal of International Law* 616 (1999).

[29] Habermas, "Why Europe needs a Constitution" supra note 6; Michael Zürn, "Democratic Governance Beyond the Nation-State: The EU and Other International Institutions," 6 *European Journal of International Relations* (2000); Joseph Weiler, *The Constitution of Europe: "Do the New Clothes Have an Emperor?" and Other Essays on European Integration* (1999); and the various contributors to Eriksen and Fossum, *supra* note 25. See also Michael Zurn and Christian Joerges eds, *Law and Governance in Postnational Europe: Compliance Beyond the Nation-State* (2005).

emerging, based in part on deliberative principles.[30] It may not constitute a single polity analogous to a domestic one, but it is one layer in a multilayered system of governance that is seen as legitimate by most Europeans.

The most enthusiastic advocates of transnational deliberation have found evidence of it at the *global* level, exemplified by but not restricted to the growing influence of nonstate actors.[31] John Dryzek sees "discursive sources of governance and order" in the power of transnational civil society to question, criticize, and shed the light of publicity on governmental action.[32] Similarly, James Bohman points to the increasing importance of informal transnational networks, who "by fostering communicative interaction. . . have produced self-regulating forms of cooperation among those affected by global processes."[33] Yet if the sphere of deliberation is opened up to the entire globe, is it possible to imagine a discursive process that is bounded in any way? Deliberative democrats see it as a virtue of their theory that it resists tying political prescriptions to foundational theory; the aim is to justify collective decisions without resorting to metaphysical truths about human nature or society.[34] They argue that reasoning about public policy and values is possible without some transcendent, prepolitical understanding of what those values mean and how to prioritize among them when they conflict. In democratic society, it is certainly plausible that one can engage in reasonable debate over matters of public policy without assuming the validity of any "self-evident" values or truths. But is it plausible at the international level? Does the heterogeneity of international society not suggest that everything is up for grabs, that any argument is as good as any other?

---

[30] The drafting of an EU constitution, the practice of seeking consensus in the Council of Ministers, the authority of the European Court of Justice, the growing power of the European Parliament, "interparliamentary discourse," the committee system, and the emergence of an EU-oriented media are among the developments identified by the various contributors to Eriksen and Fossum, (see note 6). The failure of the EU constitution does not negate the argument, as the Lisbon Treaty does for Europe almost exactly what the constitution would have done, but without the name. See also James Bohman, "Reforming the Transnational Polity: Deliberative Democracy and the European Union," in *Democracy Across Borders: From Demos to Demoi* 135–71 (2007). One scholar sees deliberative interaction at work in the expansion of the EU and NATO. Franck Schimmelfenning, *The EU, NATO and the Integration of Europe: Rules and Rhetoric* 194–280 (2004).

[31] John Dryzek *Deliberative Democracy and Beyond* (2000); John Dryzek *Deliberative Global Politics* (2006).

[32] Dryzek, *Deliberative Democracy and Beyond, id.* at 131; John Dryzek, "Transnational Democracy," 7 *The Journal of Political Philosophy* 30–51 (1999).

[33] James Bohman, "International regimes and democratic governance: political equality and influence in global institutions," 73 *International Affairs* 499, 506 (1999). See also James Bohman, "The Globalization of the Public Sphere: Cosmopolitanism, Publicity and Cultural Pluralism," LXXV *The Modern Schoolman* (1998); Bohman, *supra* note 30. See also Walter Barber and Robert Bartlett, *Deliberative Environmental Politics: Democracy and Ecological Rationality* (2005).

[34] Gutmann and Thompson (1996), *supra* note 16 at 5; Cunningham, *supra* note 9 at 170.

Not necessarily. Joshua Cohen sees an emerging "global public reason" comprised of "norms, values and forms of argument suited to justification in global politics."[35] To say that the ideal of public reason has some significance in global politics means those engaged in politics at that level feel compelled to justify their decisions on the basis of considerations that others can reasonably be expected to view as relevant. For example, scientific findings on the impact of greenhouse gases are understood to be relevant to the debate on climate change, even if there is disagreement on the significance of the findings or the policy implications. Few, if any, policy makers or competent analysts would say that scientific evidence is simply irrelevant. IOs are settings where a good deal of transnational deliberation occurs. They are places where states and increasingly nonstate actors discuss, debate, and generate shared (inter-subjective) understandings about the terms of international life. They are vehicles for the expression of global public reason:

> [A] relatively autonomous space of global politics is emerging, comprising global rule-making or governance, a politics—both within those settings and surrounding them—that contests and shapes their operations, . . . Here is the place of global public reason. It is, in the first instance, a common reason for the domain of global politics: a public reason that might provide common ground for rule-makers and for those in the wider sphere of transnational politics contesting the operation of those rule-makers.[36]

Analogous to the "demos" in a democratic society, the patterns of interaction and interdependence that emerge in and around IOs create the conditions for reasoned exchange on matters of regional or global public policy. Membership in an international organization leads to internalization of shared experiences and common understandings and—to the extent that continued membership is desired—cultivates an incentive to operate within and perpetuate the norms it embodies. (I will return to this in Chapter 3).

III. THE NATURE OF LEGAL DISCOURSE

Thus, a case can be made that transnational deliberation is possible and that a good deal of that deliberation takes place in and around IOs. Though plausible, that abstract proposition is hard to prove. Argumentation can take many forms (prudential, ethical,

---

[35] Joshua Cohen, "Democracy's Reason, Global Reason", Tanner Lecture on Human Values II, University of California at Berkeley, April 11, 2007, 21 (on file with author). See also Joshua Cohen and Charles Sable, "Global Democracy?," 37 *New York University Journal of International Law and Politics* 763–97 (Summer 2005).

[36] *Id.* Tanner Lecture at 23.

scientific, identity-based[37]), and it is hard to pin down the impact of any of them on world politics. Without dismissing the importance of these other forms of argumentation, this book focuses on legal argumentation because there is something distinctive about it. International legal discourse is a highly specialized form of argumentation, the standard techniques of which are widely recognized.[38] The Vienna Convention on the Law of Treaties identifies text, context, and the object and purpose of rules as being sources of meaning, along with negotiating history and subsequent practice when the ordinary meaning is not clear.[39] There is much debate over how much weight to give each of these various factors or whether any words have "ordinary" meanings, but they embody conventional thinking about treaty interpretation and, by extension, legal argumentation.

Moreover, as discussed in the introductory chapter, the law, by definition, embodies shared understandings. In positivist legal theory, law comes into existence if and only if the subjects of the law (states) manifest their consent to it. That means that law cannot be dismissed lightly—it is not something "out there" that is imposed on states, at least in theory. It is a reflection of state interests and will. It is not divorced from material power—if powerful states choose not to consent to the law or repeatedly iterate what they understand the law to be, that has an impact on what the law is.[40] But when legal language is used, it is not understood as invoking power: law, "if not antithetical to assertions based on power, at least is in tension with the brute use of power."[41] Even if critical theorists are right that law is the exercise of power by other means, it is not presented that way by those who engage in legal discourse.

That being said, the difference between legal argumentation and political deliberation should not be overstated. Deliberative democrats question the distinction made between courts as forums for principled deliberation and legislatures as brokers of interests.[42]

---

[37] Crawford, *supra* note 4.
[38] See Kenneth Abbott, Robert Keohane, Andrew Moravscik, Anne-Marie Slaughter and Duncan Snidal "The Concept of Legalization" in *Legalization and World Politics* 17–36 (Goldstein et al. eds., 2001). For a fuller and somewhat different account of the distinctive nature of legal argumentation, see Jutta Brunnée and Stephen Toope, *Legitimacy and Legality in International Law: An Interactional Theory* 56-125 (2010). These authors draw on Lon Fuller's criteria of legality in describing what they call the "practice of legality". See also Jutta Brunnée and Stephen J. Toope, "International Law and Constructivism: Elements of an Interactional Theory of International Law," 39 *Columbia Journal of Transnational Law* 1, 51–56 (2000).
[39] Vienna Convention on the Law of Treaties (1969), Articles 31-33. Entered into force on 27 January 1980, UN Treaty Series, Vol. 1155, p.311.
[40] Glennon, *supra* n. 3, especially Chapters 3 and 4.
[41] Kal Raustiala, "Form and Substance in International Agreements," 99 *American Journal of International Law* 581, 606. See also Paul Kahn, "Speaking Law to Power: Popular Sovereignty, Human Rights and the New International Order," 1 *Chicago Journal of International Law* 1 (2000). On the multiple meanings of power, see Michael Barnett and Raymond Duvall, "Power in Global Governance," in *Power in Global Governance* 1 (M. Barnett and R. Duvall eds, 2005).
[42] Gutmann and Thompson, *supra* note 16 at 46. See also Robert Howse, "Adjudicative Legitimacy and Treaty Interpretation in International Trade Law: The Early Years of WTO Jurisprudence," in *The EU, The WTO and*

Democratic deliberation in political forums is and should be constrained by the felt need to make impartial, mutually acceptable arguments. Conversely, legal argument is not a search for objectively right answers. It is a search for inter-subjective meaning: what the law means to the parties collectively. Thus, both processes entail the exchange of reasons, the relevance and importance of which others can be expected to acknowledge even if they disagree about the precise content of those reasons and the best way to balance them.

The distinguishing characteristic of the international legal system is that it is decentralized. There is no global legislature comparable to domestic parliaments. The number of international tribunals and quasi-judicial bodies is growing, but most legal disputes are not subject to authoritative judicial settlement. Compliance is common, but coercive enforcement is rare: even the powerful World Trade Organization (WTO) Appellate Body does not enforce the law directly, but rather determines when proportionate retaliation is permissible—a sort of structured self-help system.[43] With no global legislature, judiciary, or police force, international law operates largely through a process of justificatory discourse.

There is a substantial body of legal scholarship that supports this conception of law as fundamentally a discursive process. It starts from the observation that governments almost always claim their actions to be consistent with international law. Officials rarely state the law is irrelevant but rather seek to interpret the law in a manner that justifies their actions. The felt need to make a legal case imposes limits on the style of argument they use: it frames the choices available to them and how they explain and justify those choices to relevant domestic and international audiences.[44] Abram Chayes and Antonia Handler Chayes situate justificatory discourse in their "management model" of compliance.[45] Their central claim is that "the interpretation, elaboration, application and ultimately enforcement of international rules is accomplished through a process of (mostly verbal)

---

the NAFTA: Towards a Common Law of International Trade 35, 43 (J.H.H. Weiler ed., 2000). Cf. Brunnée and Toope *supra* note 38 at 71-72 who argue that the criteria of legality (following Lon Fuller) establish the conditions for reasoned dialogue and reciprocity. They are what make interactions 'legal' as opposed to political or social. And those conditions are demanding, they are different in kind not degree from political deliberation. Embodying what Fuller calls the "internal morality of law," they include the requirements that law must be general, promulgated, not retroactive, clear, realistic, constant and congruent with the actions of officials operating under the law. Lon Fuller, *The Morality of Law* (Revised edition, 1969).

[43] Raustiala, *supra* note 39.

[44] Chayes and Chayes, *supra* note 2 at 214, citing Friedrich Kratochwil, *Rules, Norms and Decisions: On the Conditions of Practical and Legal Reasoning in International Relations and Domestic Affairs* (1989). For a similar argument applied to domestic law, see Cass Sunstein, *Legal Reasoning and Political Conflict* 13 (1996).

[45] Chayes and Chayes, *supra* note 2. The writings of Thomas Franck (a lawyer) and Friedrich Kratochwil (an international relations theorist) figure prominently in the Chayes' theoretical analysis. For a clear and thorough account of the tradition from which *The New Sovereignty* emerged, see Harold Koh's review essay "Why Do Nations Obey International Law?" 106 *Yale Law Journal* 2599 (1997).

interchange among interested parties."[46] Similarly, Thomas Franck explains compliance with international law in terms of "fairness discourse." Fairness, he argues, is not a divine "given" but rather a contingent quality that captures a process of reasoning and negotiation on the basis of principles that combine procedural legitimacy and distributive justice.[47] Jutta Brunée and Stephen Toope state "it is through institutionally shaped rhetorical practices, and acceptances of reasoned argument, that law emerges from broader social practice."[48] States seek to interpret their obligations in a manner that is most advantageous to them, but having to do so in legal terms means making their case on grounds that are logically independent of their own interests and wishes.[49]

A legal argument is by definition inter-subjective—an appeal to standards that, at least in principle, apply to all who are similarly situated. Purely self-serving appeals ("I interpret the law this way because it is in the national interest to do so,") are never heard in settings where legal argumentation counts unless accompanied by more impartial claims. Law serves a communicative function: to express one's claims in legal terms means to signal which norms one considers relevant and to indicate which procedures one intends to follow and would like others to follow.[50] Law, by facilitating communication between states, "adds to the common grammar of statecraft."[51]

This is not to say legal argumentation must be sincere for it to have an impact on behavior. Like Elster's claim about the "civilizing force of hypocrisy" described above, states need not be persuaded of the substantive merit of a legal rule in order to be constrained by it. Ryan Goodman and Derek Jinks posit a theory of 'acculturation', which they present as an explanation for compliance with international law when persuasion and coercion are absent.[52] Acculturation, they argue, can produce "outward conformity

---

[46] Chayes and Chayes, *supra* note 2 at 118.

[47] Thomas Franck, *Fairness in International Law and Institutions* 7 and 14 (1995). For a good summary of Franck's fairness theory, see *The Foundations of International Law and Politics* 136 (Oona Hathaway and Harold Koh eds., 2005).

[48] Jutta Brunée and Stephen Toope, "International Law and Constructivism: Elements of an Interactional Theory of International Law," 39 *Columbia Journal of Transnational Law* 19-74 (2000). See also Stephen Toope, "Emerging Patterns of Governance and International Law," in *The Role of Law in International Politics: Essays in International Relations and International Law* 91 (M. Byers ed., 2000).

[49] Oscar Schachter, "International Law in Theory and Practice," *Collected Courses of the Hague Academy of International Law* 59 (1985). Andrew Hurrell, "International Society and the Study of Regimes: A Reflective Approach," in *Regime Theory and International Relations* 49 (Volker Rittberger ed., 1995).

[50] Stanley Hoffman, "Introduction" to *International Law and Political Crisis* (L. Scheinman and D. Wilkinson eds., 1968).

[51] Robert Keohane and Joseph Nye, "Power and Interdependence Revisited," 41 *International Organization* 725, 746 (1987).

[52] Ryan Goodman and Derek Jinks, "How to Influence States: Socialization and International Human Rights Law" 54 *Duke Law Journal* 621 (2004). For sympathetic critiques of Goodman and Jinks' approach, see José Alvarez, "Do States Socialize?" 54 *Duke Law Journal* 961 (2005); Harold Koh, "Internalization through Socialization", 54 *Duke Law Journal* 975 (2005); and Brunée and Toope, *supra* note 38 at 106-107.

with a rule...without private acceptance".[53] In other words, states have an incentive to claim that their behavior complies with the law even if they have no genuine commitment to it because that is what is expected in the surrounding culture. Conformity has its own rewards, even if conformity is the result of social pressure rather than internal acceptance of the rule in question.

Critical theorists acknowledge that discourse is at the heart of the legal enterprise, but they do not see it as a form of communication. Rather, legal discourse is an (ultimately futile) effort to make the policy choices it reflects seem neutral and objective—in other words, apolitical. Marti Koskenniemi, for example, describes international law as an elaborate argumentative structure, in which the enduring tension between opposite values, such as the community and individual, play out discursively.[54] The discourse cannot reconcile those competing values without appealing to principles that are outside the law. The law is nothing more than rhetoric, and the rhetoric cannot provide "objective" answers to legal disputes because the entire structure is built on contradictions. The project of critical legal studies is to expose those contradictions, to uncover the "hidden ideologies, attitudes and structures which lie behind [legal] discourse."[55] It is possible, according to David Kennedy, to distinguish good legal arguments from bad, but no one is persuaded by good arguments: "international law is a conversation without content—a ritualized exchange... Action [is] not compelled by the power of the argument."[56] Any line of argument necessarily bumps up against an equally valid line of counterargument, and there is no way of choosing between them without invoking political—and therefore contested—principles.

Theorists who are less skeptical about the communicative function of law acknowledge the contradictions but see that as a fundamental reason for the discourse. As Kennedy himself notes, Oscar Schachter argued that the antimonies in international law were not a vice, but rather a virtue to be embraced and worked with.[57] They do not render the law meaningless, but rather help to shape and construct its application to particular cases.[58] Indeed, managing the tension between competing values is at the core of Franck's fairness theory:

> [The] two aspects of fairness—the substantive (distributive justice) and the procedural (right process)—may not always pull in the same direction, because the

---

[53] *Id* at 643.
[54] Martti Koskenniemi, *From Apology to Utopia: The Structure of international Legal Argument* 40–41 and 449–50 (1989).
[55] David Kennedy, "Theses about International Law Discourse," 23 *German Yearbook of International Law* 353, 355 (1986).
[56] *Id* at 376. See also Philip R. Trimble, "International Law, World Order and Critical Legal Studies," 42 *Stanford Law Review* 811, 838 (1990).
[57] David Kennedy, "Tom Franck and the Manhattan School," 35 *New York University Journal of International Law and Politics* 397, 427 (2002).
[58] Stephen Toope, "Emerging Patterns of Global Governance," in *The Role of Law in International Politics: Essays in International Relations and International Law* 98 (Michael Byers ed., 2000).

former favors change and the latter stability and order. The tension between stability and change, if not managed, can disorder the system. Fairness is the rubric under which this tension is discursively managed.[59]

This is the point that democratic theorists make about the value of deliberation. It is precisely because societies are pluralistic, and few values are "self-evident," let alone divinely inspired, that democratic deliberation is necessary. The purpose of the deliberation may be to win political battles, or it may be to persuade and be persuaded. Either way, it is not a charade, or a mask behind which value choices are hidden. Heterogeneity and interpretative conflict are a resource, not an obstacle to deliberative problem solving; a way of thrashing out competing normative claims in any pluralistic society.[60]

Whether or not the discourse ever provides clear answers to contested cases, what all these accounts (critical and constructive) have in common is the disciplining force of legal argumentation. Legal deliberations are bounded: certain types of argument and styles of reasoning are acceptable and accepted; others are not.[61] There is a limit to which any language, including the language of the law, can plausibly be stretched.[62] The limits exist because those who use legal language are typically in a relationship of some duration, from which common meanings, values, and expectations have emerged. They share a general understanding of the purpose of the enterprise in which they are engaged (that the interpretation and application of law, for example, is not the same as the interpretation and application of religious or literary texts) and, as a result, are constrained by the conventions of argument, persuasion, and justification associated with the discipline. "While there are likely to be disagreements about the proper use of a term or the interpretation of a rule, purely idiosyncratic uses are excluded even if the use of the concepts remain contestable and contested."[63] Beyond that, legal discourse is a search for intersubjective meaning through the exchange of reasons that are distinctly "legal." This is not likely to produce single right answers to hard cases, but can rule out answers that are clearly wrong while providing a framework for discussing and debating the merits of those that are plausible.

---

[59] Franck, *supra* note 45 at 7.

[60] Patricia Nanz, "Democratic Legitimacy and Constitutionalisation of Transnational Trade Governance: A View from Political Theory," in *Constitutionalism, Multilevel Trade Governance and Social Regulation* 59, 76 (C. Joerges and E. Petersmann eds., 2006).

[61] Friederich Kratochwil, "How Do Norms Matter?" in *The Role of Law in International Politics* 35, 52 (M. Byers ed., 2000). On the disciplining force of legal argumentation generally, see Friederich Kratochwil Kratochwil, *Rules, Norms and Decisions, (1989)*. See also Schachter, *International Law in Theory and Practice (1991)*; Koskenniemi, *From Apology to Utopia (2006)*; Toope, *supra* note 58 at 98; Kennedy, *supra* note 57 at 431.

[62] Quentin Skinner, *Visions of Politics: Regarding Method* 156 (2002). For an instructive application of Skinner's theory to debates about humanitarian intervention, see Nicholas J. Wheeler, *Saving Strangers: Humanitarian Intervention in International Society* 7 (2002).

[63] Kratochwil, *supra* note 61, at 52.

Where does this legal argumentation occur? In all sorts of places, but it tends to be concentrated in IOs. IOs are often denigrated as "talk shops." In less pejorative terms, they are sites for discursive interaction among member states and interested nonmembers and nongovernmental actors. Because IOs are typically constructed through a legal act (negotiation of a constituent instrument) and operate on the basis of formal rules, much of the discursive interaction is based on law. Their charters are the starting point for argumentation about acceptable behavior by the members of the organization and the role of the various parts of the organization in regulating that behavior—like, if not necessarily the same as, a constitution. The UN Charter, according to Habermas, Franck, Bardo Fassbender, and others has constitutional features.[64] The normative framework of the Charter has been supplemented by a vast range of treaties adopted by the UN General Assembly, including all the global human rights treaties; binding decisions of the Security Council (SC), including some that are legislative in character; opinions of the International Court of Justice; "soft law" in the form of nonbinding declarations of the General Assembly and SC that nevertheless have some legal weight; decisions of other intergovernmental bodies like the Human Rights Council; and operational activities of peacekeepers, humanitarian organizations, and other agencies that have an impact on the development of the law. Similar arguments can be made about the WTO in the trade realm.[65]

These organizations operate on the basis of a normative framework that evolves but does not shift in direct proportion to the vicissitudes of international politics. The more "legalized" the organization—that is, the more it operates on the basis of precise rules and formal dispute settlement procedures—the more demanding is the discourse within it.[66] Deviations from the standard forms of argument are possible but likely to

---

[64] Jurgen Habermas, *The Divided West*, 160–66 (Edited and Translated by Ciaran Cronin, 2006); Bardo Fassbender, *The United Nations Charter as the Constitution of the International Community* (2009); Simon Chesterman, Thomas Franck and David Malone, *The Law and Practice of the United Nations* (2008), Chapter 1. On "constitutionalization" of the international system generally, see Ronald St. John MacDonald and Douglas M. Johnston, *Towards World Consitutionalism: Issues in the Legal Ordering of the World Community* (2005); Jeffrey Dunoff and Joel Trachtman eds., *Ruling the World? Constitutionalism, International Law and Global Governance* (2009); Jan Klabbers, Ann Peters and Geir Ulfstein *The Constitutionalization of International Law* (2009); Mattias Kumm, "The Legitimacy of International Law: A Constitutionalist Framework of Analysis," 15 *European Journal of International Law* 907–31 (2004).

[65] See generally Christian Joerges and Ernst-Ulrich Petersmann eds., *Constitutionalism, Multilevel Trade Governance and Social Regulation* (2006). For an argument on the constitutional nature of the international trade system, see Ernst-Ulrich Ptersmann, "The WTO Constitution and Human Rights," 3 *Journal of International Economic Law* 19 (2000). See also Joel Trachtman, "The Constitution of the WTO," 17 *European Journal of International Law* 23 (2006). For a counterargument, see Robert Howse and Kalypso Nicolaidas, "Legitimacy and Global Governance: Why Constitutionalizing the WTO is a Step Too Far," in *Efficiency, Equity and Legitimacy* (Porter et al. eds., 2001).

[66] On "legalization," see Judith Goldstein et al. eds., *Legalization and World Politics* (2001). James Bohman uses the term "juridification" to make a similar point: ". . . the tendency toward the increasing expansion of law and

be counterproductive if the goal is to persuade. Moreover, any argument, even one made hypocritically, is more likely to succeed if pure self-interest is diluted. Having to pay lip service to the collective interest and shared principles forces states to moderate the rhetorical positions they take. This, in turn, can lead to what Risse calls "argumentative self-entrapment."[67] Once governments accept a norm rhetorically, they begin to argue over its interpretation and application to the particular case at hand, rather than the validity of the law itself. This creates a "discursive opening" for their critics—"if you say you accept human rights, then why do you systematically violate them?"—which eventually induces governments to match deeds with words.[68] The deeds may either be tactical concessions in order to give their claims the ring of plausibility, or they may reflect major policy choices. David Rieff's comment on the intervention in Kosovo (discussed in Chapter 4) is suggestive: "hoist on the petard" of their professed commitment to human rights, Western states could not easily avoid acting.[69] Whether the leaders who ultimately made the decision genuinely wanted to act is, in many respects, beside the point.

IV. DELIBERATION, ARGUMENTATION, AND LEGITIMACY

All of this suggests that deliberation and legal argumentation are a measure of the legitimacy of decision making in IOs. Concerns about the legitimacy of international institutions have grown in proportion to their growing autonomy. If IOs are nothing more than coordination devices for states, then no question of legitimacy arises.[70] The power and influence that the organizations wield resides with the governments of member states, so all that matters is whether those governments are legitimate. But if the organization wields influence separate from the collective will of its members, questions must be asked about what gives those wielding the power the authority to do so, how they wield

---

law-like methods of formal rules and adjudication to new domains of social life." Bohman, *supra* note 30, at 152. John Dryzek worries that the juridification of IOs can make them less democratic, either because the rules can become overly rigid and impossible to apply to complex issues or too much administrative discretion is left to unelected officials. Dryzek, *Deliberative Global Politics* 136–45 (2006).

[67] Risse, "Let's Argue," *supra* note 5, at 32. For a more recent explanation of the notion of argumentative entrapment, see Risse, "Global Governance", supra note 4.

[68] Id at 32–33. See also Louis Henkin: "the fact that nations feel obliged to justify their actions under international law, that justifications must have plausibility, that plausible justifications are often unavailable or limited, inevitably affects how nations will act." Louis Henkin, *How Nations Behave* 45 (1979).

[69] David Rieff, "A New Age of Liberal Imperialism," 1 *World Policy Journal* 7 (Summer 1999).

[70] Allen Buchanan and Robert Keohane, "The Legitimacy of Global Governance Institutions," 20 *Ethics and International Affairs* 405, 408 (2006); Daniel Bodansky, "The Legitimacy of International Governance: A Coming Challenge for International Environmental Law," 93 *American Journal of International Law* 596 (1999).

it, and to whom they are accountable. From the perspective of the "democratic deficit," these questions become even sharper if individuals are directly affected by the activities of the organization. To what extent, if any, do the individuals have any influence over decisions that impact their lives?

The legitimacy of international institutions is increasingly a concern of both international law and international relations theorists.[71] This is in part because IOs are producing more law, and in part because legitimacy is sometimes invoked as an alternative to law in assessing what the institutions do (or do not do).[72] The starting point for contemporary discussion of legitimacy in the international legal field is Thomas Franck's influential work on procedural fairness.[73] Compliance with the law can be explained by the belief among those addressed that a "rule or an institution has come into being and operates in accordance with generalized principles of right process."[74] Franck later added distributive justice as a substantive dimension of "fairness," to come up with a fully developed theory of compliance: "The fairness of international law, as of any other legal system, will be judged, first by the degree to which the rules satisfy the participants' expectations of a justifiable distribution of costs and benefits, and secondly by the extent to which the rules are made and applied in accordance with what the participants perceive as right process."[75] Rules that are both procedurally legitimate and substantively just exert a compliance pull on states, even in the absence of enforcement.

Franck's concept of legitimacy is subjective—it depends on the beliefs, expectations, and perceptions of those to whom the rules are addressed.[76] This subjective understanding is echoed in contemporary international relations theory. As Ian Hurd claims, "legitimacy

---

[71] Leading works in the international law field are Thomas Franck, *The Power of Legitimacy among Nations* (1990); Thomas Franck, *Fairness in International Law and Institutions* (1998); Allan Buchanan, *Justice, Legitimacy and Self-Determination: Moral Foundations of International Law* (2003); Brunée and Toope, *supra* note 38; Daniel Bodansky *id*. Leading works in the international relations field are Buchanan and Keohane *id*.; Ian Clark, *Legitimacy in International Society* (2005); Ian Hurd, *After Anarchy: Legitimacy and Power at the United Nations* (2007); and Jean-Marc Coicaud and Veijo Heiskanen eds., *The Legitimacy of IOs* 259 (2001). For an argument that rationalist explanations for powerful states using IOs are more persuasive than legitimacy-based arguments, see Alexander Thompson, "Coercion through IOs: The Security Council and the Logic of Information Transmission," 60 *International Organization* 1 (2006).

[72] For example, the Independent International Commission on Kosovo declared NATO's intervention in 1999 without UN Security Council authorization to be illegal but legitimate.

[73] Thomas Franck, *The Power of Legitimacy Among Nations* (1990).

[74] Four key indicators of legitimacy are determinacy (the clarity of the rule), symbolic validation (the extent to which the rule communicates authority), coherence (how the rule relates to other rules and whether its application treats like cases alike), and adherence (the rule's connection to the system's over-arching institutional and procedural framework). *Id* at 24.

[75] Franck, *Fairness, supra* note 45.

[76] Brunée and Toope agree with Franck's view that certain internal features of law explain its compliance pull, but object to the explicitly positivist basis for his argument – namely that it is tied to state consent. They claim that law is legitimate only when it is produced through an "interactional framework" that entails broad participation in the construction and maintenance of legal regimes. Brunée and Toope, *supra* note 38 at 53 and Chapter 3.

refers to the belief by an actor that a rule or institution ought to be obeyed. It is necessarily a normative and subjective belief, and not one that is necessarily shared with any other actor."[77] As an explanation for compliance with norms, legitimacy is distinct from coercion and self-interest. Actors (states in the international system) follow rules not only because they fear sanctions for failing to do so or calculate compliance is in their interest but out of an internal sense of obligation.[78] To say that an institution is legitimate implies that it deserves support even if it does not always advance the interests of everyone subject to its rule.[79] Thus, legitimacy makes an institution—or the rules that emanate from it—more stable because support does not fluctuate in direct proportion to changes in self-interest or the ability to credibly threaten coercion.[80]

Connected to political authority, legitimacy is recognition of the right to govern.[81] As such, it necessarily has a collective dimension. It depends on the *shared beliefs* among those ruled of the ruler's rightful authority. Thus, legitimacy is "a generalized perception or assumption that the actions of an entity are desirable, proper or appropriate within some socially constructed system of norms, values, beliefs and definitions."[82] For legitimacy to have collective effects, it cannot be entirely subjective; if it were, every individual's sense of what is right and proper would be equally valid, and the notion of exercising legitimate power would be meaningless. To regulate social behavior, it must be *inter-subjective*. And these inter-subjective beliefs are not purely coincidental (they do not arise simply because a group of individuals happen to share them) but rather through social interaction.

---

[77] Hurd, *supra* note 71. See also Ian Hurd, "Legitimacy" in *Encyclopedia Princetoniensis: The Princeton Encyclopedia of Self-Determination* (2006). For a contrary perspective, see Buchanan and Keohane *supra* note 70 at 405. They distinguish normative and sociological meanings of legitimacy as follows: "To say that an institution is legitimate in the normative sense is to assert that it has the right to rule. . . An institution is legitimate in the sociological sense when it is widely believed to have the right to rule. When people disagree over whether the WTO is legitimate, their disagreements are typically normative. They are not disagreeing about whether they or others believe that this institution has the right to rule; they are disagreeing about whether it has the right to rule."

[78] Hurd, *After Anarchy, id.* at 51. This corresponds to H.L.A. Hart's theory of law and the legal process theory of Harold Koh that builds on Hart. H.L.A Hart, *Concept of Law* (2d ed., 1994); Harold Koh, "Why Do Nations Obey International Law?," 106 *Yale Law Journal* 2599 (1997); Harold Koh, "Bringing International Law Back Home," 35 *Houston Law Review* 623 (1998).

[79] Moreover, the felt sense of obligation to comply is independent of the content of the rules themselves: "I have a content-independent reason to comply with the rules of the club to which I belong if I have agreed to follow them and this reason is independent of whether I judge any particular rule to be a good or useful one." Buchanan and Keohane, *supra* note 70 at 409–11.

[80] Clark, *supra* note 71, at 15–16.

[81] Jean-Marc Coicaud, "International Democratic Culture and Legitimacy," in *The Legitimacy of IOs, supra* note 71, at 259; Bruce Cronin and Ian Hurd, "International Authority and the UN Security Council," in *The UN Security Council and the Institution of International Authority* (B. Cronin and I. Hurd eds., 2008).

[82] Mark Suchman, "Managing Legitimacy: Strategic and Institutional Approaches" 20 *Academy of Management Review* at 571, 574 (1995). "Legitimate," it should be stressed, means appropriate behavior within a social context, not necessarily normatively good. Nazi law, for example, could have been seen as legitimate.

This social interaction is a political, contested process. "Actors and institutions constantly work to legitimize their power, and challengers to that power work to delegitimate it."[83] Legitimation and delegitimation is done by drawing on prevailing norms. The *practice* of legitimacy is an attempt to reconcile tensions among competing norms—the process by which they are "interpreted, developed, reconciled, transcribed and consensually mediated" in international society.[84] Because the norms that have currency at a particular historical moment may pull in different directions (for example, positive law may dictate one response to massive human rights violations while moral conceptions may suggest another), legitimation is a dynamic, negotiated process:

> The practice of legitimacy describes political negotiation amongst the members of international society as they seek out an accommodation between. . . seemingly absolute values and attempt to reconcile them with a working consensus to which all can feel bound.[85]

The political negotiation is heavily influenced by prevailing distributions of material power but is tempered by a search for consensus. Echoing Ian Clark's emphasis on contestation and consensus-building, Buchanan and Keohane argue that the legitimacy of international institutions depends upon whether there is ongoing, principled contestation of their goals, which requires engagement with actors outside the institution:

> [I]n the absence of global democracy. . . legitimacy depends crucially on the activities of external epistemic actors. Effective linkages between the institution and external epistemic actors constitute what might be called the transnational civil society channel of accountability. . . . Every feature of the institution becomes a potential object of principled, informed, collective deliberation, and eligibility for participation in deliberation will not be restricted by institutional interests.[86]

In a similar vein, Charles Sabel and Joshua Cohen claim that accountability "generally understood means presenting the account of one's choices that is owed to others in comparable situations."[87] When an actor is required to explain and justify its actions, accountability is enhanced. They argue that this form of accountability is analogous to the accountability provided by domestic administrative law (the requirements of hearings, transparency, notice and reason-giving, perhaps with judicial review). It is analogous and

---

[83] Hurd, "Legitimacy," *supra* note 71, at 1.
[84] Clark, *supra* note 71, at 4. See also Brunnée and Toope, *supra* note 38 at 6-19, 27-28 and 70-77 where they describe the "practice of legality" in similar terms.
[85] Clark, *id.* at 29–30.
[86] Buchanan and Keohane, *supra* note 70, at 432 and 434.
[87] Cohen and Sable, *supra* note 35, at 779.

not the same, because there is no global state to enforce global administrative law,[88] but it serves a similar purpose through systems of reporting, mutual reason-giving, and peer review. The EU, for example, does not have a coherent body of administrative law structuring how broad policy objectives are translated into specific regulations at that national level or in EU institutions, but decision making at key steps is "transparent, accessible to relevant parties in civil society as well as affected administrators, and deliberative in the sense of providing reasons for decisions."[89] In a consent-based international legal system, those who make the rules and those who are subject to them are one and the same (states). But as international law begins to have a more direct effect on individuals, communities, and corporations, then expectations grow that these nonstate actors should be able to participate more actively in making, interpreting, and applying the law. And as the value of democratic deliberation to sound decision making gains traction internationally, the overlap with transnational legal discourse—engaging individuals, nongovernmental organizations, corporations, and levels of government other than the executive branch—becomes apparent.

V. CONCLUSION

To summarize, argumentation matters to world politics. International legal and international relations theorists have converged on this insight and have begun to explore why that is the case and how much it matters. The line of thinking comes more naturally to lawyers because argument is their stock in trade, and because international legal scholars have spent decades trying to understand and explain why law matters in a decentralized legal system where enforcement and authoritative dispute settlement are rare. What is striking in this story is the compatibility of the case for transnational democratic deliberation with that for legal argumentation. Returning to Habermas, deliberation is the process by which rules and institutions are legitimated *discursively*:

> A discourse theory of law. . . might not solve the tension [between the ideal of single right answers and the fallibility of actual decision-making], but at least it takes it seriously. Such a theory relies on a strong concept of procedural rationality that locates the properties constitutive of a decision's validity not only to the logicosemantic dimension of constructing arguments and connecting statements,

---

[88] Cohen and Sabel were strongly influenced by the "global administrative law" project of Kingsbury, Krisch and Stewart, which sees the emergence of a relatively autonomous body of regulatory programs at the global level and asks whether global administrative law principles can be or are being developed to ensure the accountability of those making these rules. See Benedict Kingsbury, Nico Krisch and Richard Stewart, "The Emergence of Global Administrative Law," 68 *Law and Contemporary Problems* 3–4, 15–61 (2005).

[89] Cohen and Sable, *supra* note 35, at 782.

but also in *the pragmatic dimension of the justification process itself*. . . . [O]ne cannot exclude the possibility that new information and better reasons will be brought forward. Under favorable conditions, we bring argumentation to *de facto* conclusion only when the reasons solidify against the horizon of unproblematic background assumptions into such a coherent whole that an uncoerced agreement on the acceptability of the disputed validity claim emerges.[90]

Legal argumentation, like democratic deliberation, will not lead to objectively right answers or compel agreement, let alone action, but it does help to solidify agreement until new, better arguments and reasons are introduced. The "force of the better argument" can never completely supplant the influence of material power—those with the most power will, if nothing else, be able to shape the agenda and terms of discourse, pressing arguments that work to their advantage and suppressing others. But the felt need to engage in reasoned exchange levels the playing field. To the extent that IOs are conducive to that kind of reasoned exchange, their legitimacy is enhanced.

---

[90] Habermas, *Between Fact and Norms,* 226–27 (William Rehg translator, 1996).

3

INTERPRETIVE COMMUNITIES

I. INTRODUCTION

IN CHAPTER 2, I discussed the connection between democratic deliberation and legal argumentation, drawing on Habermas's theory of communicative action. In this Chapter, I develop the concept of an interpretive community to explain how and why argumentation structures international order and affects state behavior. I do so in several steps. I begin by discussing the nature of interpretation and interpretive communities. In the second part, I consider the composition of interpretive communities and how they relate to formal international organizations. Then I explain two principal functions that interpretive communities serve: they set the parameters of legal discourse and, in effect, pass judgment on legal claims (thereby impacting compliance with law); and they define/interpret/extend the rules of international life (thereby impacting evolution of the law). I conclude with a discussion of the legitimacy of interpretive communities, parallel to the argument at the end of Chapter 2 on the legitimacy of international organizations.

II. THE CONCEPT OF AN INTERPRETIVE COMMUNITY

States feel compelled to justify their actions on the basis of law. *Why* they feel so compelled is a difficult question. The reasons are both interest-related (instrumental) and identity-related (constructivist). To summarize an argument that I expand on below, states have an interest in appearing to be law abiding because reciprocal compliance by other states is more likely, longer-term cooperation in the same and other areas is more likely, and almost all states benefit from the predictability and stability of a law-based international system. The constructivist explanation is that states develop a sense of obligation through participation in international regimes. The law becomes internalized in various ways, and compliance becomes a matter of habit, or at least the burden of persuasion shifts to those who would seek to defy norms as conventionally understood.

Before elaborating on why, a preliminary question is: Who decides whether the legal justification is sound? Who renders authoritative interpretations of the law? A skeptic could concede that states have an interest in *appearing* to be law abiding, but international law is so vague and malleable that a legal justification can be found for virtually any position. If that is true, then the law cannot possibly be a constraint. Yet there is a logical flaw in that position. If any legal argument is as good as any other, then no purpose would be served by trying to justify one's acts in legal terms. Nothing would be gained or lost from doing so. Yet, empirically, states almost always try to claim that their actions are consistent with the law. It is extremely rare to hear a leader say, "we don't care about international law"; what he or she says when challenged is, "this is how we interpret the law, and our interpretation is correct." The United States worked hard to present the best legal case it could for military action against Iraq. Those making the arguments must have seen some purpose in doing so and, by logical extension, they must have assumed there was a way of distinguishing good claims from bad (knowing the issue was unlikely ever to be decided by a court). Then the question becomes, who makes that distinction? My answer is: the interpretive community.[1]

---

[1] See Ian Johnstone, "Security Council Deliberations: The Power of the Better Argument," 14 *European Journal of International Law* at 437–80 (2003). The idea of interpretive communities comes from Stanley Fish, a literary theorist who has written extensively on interpretation of domestic but not international law. See especially, *Is There a Text in this Class? The Authority of Interpretive Communities* (1980) and *Doing What Comes Naturally: Change, Rhetoric, and the Practice of Theory in Literary and Legal Studies* 141–42 (1989). The first time the term was applied to international law was Ian Johnstone, "Treaty Interpretation: The Authority of Interpretive Communities," 12 *Michigan Journal of International Law* 371 (1991). The main intellectual debt in the international legal field is Oscar Schachter, "The Invisible College of International Lawyers" 72 *Northwestern University Law Review* (1997). For other references to the concept by international relations and law scholars, see Robert Keohane, "International Relations and International Law: Two Optics," 38 *Harvard International Law Journal* 487, 491 (1997); Abram Chayes and Antonia Handler Chayes, *The New Sovereignty: Compliance with International Regulatory Agreements*, 279 (1995); Jutta Brunnée and Stephen Toope, *Legitimacy and Legality in International Law: An Interactional Account* 80 (2010); José Alvarez, "Constitutional Interpretation in International Organizations," in *The Legitimacy of International Organizations* 133–35 (Jean-Marc Coicaud and Veijo Heiskanen eds., 2001); Harold Koh, "Why do Nations Obey International Law?," 106 *Yale Law Journal* 2599, 2639 (1997); Andrew Hurrell, "International Law and the Changing Constitution of International Society," in *The Role of Law in International Politics* 331 (M. Byers ed. 2001); Michael Van Alstine, "Dynamic Treaty Interpretation," 146 *University of Pennsylvania Law Review* 687, 776 (1998); Robert Howse, "Adjudicative Legitimacy and Treaty Interpretation in International Trade Law: The Early Years of WTO Jurisprudence," in *The EU, the WTO and the NAFTA: Towards a Common Law of International Trade* 35, 57 (J.H. Weiler ed., 2000).

The starting point for understanding the power of interpretive communities is the idea that legal practice, as Ronald Dworkin and others have argued persuasively, is fundamentally an exercise in interpretation.[2] In a domestic legal system, judges are the primary interpreters. In the decentralized international legal system, much law is interpreted not by a disinterested, impartial arbiter but by domestic officials who are institutionally and politically predisposed to interpretations that favor their government or state. This could be taken as proof that legal interpretation is an unconstrained activity driven entirely by calculations of interest and power politics. Consistent with a subjective theory of legal interpretation, this perspective emphasizes the creative role of the interpreter and denies that objectivity is possible, given the inherent ambiguity of words. It is the polar opposite of a "textualist" approach, according to which language is determinate, and meaning can be extracted from a text by a reader who employs the correct process. The notion of interpretive communities splits the difference between these two positions. It sees interpretive authority as residing in neither reader nor text but in the community of experts and interested participants engaged in the field of practice in which the interpretive dispute arises.

The concept of interpretive communities was developed by Stanley Fish, a literary theorist, who claims it has explanatory power both in his field and in the field of legal interpretation. Designed to avoid the pitfalls of both pure objectivity (meaning resides in the text) and pure subjectivity (meaning resides in the reader), it is best understood as a way of speaking about the power of institutional settings, within which assumptions, beliefs, and modes of argument are so deeply entrenched that they come to be seen as matters of common sense.[3] According to Fish, "interpretive communities" explain both the fact of disagreement (if texts have their own meaning, why do so many readers disagree?) and agreement (if texts mean what each reader wants them to mean, why do so many agree?). An interpretive community provides "the assumed distinctions, categories of understandings and stipulations of relevance and irrelevance" that make agreement possible, not because meaning can be extracted from texts but because of the communal

---

[2] Ronald Dworkin, "Law as Interpretation," 60 *Texas Law Review* 27 (1982). See also Cass Sunstein, *Legal Reasoning and Political Conflict* 167 (1996) ("interpretation is a pervasive part of legal thinking"); Cass Sunstein, *The Constitution of Many Minds: Why the Founding Document Doesn't Mean What it Meant Before* (2009); Friedrich Kratochwil, "How do Norms Matter?," in *The Role of Law in International Politics* 42 (M. Byers ed.,2000); Richard Fallon Jr., "Reflections on Dworkin and the Two Faces of Law," 67 *Notre Dame Law Review* 553 (1992). For a critique of the view that law is fundamentally an interpretive practice, see Dennis Patterson, "The Poverty of Interpretive Universalism: Toward the Reconstruction of Legal Theory," 72 *Texas Law Review* (1993).

[3] These assumptions and beliefs are, for the community associated with the particular institutional setting, "facts," which are not immutable but provide objectivity within a community of interpretation where they need not be questioned. Kenneth Abraham, "Statutory Interpretation and Literary Theory: Some Common Concerns of an Unlikely Pair," in *Interpreting Law and Literature: A Hermeneutic Reader* 115, 122–24 (S. Levinson and S. Mailloux eds., 1988).

nature of the interpretive act.[4] It constrains interpretation by providing the mode of argumentation that is embedded in the relevant practice or enterprise. All professional interpreters, Fish argues, are situated within an institutional context, and interpretive activity only makes sense in terms of the purposes of the enterprise in which the interpreter is participating.[5] Texts do not have properties before they are encountered in situations or fields of practice; the meanings they have are always a function of the circumstances in which they are encountered.[6] Thus, interpretation is constrained not by the language of the text, or its context, but by the "cultural assumptions within which both texts and contexts take shape for situated agents."[7] Meaning is produced by neither the text nor the reader but by the interpretive community in which both are situated.

The idea of interpretive communities runs counter to the view that meaning is radically indeterminate. Rational discourse about competing interpretations within an enterprise is possible as long as there is an understanding, largely tacit, of the enterprise's general purpose.[8] Disputes over meaning are resolvable through the conventions of argument, judgment, and persuasion as they operate in the relevant discipline.[9] The professional interpreter is a participant in a particular field of practice and is engaged in interpretive activity that must be persuasive to others. In that capacity, he or she acts as an extension of an institutional community; failure to act in that way would be stigmatized as inconsistent with the conventions and purposes of that community. In other words, if the interpreter proffers an interpretation that reaches beyond the range of responses dictated by the conventions of the enterprise, he or she is not likely to be persuasive within that community.

---

[4] Fish, *Doing What Comes Naturally*, *supra* note 1.

[5] Cass Sunstein makes the same point: "Knowledge of the law consists in large part of prevailing interpretive practices within the legal community... In any field interpretive practices should be chosen because of the setting in which interpretation occurs... Interpretive practices are a function of the role in which interpreters find themselves." Sunstein, *supra* note 2, at 33 and 169.

[6] Stanley Fish, "Fish v. Fiss," 36 *Stanford Law Review* 1325, 1335 (1984). Stanley Fish and Owen Fiss engaged in a sustained debate over the way in which interpretation is constrained in domestic legal systems. Fiss, borrowing the idea of interpretive communities from Fish, posited a concept of "bounded objectivity" and argued that judges are constrained by "disciplining rules" to which they are committed by virtue of the office they occupy. Owen Fiss, "Objectivity and Interpretation," 34 *Stanford Law Review* 739 (1982). Fish responded that appeals to the authority of the judicial office do not help, because the disciplining rules to which judges are presumably committed are in need of interpretation themselves. The constraints on interpretation are not external but rather are embedded in the practice or enterprise of judicial interpretation itself. Stanley Fish, *Doing What Comes Naturally supra* note 1, at 141–42.

[7] Fish, *supra* note 1, at 300.

[8] *Fish v. Fiss*, *supra* note 6, at 1343.

[9] Fish, *Doing What Comes Naturally*, *supra* note 1, at 116. "Interpreters are constrained by their tacit awareness of what is possible and not possible to do, what is and is not a reasonable thing to say, what will and will not be heard as evidence, in a given enterprise; and it is within those same constraints that they see and bring others to see the shape of the documents to whose interpretation they are committed." Stanley Fish, "Working on the Chain Gang: Interpretation in Law and Literature," 60 *Texas Law Review* 551, 562 (1982).

Fish's theory of interpretation has much in common with Ronald Dworkin's theory of law, although the two have debated each other in print.[10] Dworkin puts interpretation at the center of his theory and, like Fish, seeks a middle ground between pure objectivity and pure subjectivity. He, too, stresses that interpretation is enterprise specific and claims that constraints are inherent in the enterprise.[11] He describes law as an "argumentative attitude"[12] and, in the simplest formulation of his thesis, states that "constructive interpretation is a matter of imposing purpose on an object or practice in order to make of it the best possible example of the form or genre to which it is taken to belong."[13] In short, the goal of interpretation is to make a text the best it can be.

Dworkin divides interpretation into three stages in which different degrees of consensus are needed if the interpretive attitude is to flourish.[14] In the first, "pre-interpretive" stage, there must be a great degree of consensus within a community about the rules and standards taken to provide the tentative content of the practice.[15] To illustrate the

---

[10] In a nutshell, Dworkin argues that the constraints imposed by the practices of the professional literary community are so weak that interpretation is rendered wholly subjective by Fish's theory. Fish, on the other hand, finds Dworkin's account of interpretation to be generally attractive but accuses him of falling away from his own best insights about the fallacies of pure objectivity by assuming that existing law in the form of a chain of decisions has, at some level, the status of "brute fact" and is not the product of interpretation. See Dworkin, "Law as Interpretation," *supra* note 2; Fish, "Working on the Chain Gang," *supra* note 9; Dworkin, "My Reply to Stanley Fish (and Walter Benn Michaels): Please Don't Talk about Objectivity Any More," in *The Politics of Interpretation* 287 (1983); Fish, "Wrong Again," 62 *Texas Law Review* at 299 (1983); and Ronald Dworkin, *Law's Empire* 77 and 425 note 23 (1986). An article that compares and criticizes both theories is Dennis Patterson, "The Poverty of Interpretive Universalism: Toward the Reconstruction of Legal Theory," 72 *Texas Law Review* (1993). For Fish's response to Patterson, see "How Come You Do Me Like You Do? A Response to Dennis Patterson," 72 *Texas Law Review* 57 (1993). Patterson's counter-reply is "You Made Me Do It: My Reply to Stanley Fish," 72 *Texas Law Review* 67 (1993).

[11] "The history or shape of a practice or object constrains the available interpretations of it." Dworkin, *Law's Empire, id.* at 52. "Participants in a practice: share a vocabulary, must understand the world in similar ways and have interests and convictions sufficiently similar to recognize the sense in each other's claims, to treat them as claims rather than just noises. That means not just using the same dictionary but sharing what Wittgenstein called a form of life sufficiently concrete so that the one can recognize the sense and purpose in what the other says and does." *Id.* at 63.

[12] "Law's empire is defined by attitude, not territory or power or process... It is an interpretive, self-reflective attitude addressed to politics in the broadest sense... Law's attitude is constructive: it aims, in the interpretive spirit to lay principle over practice, to show the best route to a better future, keeping the right faith with the past. It is, finally, a fraternal attitude, an expression of how we are united in community though divided in project, interest and conviction." *Law's Empire, supra* note 10 at 413.

[13] *Id.* at 52.

[14] The following account is from *id.* at 65–68.

[15] "Law cannot flourish as an interpretive enterprise in any community unless there is enough initial agreement about what practices are legal practices so that lawyers argue about the best interpretation of roughly the same data... I do not mean that all lawyers everywhere and always must agree on exactly which practices should count as practices of law, but only that lawyers of any culture where the interpretive attitude succeeds must largely agree at any one time. We all enter history of an interpretive practice at a particular point; the necessary pre-interpretive agreement is in that way contingent and local." *Id.* at 90–91. Note that Dworkin states explicitly

point, Dworkin states the following about the concept of justice: "the thesis that abstract art is unjust is not even unattractive, it is incomprehensible as a theory about justice because no competent pre-interpretive account of the practice of justice embraces the criticism and evaluation of art."[16] At the second, interpretive stage, interpreters share some convictions about the standard features of the practice and why it is worth pursuing; if one advances justifications or interpretations that go beyond the accepted boundaries of a practice, one is marked "as outside the community of useful or at least ordinary discourse about the institution." At the third, post-interpretive stage, the interpreter needs more substantive convictions about what kinds of justifications really would show the practice in the best light.[17] According to Dworkin, what matters at the post-interpretive stage is not so much the conventions of an interpretive community but rather the coherent set of principles that reside in the "political structure and legal doctrine of the community" as a whole.[18] Hard cases arise when the threshold test of fit (at the second stage) does not discriminate between two or more competing interpretations. To decide which of those interpretations is "right" (in Dworkin's theory, there is only one right answer), his ideal judge, Hercules, must ask "which shows the community's structure and institutions and decisions—its public standards as a whole—in a better light from the standpoint of political morality."[19]

Thus, Dworkin and Fish share the view that law is an interpretive practice and that all interpretation is enterprise specific, in the sense that different standards and techniques of interpretation apply in different enterprises. They also agree that legal interpretation is constrained in some way (it is not purely subjective or discretionary), but they disagree about the source of the constraint. Fish sees interpretation as an inter-subjective enterprise, whereas Dworkin's Hercules is engaged in a more private exercise—a "conversation with himself, as joint author and critic."[20] Moreover, Dworkin believes that Hercules can and should appeal to something external to the law—moral and political philosophy—to decide what puts it in its best light. Cass Sunstein is troubled by this feature of Dworkin's theory. He argues that lawyers' inquiry into what is the best interpretation of the law draws from principles already internal to the legal culture. It centers not on political philosophy but on "what positions now within the legal culture can be supplied by good arguments."[21] Friederich Kratochwil makes the more pointed critique that attempting to

---

that some interpretation is necessary even at the preinterpretive stage. But because the degree of consensus is so great, the classifications it yields are treated as given in day-to-day reflection and argument. *Id.* at 66.

[16] *Law's Empire, supra* note 10, at 75.
[17] *Id.* at 68.
[18] *Id.* at 255.
[19] *Id.* at 256.
[20] This is Dworkin's metaphor for interpretation. *Law's Empire, supra* note 10, at 58.
[21] Cass Sunstein, *The Partial Constitution* 113 (1993). In this respect, Sunstein's position is closer to that of Stanley Fish although he also criticizes the latter's approach on the grounds that it amounts essentially to a rejection of

show there are single right answers, even in hard cases, is virtually impossible because in a pluralist environment, those principles are deeply contested.[22] Fish insists that his account of interpretation cannot be faulted on the grounds that it is a private affair—that it is a "conversation with oneself"[23]—but his notion of a professional community of interpreters has been criticized for being too insular, too little open to critical reflection and influences from outside the community.[24]

Habermas, in considering this problem, emphasizes the importance of *argumentation* to legal interpretation.[25] Normative judgments, he argues, are made not by logical inference or conclusive evidence but "discursively. . . by way of a justification that is carried out with arguments."[26] From this perspective, legal discourse is interactive, and the political

---

the idea that interpretive disputes can be settled through reason or argument (at 114). Sunstein later extends the argument to suggest that the US constitution is the product of "many minds" and that more than one approach to interpretation is acceptable (indeed necessary), but reaching for answers beyond the US legal culture is inappropriate because it will simply add complexity without producing better outcomes. Sunstein, *The Constitution of Many Minds, supra* note 2 at 209.

[22] Kratochwil, *supra* note 2, at 42. See also Howse, *supra* note 1, at 41 Although this critique of the one right answer thesis would seem to carry particular weight in the international legal order, Thomas Franck finds much in Dworkin's theory of law as integrity that is useful for his own analysis of fairness discourse in international law and institutions. See Thomas Franck, *Fairness in International Law and Institutions* 7, 14 and 26–46 (1995).

[23] In responding to Patterson, Fish strongly and persuasively counters the charge that his theory does not give due account to the role of inter-subjectivity in the constitution of meaning: "but that's all I do; that's what interpretive communities are all about." "How Come You Do Me Like You Do?," *supra* note 10, at 60.

[24] Andrew Goldsmith, "Is there Any Backbone in This Fish? Interpretive Communities, Social Criticism and Transgressive Legal Practice," 23 *Law and Social Inquiry* 373 (1998). See also Patterson, *supra* note 10. Fish does offer an account of how members of an interpretive community may change their mind or views (*Doing What Comes Naturally, supra* note 1, at 146), but some of his explanations of the internal constraints on interpretation seem to suggest that it is intellectually impossible for an interpreter to diverge from the conventions of his or her community. For example, he says that the interpreter is "possessed by. . . a tacit knowledge that tells him not so much what to do, but already has him doing it as a condition of perception and even thought." *Fish v. Fiss, supra* note 6, at 1333.

[25] Habermas questions whether Dworkin's "monological" or single author model of Judge Hercules, distinguished by his privileged access to the truth, should be held up as a political ideal. Habermas, *Between Facts and Norm.* Trans. by William Rehg (1966). He cites approvingly Frank Michaelman's complaint that Hercules is a loner: "What is lacking is dialogue. . . His narrative constructions are monologous. He converses with no one except through books. He has no encounters. He meets no otherness. Nothing shakes him up. No interlocutor violates the inevitable insularity of his experience and outlook." Frank I. Michaelman, "The Supreme Court 1985 Term–Foreword: Traces of Self-Government," 100 *Harvard Law Review* 76 (1986).

[26] Habermas, *Between Facts and Norms, id.* at 226. Substantial reasons cannot "compel" an end to normative argument. The discourse rather, is an unending process of argumentation striving toward a limit, which is only reached provisionally when an uncoerced agreement on the acceptability of the disputed claim emerges (at 227). "The practice of argumentation is characterized by the intention of winning the assent of a universal audience to a problematic proposition in a non-coercive but regulated contest for the better arguments based on the best information and reasons. . . Whether norms and values could find the rationally motivated assent of all those affected can be judged only from the intersubjectively enlarged perspective of the first-person plural" (at 228).

ideal is "an open society of interpreters."[27] In the international legal system, it seems that something approximating an open society of interpreters actually exists. There are institutions whose legal opinions carry special weight, such as the International Court of Justice, but because the system is non-hierarchical, no single institution has ultimate interpretative authority. The influence of court judgments and advisory opinions, decisions of intergovernmental bodies, statements of governmental officials, scholarly articles, op-ed pieces, and the views of the many other participants in the international legal process depend as much on their persuasive power as institutional authority.[28]

Thus, legal discourse is not simply the search for a negotiated agreement on the meaning and application of legal terms. Nor is it the search for some legal truth "out there," waiting to be discovered. It is an inter-subjective practice that operates on the basis of common understandings about the relationship governed by the rules in question and the manner in which those rules should be interpreted. Gerald Postema's description of friendship as a social practice helps illustrate what inter-subjective interpretation means:

> The history of the friendship is a common history and the complex meaning of the relationship is collectively constructed [by the friends] over the course of the history. When friends share a common history, Aristotle points out, it is not like cows sharing a pasture, for the shared life of friends engenders common perception, a common perspective, and common discourse. Friendship is characterized, ultimately, not by sympathy or consensus, but by common deliberation and thought. . . A friend's understanding of the relationship could only be achieved through interaction with the other. . . To regard the meaning of that relationship as the private interpretive construct of one or the other, or some ideal limit of such constructs, fails to recognize the common perspective and discourse which structures the relationship.[29]

Although legal interpretation is not based on trust in the way friendship is, the interactive nature of the enterprise is analogous. The interpretive task is to ascertain what the law means to the lawmakers collectively, rather than to any one of them individually. The interpretive community is the device through which that collective understanding is derived and expressed, not in a mechanical way but through a diffuse discursive process that can be observed, if not pinned down with precision. Because there is tacit agreement

---

[27] *Id.* at 223.
[28] Thomas Franck argues that the weight of even a court judgment in a domestic legal system comes down to persuasive power: "The power of the court to do justice depends on the persuasiveness of the judge's discourse, persuasive in the sense that it reflects not their own but society's value preferences." Franck, *supra* note 22.
[29] Gerald J. Postema, 'Protestant' Interpretation and Social Practices," 6 *Law and Philosophy* 283, 309–10 (1987).

among members of the interpretive community, rational discourse is possible, and they can distinguish good legal arguments from bad ones.

III. INTERPRETIVE COMMUNITIES AND INTERNATIONAL ORGANIZATIONS

While the term "interpretive community" is meant to describe the nature of interpretation and not an actual collection of people with membership cards, it is useful to consider who might belong to this community to appreciate that the concept is not a mere abstraction. It is like, but not identical to, an epistemic community[30]—the main difference being that an interpretive community offers not only knowledge and policy advice but more importantly, passes judgment. Like the "communities of practice" posited by Emanuel Adler, members of an interpretive community are engaged in a shared enterprise with broadly similar understandings of what they are doing and why they are doing it.[31] It is easiest to imagine a community composed of two, and perhaps three, concentric circles. The inner circle consists of individuals responsible for the creation and implementation of a particular legal norm. It is surrounded by a second circle of government officials, lawyers, and other experts engaged in professional activities associated with the practice or issue area regulated by the norm. The line between the inner and second circle is blurred. Thus, for example, in the case of NATO's intervention in Kosovo (see Chapter 4), representatives of governments who were not on the Security Council (SC) but who participated in the deliberations, and had been involved in Council debates on humanitarian intervention in the past (like India), or had a special stake in the outcome (like Bosnia) are in both the inner and second circles. Around these two concentric circles is an even more amorphous constellation of actors whose interests are affected and—to the extent that deliberative principles have traction at the transnational level—accounted for by those in the two inner circles.

To be more precise, the inner circle (the narrow interpretive community) consists primarily of a network of government and intergovernmental officials who, through the process of formulating, negotiating, adopting, and applying rules, come to share a set of assumptions, expectations, and a body of consensual knowledge. This consensual knowledge yields understandings and stipulations of relevance and irrelevance that enables them to interpret a text in common. Thus, for example, in the debate over the interpretation of the Anti-Ballistic Missile Treaty sparked by the Reagan Administration's desire to develop and test its Strategic Defense Initiative (known as "star wars"), the inner circle

---

[30] Peter Haas, "Introduction: Epistemic Communities and International Policy Coordination" 46 *International Organization* 1–35 (Winter 1992).

[31] Emanuel Adler, *Communitarian International Relations: The Epistemic Foundations of International Relations* 22 (2005). See also Brunnée and Toope, *supra* note 1 at 80.

included U.S. negotiators of the treaty, such as Gerard Smith and Paul Nitze, senators involved in its ratification such as Sam Nunn, and government officials in power at the time of the proposed reinterpretation, such as legal adviser Abraham Sofaer.[32]

The second circle (or broader community) is an amorphous group of all those regarded as possessing expertise in international law and/or special knowledge in the relevant field. It includes what Oscar Schachter has called the invisible college of international lawyers—a group of professionals dispersed throughout the world who are dedicated to a common intellectual enterprise and engage in a continuous process of communication and collaboration.[33] It also includes political leaders, diplomats, government officials, international civil servants, scholars, and experts who participate in some way in the particular field of international law or practice in which the interpretive dispute arises. Their competency or expertise comes from training and immersion in the law or practice. As participants in the field, they have come to understand its purpose and conventions, learned not merely as a set of abstract rules but through the acquisition of know-how, a mastering of discipline or technique.[34] They may not share all the same values, but the members of the legal interpretive community share a perspective and way of understanding the world acquired through their immersion in the law and interaction with one another. A legal adviser, either to a government or international organization, is an important member of both the inner and second circles. Her job is to serve a client, but performing that job well requires her to provide opinions based on her best judgment of what the law is. The opinion of a legal adviser to a government is a gauge of what the judgment of the interpretive community is likely to be on a particular course of action. The opinion of a legal adviser to an international organization is that plus an element of community judgment itself.

The third, outermost circle is analogous to the public sphere discussed in Chapter 2. It encompasses social movements, the media, and informal networks or what may be called transnational civil society.[35] These are not necessarily experts in the field of practice, but rather people who are affected by the legal issues at stake and/or who purport to speak for those who are affected. They are the broad audience who listen to and critique the reasons given by policy makers for the decisions they make, on the basis of values as well as

---

[32] Johnstone, "Treaty Interpretation" *supra* note 1, at 399–402. See also Harold Koh, "Transnational Legal Process," 75 *Nebraska Law Review* 181 (1996).

[33] Schachter, *supra* note 1, at 217.

[34] Postema, *supra* note 29, at 304.

[35] The seminal book on transnational civil society is Ann Florini ed., *Third Force: The Rise of Transnational Civil Society* (2000). Two good accounts of transnational civil society in global governance are Jen Steffeck, Claudia Kissging and Patrizia Nanz eds., *Civil Society Participation in European and Global Goverance: A Cure for the Democratic Deficit* (2008), and Jan Aart Scholte, "Civil Society and Democratically Accountable Global Governance," in *Global Governance and Public Accountability* 87 (D. Held and M. Koenig-Archibugi eds., 2005).

technocratic considerations. The legitimating impact of this outermost circle is discussed at the end of this chapter.

Interpretive communities tend to coalesce around international organizations (IOs), in part because a good deal of international law is made there. Treaties are negotiated in the UN General Assembly, the WTO, the International Labor Organization, and the plenary bodies of regional organizations; binding decisions are made in the UN Security Council and European Union Council; regulations are adopted by the European Commission and in some specialized agencies like the International Civil Aviation Organization; and customary law crystallizes in the practices and declaratory resolutions of a host of organizations.[36] Many of the government officials directly involved in the making of law are diplomatic representatives to IOs. Secretariat officials are often involved in drafting treaties and resolutions or at least participating in the negotiations that lead to them. IOs often oversee implementation of the law, and so committees like the human rights treaty bodies form for the purpose of interpreting the law and monitoring compliance. Even when there is no formal oversight mechanism, the diplomatic representatives, intergovernmental officials, and associated experts in these organizations develop the "know-how" that gives their opinions special weight.

Moreover, international secretariats can serve as focal points for governmental and nongovernmental networks to form and mobilize in support of particular objectives. Neo-functionalist theory imagined that the European Commission would become the motor or driving force for European integration—the place where interest groups and policy elites would forge alliances to exert pressure for community-wide policies. That never happened in quite the way the neo-functionalists predicted, but the Commission is the heart of vast network of intergovernmental, governmental, and nongovernmental actors that share some common ground in their understanding of the object and purpose of European law. Similarly, the International Labour Office (ILO) is at the core of a group of governmental, labor, and business representatives who dedicate their professional lives to making, interpreting, and applying labor law. The United Nations Environment Programme (UNEP) played that role in respect of environmental treaties in the past, and one of the arguments for upgrading it to a specialized agency (or even a "World Environment Organization") is to recapture some of that glory.[37] As incubators of coalitions, IOs are places where transnational advocacy networks of nongovernmental organizations (NGOs), social movements, and activists go to make their influence felt.

---

[36] On the range of ways in which international organizations make law, see José Alvarez, *International Organizations as Law-Makers* (2006).

[37] See generally Frank Bierman and Steffen Bauer eds., *A World Environment Organization: Solution Or Threat For Effective International Environmental Governance?* (2005); James Gustave Speth and Peter Haas, *Global Environmental Governance: Foundations of Contemporary Environmental Studies* (2006); Regina Axelrod, Stacy Van Deveer and David Leonard Downie eds, *The Global Environment: Institutions, Law and Policy* (3rd ed., 2010).

And they are places where transgovernmental networks of legislators, judges, and bureaucrats find common cause.[38]

When legal disputes arise on issues that fall within the scope of the organization's competence, these coalitions configure as diffuse interpretive communities that pass legal judgment. How cohesive the judgment is varies across organizations. Functional organizations in heavily regulated areas are more likely to serve as incubators of a unified interpretive community rather than multipurpose organizations—especially where developing law and policy requires a high degree of expertise (environmental science, for example, or health). But even in multipurpose organizations like the EU and UN, government officials and attentive publics invest a good deal of effort in trying to shape and influence events, creating the conditions for a vibrant interpretive community. Moreover, the more the organization operates on the basis of "hard law"—precise, obligatory norms that provide for some impartial, third-party oversight[39]—the more influential the interpretive community is likely to be because there is a more solid foundation on which to base legal judgments.

To summarize, an interpretive community loosely composed of three concentric circles of officials, professionals, and civil society representatives associated with a field of legal practice sets the parameters of discourse surrounding that practice and affects how the law is interpreted and applied. It is the arbiter of what constitutes a good legal claim; it represents the institutional mechanism closest to an impartial arbiter that most international disputes provide. Its influence derives from its ability to issue credible legal judgments. It wields that influence directly by evaluating particular interpretations and applications of the law, and indirectly in the way that states measure their own interpretations against anticipated judgment of the community. The extent of influence depends on how unified the interpretive community is, which varies with the setting. If after extensive deliberation on an issue international legal opinion is sharply divided, then almost by definition no interpretive 'community' exists, or perhaps there are multiple communities. They tend to be most unified when coalesced around a valued international organization that operates on the basis of formal rules and procedures (like the EU), as opposed to less "institutionalized" organizations that serve mainly as venues for intergovernmental meetings and broad policy making (like the G20).

---

[38] On networks generally, see Chayes and Chayes, *supra* note 1, citing with approval Robert Keohane and Joseph Nye's seminal work, "Transgovernmental relations and international organizations," 27 *World Politics* 51 (1974). See also, Margaret Keck and Katherine Sikkink, *Activists Beyond Borders: Advocacy Networks in International Politics* (1998) on transnational advocacy networks; and Anne-Marie Slaughter, *A New World Order* (2004) on transgovernmental networks.

[39] Goldstein et al. eds., *Legalization and World Politics* (2001). But see the critique by Martha Finnemore and Stephen Toope, "Alternatives to Legalization: Richer Views of Law and Politics," 55 *International Organizations* 743 (2001).

IV. THE FUNCTIONS OF INTERPRETIVE COMMUNITIES

Interpretive communities impact both compliance with the law and its evolution. They achieve the first mainly by extracting reputational costs for noncompliance; they achieve the second mainly by serving as vehicles for transmitting new norms and promoting their internalization. In the next subsections, I address each function in turn.

A. Inducing Compliance

The power of interpretive communities is tied to the felt need to justify actions on the basis of law. At one level, this felt need comes down to instrumental calculations of interest. Governments cannot escape collective judgment of their conduct by other governments (expressed either bilaterally or in multilateral institutions), international lawyers, and organs of public opinion.[40] These appraisals matter because states have an interest in reciprocal compliance by others; they have a stake in preserving a reputation for reliability—to remain a member in "good standing in the regimes that make up the substance of international life"[41]; and because they have a long-term interest in the predictability and stability of a law-based international system.[42] Reputation is central to this instrumentalist account of compliance. Policy makers are concerned about preserving a reputation for honoring commitments.[43] International organizations play a role here because they create an incentive to cultivate a reputation for fidelity to the law. They both lengthen and broaden the "shadow of the future,"[44] meaning they are places where cooperation is institutionalized over time and across a range of issues. The more a state cares about future relations or cooperation on other issues, the more likely it is to play by the rules, even if it calculates that violating a particular rule would serve its short-term interests.

But a reputation for fidelity to the law is not the only kind of reputation that matters in international affairs. Powerful states also have a stake in preserving a reputation for

---

[40] Oscar Schachter, *International Law in Theory and Practice* (1991).

[41] Chayes and Chayes, *supra* note, 1 at 27. See also Thomas Franck, *The Power of Legitimacy Among Nations* 38 (1990).

[42] Andrew Hurrell argues that both weak and strong states have an interest in the maintenance of "a law-impregnated international community." For weak states, the "fabric of the international legal order bolsters their very ability to maintain themselves as 'states.'" Strong states, on the other hand, have a disproportionate influence in making the rules of the international order and have a stake in preserving the stability of the system from which they clearly benefit. Hurrell, *supra* note 1, at 60–61. Hurrell relies on Schachther, *supra* note 38, at 30.

[43] Keohane, "Two Optics," *supra* note 1. The most important recent work on reputation is by a lawyer, Andrew Guzman, *How International Law Works: A Rational Choice Theory* 71-117 (2008). But see Rachel Brewster, "Unpacking the State's Reputation", 50 *Harvard International Law Journal* 231 (2009) who claims that the impact of reputation is more complicated that Guzman suggests.

[44] Robert Axelrod, *The Evolution of Cooperation* (Revised Edition, 2006).

vigorously pursuing their interests, for helping their allies, and punishing their enemies.[45] That kind of reputation does not necessarily push in the direction of compliance with the law. Regarding Iraq in 2003, the Bush Administration may well have felt it was important to establish and uphold a reputation for toughness in dealing with "rogue states," even if that meant breaking the law (in Chapter 5, I consider whether the invasion really did break the law). IOs have a moderating effect because interaction within them is not a one-time event. There are situations in which a state will want to appear tough. But to the extent that it believes it benefits from participating in the institution, it has an incentive to preserve a reputation for playing by the rules. Institutions alter the incentives for cooperation by affecting the kind of reputation a state wants to cultivate.

This emphasis on reputation illustrates that the prospects for compliance with the law do not turn *entirely* on a straightforward calculation of interests. As important is the sense of internalized obligation that comes through the conduct of international relations and the practice of international law. Lawyers who draw on social constructivist international relations theory have offered alternative explanations of how this sense of obligation emerges and functions. Ryan Goodman and Derek Jinks have a developed a socialization theory that ties compliance to a process of acculturation whereby states adopt "the beliefs and behavior patterns of the surrounding culture."[46] Jutta Brunné and Stephen Toope present an "interactional" theory of legal obligation that ties the compliance pull of law to its congruence with shared understandings, specified criteria of legality, and enmeshment in an "interactive practice of legality".[47] Thomas Franck claimed, more straightforwardly, that pressure to comply comes from a common sense of being part of the community of states and a desire to remain a member in good standing of that community.[48] Obviously, the sense of obligation is not felt equally by all states, but it is pervasive enough that it impacts the conduct of international affairs. Most states participate in international regimes and, through that participation, internalize the norms they embody.[49] This internalization may well occur in the minds of decision makers; they may

---

[45] Keohane, "Two Optics", *supra* note 1; George Downs and Michael Jones, "Reputation, Compliance and International Law", XXXI *Journal of Legal Studies* 95 (2002).

[46] Ryan Goodman and Derek Jinks, "International Law and State Socialization: Conceptual, Empirical and Normative Challenges", 54 *Duke Law Journal* 983, 992 (2005).

[47] Brunnée and Toope, *supra* note 1 at 100-125.

[48] See Franck, *The Power of Legitimacy*, *supra* note 41, at 196. As the Chayes' put it, states are literally *bound up* in the international system and they want to remain in good standing in that system. "Sovereignty no longer exists in the freedom of states to act independently in their perceived self-interest but in membership in reasonably good standing in the regimes that make up the substance of international life". Chayes and Chayes, *supra* note 1 at 27. The *need* to remain an accepted member of the system is what ensures an acceptable level of compliance with international agreements.

[49] The most thoughtful recent work on socialization and internalization of norms is by legal scholars Ryan Goodman and Derek Jinks. See, for example, "Toward an Institutional Theory of Sovereignty", 55 *Stanford Law Review* 1749 (2003); "How to Influence States: Socialization and International Human Rights Law," 54 *Duke*

genuinely come to believe in the value of the norms. But even without that psychological dimension, socialization occurs when norms become embedded in domestic political, legal, and social systems. As Harold Koh explains,

> Social internalization occurs when a norm acquires so much public legitimacy that there is widespread general obedience to it. Political internalization occurs when political elites accept an international norm, and adopt it as a matter of government policy. Legal internalization occurs when an international norm is incorporated into the domestic legal system through executive action, judicial interpretation, legislative action or some combination of the three.[50]

Calculations of interest are still at work but filtered through political habits and bureaucratic routine. Breaking out of the routines is possible, but the burden of persuasion is on those who would act contrary to the norm as conventionally understood. And because this internalization of the law occurs in all states that participate in a regime, a multinational network emerges that operates roughly in harmony. The participants in the network operate more or less in parallel as an institutional check on less-cooperative forces within each state.

Reverting back to the types of communicative behavior discussed in Chapter 2, whether driven by the "civilizing" force of strategic argumentation or the logic of true reasoning and mutual persuasion, arguments can have an independent impact on behavior. According to the first logic, legal arguments advance interests because both the speaker and target of the argument see instrumental benefits from preserving a reputation for norm-guided behavior. According to the second logic, as Kratochwil explains: "Actors are not only programmed by rules and norms, but they reproduce and change by their practice the normative structures by which they are able to act, share meanings, communicate intentions, criticize claims and justify choices."[51] In other words, the practices of

---

Law Journal 621 (2004); "International law and state socialization", *supra* note 46; "Incomplete Internalization and Compliance with Human Rights Law," 19 *European Journal of International Law* 725 (2008).

[50] Harold Koh, "Why do Nations Obey International Law?," *supra* note 1. See also Harold Koh, "Bringing International Law Back Home," 35 *Houston Law Review* 623 (1998).

[51] Friederich Kratochwil, *Rules, norms and decisions: on the conditions of practical and legal reasoning in international relations and domestic affairs* 61 (1989). See also Thomas Risse "'Let's Argue': Communicative Action in World Politics," 54 *International Organization* 1, 10 (2000); Chayes, *supra* note 1 at 228; Keohane, "Two Optics," *supra* note 1 at 487. More fundamentally, Kratochwil questions the causal connection between norms and behavior that instrumental accounts try to make. In answering the question "how do norms matter?," he states that the causal connection is not necessarily one of mechanics. Instead, "a connection is established if we think along the lines of 'building a bridge' which allows us to get from 'here' to 'there.' This is what we do when we provide an account in terms of purposes or goals, or when we cite the relevant rule that provides the missing element, showing us the reasons which motivated us to act in a certain way. No 'mechanism,' no hammer hitting a lever, no springs, no billiard balls are involved here... We reconstruct a situation, view it from the perspective

states are affected by the normative environment in which they operate, but those practices can also change that normative environment.

B. Lawmaking

The above quote suggests that the line between implementation of existing law and "interstitial lawmaking" is blurry. It also serves as a starting point for explaining the role of interpretive communities in creating new law. The notion of norm entrepreneurship helps to illuminate the process.[52] Social constructivists define norms as "collective expectations for the proper behavior of actors with a given identity,"[53] a definition that captures legal and other sorts of norms (social, moral. . .).[54] Norm entrepreneurs are actors who seek to mobilize support for a cause and see it crystallized as an accepted standard of behavior. They are often leaders of powerful states. Thus U.S. presidents, post-WWII, were entrepreneurs in creating a normative and institutional architecture (in the UN, the Bretton Woods institutions, NATO, and even the European Economic Community) based on ideas they held about world order.[55] But not all norm entrepreneurs possess as much material power to back up their visions. The concept has its origins in the notion of "moral entrepreneurs," relatively powerless nonstate actors with a proselytizing mission.[56] Henri Dunant, founder of the International Committee of the Red Cross and father of international humanitarian law, is a prime example.[57]

Martha Finnemore and Katherine Sikkink have offered the most fully developed account of norm entrepreneurship. They describe a three-stage process.[58] Norms emerge in the first stage when individuals with strong ideas about appropriate behavior call

---

of the actor, and impute purposes and values based on the evidence provided by the actor himself (although not necessarily limited to his own testimony). This, in turn, provides us with an intelligible account of the reasons for acting. . ." Kratochwil, "How do Norms Matter," *supra* note 2 at 66.

[52] I develop this notion of norm entrepreneurship more fully in Ian Johnstone, "The Secretary-General as Norm Entrepreneur" in *Secretary or General?: The UN Secretary-General in World Politics* 123–38 (Simon Chesterman ed., 2007).

[53] Peter Katzenstein ed., "Introduction: Alternative Perspectives on National Security," in *The Culture of National Security* 5 (1996); Martha Finnemore and Kathryn Sikkink, "International Norm Dynamics and Political Change," 52 *International Organization* 887–917 (1998); Audi Klotz, *Norms in International Relations: The Struggle Against Apartheid* (1995); Martha Finnemore, *National Interests in International Society* (1996); Ann Florini, "The Evolution of International Norms," 40 *International Studies Quarterly* 363–89 (1996).

[54] IR theorists tend not to draw a sharp distinction between legal and other norms, to the dismay of lawyers Jutta Brunnée and Stephen Toope, "International Law and Constructivism: Elements of an Interactional Theory of International Law," 39 *Columbia Journal of Transnational Law* 19–74 (2000).

[55] John Ruggie, "The Past as Prologue? Interests, Identity and American Foreign Policy", 21 *International Security* (1997).

[56] Ethan Nadelmann, "Global Prohibition Regimes: The Evolution of Norms in International Society," 44 *International Organization* 479–526 (1990).

[57] Finnemore and Sikkink, *supra* note 53.

[58] *Id.*

attention to issues and try to persuade state leaders to embrace the norm. These norm entrepreneurs tend to use "organizational platforms"—sometimes NGOs, but often intergovernmental organizations like the World Bank, UN, or ILO—to induce state actors to endorse their norms, ideally but not necessarily in the form of specific rules. The second stage begins when a "tipping point" is reached, and a critical mass of leaders has been persuaded to promote the norm. At that point, the norm spreads rapidly in what the authors call a "norm cascade." This process of international socialization tends to be led by states but also involves networks of individuals, NGOs, and IOs who pressure targeted actors to adopt new policies and laws. It is largely an exercise in persuasion, not coercion, although the persuasion can be reinforced by sanctions and material incentives. In the final stage, the norms become internalized in the habits and minds of political elites and in the practices of national and international institutions. Through "iterated behavior," the norms solidify and become more widespread.[59]

Harold Koh's transnational legal process traces a similar pattern. Through a process of "interaction," "interpretation," and "internalization," the law acquires "stickiness": "as nations participate in transnational legal process, through a complex combination of rational self-interest, transnational interaction, norm-internalization and identity-formation, international law becomes a factor driving their international relations."[60] New norms emerge and take shape through interaction within and between states, and in a transnational process that involves representatives of NGOs, the private sector, and officials of IOs, as well as states. IOs provide a platform for some of that interaction, and interpretive communities that coalesce around them provide the context in which the rules of international life are defined, interpreted, and extended.

New norms rarely emerge out of whole cloth; norm entrepreneurs succeed best when they tap into emerging standards and expectations. Thus, normative evolution occurs through interpretation of the law and its application to particular cases—the interstitial lawmaking referred to by Kratochwil. Interpretation may be explicit, in the form of judicial or quasi-judicial opinions given by authoritative bodies, like the International Court of Justice, or public statements made by organization officials. When the United States and the United Kingdom launched airstrikes against Iraq in January 1993, Secretary-General Boutros Boutros-Ghali took the controversial position that the raid was authorized on the basis of resolutions 678 and 687: ". . . as Secretary-General of the United Nations, I can say that this action was taken and conforms to the resolutions of the Security Council and conforms to the Charter of the United Nations."[61] This statement was referred to in the letter the permanent representative of the United States sent to the president of the SC on March 20, 2003, setting out the legal case for military action

---

[59] *Id.* at 905.
[60] Koh, *supra* note 1.
[61] UN Department of Public Information Briefing, January 14, 1993, p. 2.

against Iraq.[62] The SG's interpretation of resolution 687 was helpful to the United States in making a plausible case for the intervention in 2003. Indeed, because the case was more plausible than self-defense on the basis of the doctrine of preemption, the official U.S. and UK justifications were based entirely on the enforcement of existing SC resolutions, as I discuss further in Chapter 6.

Interpretation may also occur implicitly, through the operational activities of IOs.[63] Those responsible for managing the activities are "norm entrepreneurs" if they must interpret the mandate given by intergovernmental bodies and exercise their discretion in carrying them out. Thus, for example, electoral assistance activities engaged in by international organizations like the UN, OAS, OSCE, and EU are implicit interpretations of the right to political participation.[64] When Kofi Annan departed Nigeria after his visit aimed at facilitating the transition to civilian rule there, he spoke of the importance of a speedy return to democracy. In view of the successful transition, culminating in the election of President Obasanjo in May 1999, the SG's trip could be seen as a significant step in reinforcing the sense of an emerging entitlement to democratic governance.[65] Chapter 8 traces a similar evolution with respect to the Guiding Principles for Internal Displacement.

Thus, interpretive communities not only pass judgment, they also shape the context for the making of new law through the practices of IOs. Normative evolution tends to succeed best when old rules are extended incrementally rather than torn down and replaced; interpretive communities set the parameters of discourse within which that incremental normative process occurs.

V. THE LEGITIMACY OF INTERPRETIVE COMMUNITIES

If interpretive communities do wield power, this raises legitimacy questions like those raised about IOs in Chapter 2: whose voices are heard loudest, what perspectives come to be taken for granted as matters of common sense, and whose interests are accounted for? Two arguments can be raised against the legitimacy of interpretive communities: (a) they are dominated by a hegemon, and/or (b) they are purely technocratic. In this subsection, I will elaborate on each critique and then offer an alternative perspective: that interpretive

---

[62] S/2003/351, March 21, 2003.
[63] Ian Johnstone, "Lawmaking through the operational activities of international organizations," 40 *George Washington International Law Review* 87 (2008).
[64] Gregory Fox, "The Right to Political Participation," in "International Law" 17 *Yale Journal of International Law* 539 (1992).
[65] Johnstone, *supra* note 63.

communities are nascent forms of *democratic* deliberation, open, inclusive, and penetrable by voices other than those of dominant players and technocrats.

As noted, critical legal theorists do not see legal discourse as an open exchange of arguments among equals but as a rhetorical edifice designed to give the impression that the rules are neutral and objective—that decisions can be made and conflicts resolved by appeals to "nonpolitical" standards. According to Marti Koskenniemi, modern international law is an elaborate argumentative structure rife with contradictions. All process and no substance, it fails to set down any determining legal standards: "it is impossible to make substantive decisions within the law which would imply no political choice. . . In the end, legitimizing or criticizing state behavior is not a matter of applying formally neutral rules but depends on what one regards as politically right or just."[66] Moreover, the form and substance of the legal discourse is so determined by powerful voices that all who participate in it have "internalized the hegemonic conception of what constitutes 'the better argument.'"[67] This Gramscian notion of hegemony sees the world as ruled not by brute force but by the dominant group developing an ideology based on values and understandings that come to be seen as legitimate by subordinate groups.[68] The main task that Gramscian international relations theorists have set for themselves is to identify the hidden normative agenda that underlies the existing order in order to challenge, undermine, and hopefully transform it.[69] From this perspective, interpretive communities are dominated by hegemonic voices. The rules on the use of force, for example, were essentially written by the United States, and debates over the application of those rules in particular cases are dominated by the United States. Even more disturbingly, the language of law is becoming an instrument of war, according to David Kennedy.[70] The interpretive community is not a check on power but rather mirrors the existing power structure. It does not constrain self-serving interpretations of the law but rather legitimizes them by making them seem to be a reflection of community standards.

---

[66] Martti Koskenniemi, "The Politics of International Law," 1 *European Journal of International Law* 1 (2000); Martti Koskenniemi, "The Politics of International Law–Twenty Years Later," 20 *European Journal of International Law* 7 (2009).

[67] Dan Villa, "Postmodernism and The Public Sphere," 86 *American Political Science Review* 712, 715 (1992). In the quoted passage, Villa is setting out Michel Foucault's objection to Habermas's quest for a coercion-free consensus, which he says is not possible.

[68] For an influential application of Gramscian thought to international relations, see Robert W. Cox, *Approaches to World Order* (1996). For an important reminder of what "international hegemonic law" has looked like in the past and a provocative account of what it might look like today, see Detlev Vagts, "International Hegemonic Law," 95 *American Journal of International Law* at 843 (2001).

[69] See, for example, E. Augelli and C. Murphy, *America's Quest for Supremacy and the Third World: A Gramscian Analysis* (1988).

[70] David Kennedy, *Of War and Law* 99–172 (2006). See also Nathaniel Berman, "Privileging Combat? Contemporary Conflict and the Legal Construction of War", 43 *Columbia Journal of Transnational Law* 1 (2004).

This notion of hegemony has done a great deal to illuminate how international law works, but it does not fully capture the inter-subjective nature of legal discourse. To engage in international law formation and interpretation is to engage in a collectively meaningful activity. When disputes arise, the interpretive task is to ascertain what the law means to the parties collectively rather than to each individually. The distribution of material power has a profound influence on the development and implementation of international law, but dominant states cannot simply impose or project their norms on others; the process requires the offering up of arguments that fit within a wider context of shared understandings about the rules of international life. Those understandings are themselves the product of interaction and contestation among so wide a range of governmental and nongovernmental actors that it is unreasonable to assume the "hegemon" can reset the terms of debate whenever its interests change. Normative evolution takes time, even when the norm entrepreneur is disproportionately powerful.[71] If new arguments and interpretations reach too far beyond the parameters of accepted discourse, they are not likely to be persuasive, and no amount of material power is going to change that. Those who would seek to adapt the law in response to new threats and changing circumstances are more likely to persuade the interpretive community to go along if their initiatives are presented—and can be internalized by others—as attempts to *stretch* and *bend* the law rather than abrogate and replace it.

The other objection is that an interpretive community can be overly technocratic. Indeed, its disciplining force depends to a certain extent on expertise in the techniques and substance of legal argumentation. The problem with technocracy is that it assumes politics and value choices can be removed from policy decisions. Both David Kennedy and Marti Koskenniemi have turned their attention to this problem.[72] In Chapter 9, I consider the claim that a large group of experts within the international trading system (WTO Secretariat officials, former and current government trade officials, GATT-friendly academics, and international civil servants in other organizations), dominated thinking about trade and made "highly contingent and contested social and political notions" seem to be a matter of technocratic management and not political debate.[73] Similarly, the IMF and World Bank thrive on the expertise of their staff—in many ways

---

[71] Michael Byers, *War Law: Understanding International Law and Armed Conflict* 147-156 (2007). See also, Michael Byers, *Custom, Power and the Power of Rules: International Relations and Customary Law* (1999).

[72] David Kennedy, "Challenging Expert Rule: The Politics of Global Governance", 27 *Sydney Law Review* 5 (2005); David Kennedy, "The Mystery of Global Governance," in *Ruling the World?: Constitutionalism, International Law and Global Governance* 37 at 53–54 (J. Dunoff and J. Trachtman eds., 2009); David Kennedy, *Of War and Law* (2006) 25–26. Martti Koskenniemi, "The Fate of International Law: Between Techniques and Politics," 70 *The Modern Law Review* 1, 8 (2007); Martti Koskenniemi, "The Politics of International Law— Twenty Years Later," 20 *European Journal of International Law* 7 (2009).

[73] Robert Howse, "From Politics to Technocracy–and Back Again: The Fate of the Multilateral Trading Regime," 96 *American Journal of International Law* 94, 98 and 104 (2002).

it is the source of their authority—but as they became drawn more deeply into the social, economic, and political life of countries and away from core macroeconomic competencies, calls for a better balance between expertise and democratic accountability were heard, even from within the organizations.[74] Other than in highly technical areas, or on narrow technical decisions, an overly technocratic interpretive community lacks legitimacy because experts wield all the discursive power, immune to voices and perspectives that represent values the experts may not hold.

Yet an interpretive community need not be viewed as a closed club, accessible only to an elite group of specialists. The community forms and evolves through interaction in the conduct of international affairs.[75] The networks that engage in this interaction are not composed only of legal technocrats. They often coalesce around IOs, where perceived knowledge and expertise is much broader than international law, like those that deal with human rights. Moreover, the third concentric circle of an interpretive community looks not so much like a closed loop but rather a constellation of actors who serve as an audience for and occasionally find a way of penetrating the two inner circles. Thus "outsiders"— constituencies that represent interests and values other than global free trade—have penetrated WTO negotiations and the Secretariat itself.[76] Even the UN Security Council is a more open and transparent institution than meets the eye, as I elaborate in Chapter 4. By opening up "the possibility of public accountability and accessibility" to political influence, international organizations serve as venues for nascent forms of transnational democratic deliberation.[77]

Indeed, Habermas's ideal of legal argumentation is not insular: "Legal discourse cannot operate self-sufficiently inside a hermetically sealed universe of existing norms but must rather remain open to arguments from other sources. In particular, it must remain open to the pragmatic, ethical, and moral reasons brought to bear in the legislative process. . ."[78] But if it is thrown too wide open, the disciplining force of legal argumentation would lose

---

[74] See, for example, World Development Report 1997, *The State in a Changing World*, authored by Joseph Stiglitz, Chief Economist of the World Bank at the time who left the Bank shortly thereafter. On the influence of expertise in the global economic institutions generally, see Ngaire Woods and Amrita Narlikar, "Governance and the Limits of Accountability: the WTO, the IMF and the World Bank," UNESCO 2001; Michael Barnett and Martha Finnemore, "Expertise and Power at the International Monetary Fund," in *Rules for the World: International Organizations in Global Politics* 45–72 (2001).

[75] My argument here parallels that of Brunnée and Toope who argue that "communities of practice" can accommodate a plurality of actors. Brunnée and Toope, *supra* note 1 at 81.

[76] Howse, "From Politics to Technocracy and Back Again", *supra* note 68, at 117.

[77] James Bohman, "International regimes and democratic governance: political equality and influence in global institutions" 73 *International Affairs* 499 506 (1999); Jennifer Mitzen "Reading Habermas in Anarchy: Multilateral Diplomacy and Global Public Spheres," 99 *American Political Science Review* 15 (2005); Howse, *supra* note 68 at 117.

[78] Habermas, *Between Facts and Norms*, *supra* note 25, at 230.

its bite; any argument would be as good as any other. As a reform project, the challenge is to strike the appropriate balance between the constraining force of discursive interaction on the basis of shared disciplinary standards and the need to open up that interaction to new perspectives from beyond the conventions of argumentation and understanding that operate in the discipline. In other words, the interpretive community has to be both closed enough for its supposed "expertise" to be recognized, but open enough that it does not operate (and is not seen as operating) as a technocratic, hegemonic device that serves to shut out voices other than those that dominate the discipline or field of practice.

TWO

The Practice of Deliberation

4

RESPONSIBILITY TO PROTECT

I. INTRODUCTION

NATO'S INTERVENTION IN Kosovo was an international incident of historic significance which, among other things, galvanized legal debate on the doctrine of humanitarian intervention. That debate was conducted in part in the Security Council of the United Nations, highlighting the role of the Council as a venue for heated, deeply political but often principled argumentation about appropriate standards of international behavior. In the debates over Kosovo, legal arguments were used extensively to explain and justify positions.[1] They were pressed with varying degrees of vigor by most members of the SC, including the permanent five and many others with a stake in the outcome. From a realist point of view, the extent of reliance on legal arguments in a political forum deliberating on such a sensitive issue is hard to explain.[2] Drawing on the theoretical framework set out in Chapters 2 and 3, this chapter argues that the use of legal arguments is part of a broader discursive process in which norms are invoked to explain, defend, justify, and persuade—a process that is not inconsequential, even for the most powerful states. While legal arguments are never decisive in Council deliberations, they do shape the debates and have an

---

[1] The public versions of these claims came mostly on the day the bombing began or afterwards, but the legal issues were considered—and to an extent debated—within and between governments before the event.

[2] Leading examples of structural realist literature are Kenneth Waltz, *Theory of International Politics* (1979); John Mearsheimer, "The False Promise of International Institutions," 19 *International Security* 329 (1994/95).

impact on positions taken. They can also change the law. Thus, the Kosovo case illustrates the dual functions of the interpretive community as judge of compliance with the law and as lawmaker by setting the parameters for discourse within which incremental extension of the rules may occur.

The chapter begins by describing the SC as a four-tier deliberative setting, where at least minimal preconditions for reasoned argumentation exist. It then turns to an examination of the debates over the Kosovo intervention. I do not claim that legal considerations affected the decision to intervene itself, but rather that the positions taken in those debates can only be explained by the notion of discourse within an interpretive community, and that ultimately the discourse affected how the Kosovo episode played out. In the third section, I consider the broader normative impact of that episode, focusing on the "responsibility to protect" (R2P). I devote special attention to the role of the UN Secretary-General as norm entrepreneur—an influential voice who not only participated in the debates over the legality of intervention but mobilized international support for the emerging norm. While that story is far from over, it illustrates how legal argumentation within an interpretive community can generate soft law that may someday crystallize as hard law.

II. THE UN SECURITY COUNCIL AS A DELIBERATIVE SETTING

Deliberative democrats, as noted in Chapter 2, argue that makers of public policy should and do give principled reasons for their decisions, and add that domestic legislators should be required to do that more as a way of deepening democracy.[3] The same logic applies to international institutions. Courts and quasi-judicial tribunals are erroneously seen as the exclusive domain for deliberation, based on rules and principles, when, in fact, international legal discourse takes place in a variety of settings. It occurs through diplomatic correspondence; the speeches and statements of government officials; meetings within and between governments; and in public, press, and academic commentary. It is especially intense in international organizations, including the Security Council (SC) of the United Nations.[4]

The SC is far from Habermas's ideal deliberative setting, where participants have equal standing and equal voice in public debates, no speaker can be prevented from joining the debate, and they inhabit a "common lifeworld" (see Chapter 2). In democratic theory, deliberative legitimacy requires that all those affected by a decision have an opportunity

---

[3] Amy Gutmann and Dennis Thompson, *Democracy and Disagreement* 46 (1996).

[4] My description of the SC as a deliberative setting draws on Ian Johnstone, "Legislation and Adjudication in the UN Security Council: Bringing Down the Deliberative Deficit", 102 *American Journal of International Law* 275 (2008). See also Ian Johnstone "The Security Council as Legislature," in *The UN Security Council and the Politics of International Authority* (B. Cronin and I. Hurd eds., 2008).

to participate, or at least witness, the making of decisions. On the surface, it would seem that none of these preconditions are met in the UN Security Council. Members do not share values, a history or even a language; the participants are anything but equal; and the proceedings are hardly public. Indeed, the SC is designed to be as heterogenous as possible, with balanced representation from each geographical region and 10 of its 15 members rotating every two years. Five of its members have permanent status and the veto power, which gives them disproportionate influence in the deliberations, even when they do not use the veto. The ability to participate meaningfully varies among members, based on access to intelligence and information, and even mundane matters like mission size and time zones. More to the point, the Council is composed of only a small fraction of the total UN membership, and participation by nonmembers is severely restricted. The outcomes of deliberations—the resolutions and statements adopted or defeated—are public and are usually accompanied by explanations of votes, but most of the debates themselves take place in semiprivate informal consultations. The ideal of deliberation free from relationships of power and coercion would seem to be so far from reality that it offers no help in understanding how decisions are actually made.

On closer inspection, however, the situation is more complex. To begin with, perfect consensus on values and conceptions of interest is not a precondition for meaningful discourse (if such consensus existed, there would be no need to deliberate). What is necessary is a sense of being in a relationship of some duration from which common meanings and expectations have emerged, and of being engaged in an enterprise the general purpose of which all understand in roughly the same way.[5] To a greater extent than conventional wisdom holds, the SC meets that condition. Its mission is to "maintain international peace and security," and debates are structured by a normative framework embodied in the UN Charter. That normative framework has been supplemented by the SC's own decisions and operational activities, as well as treaty law, opinions of the International Court of Justice and other judicial bodies, "soft law" in the form of GA resolutions, and decisions of other intergovernmental bodies.

In the field of human rights, the normative climate has clearly changed since the founding of the UN. In 1945, international peace and security was conceived largely in terms of the military threat that states posed to each other. But the UN Charter contains the seeds of a broader conception of security, that of human security. The seed has sprouted in a web of international human rights instruments, starting with the Universal Declaration of Human Rights and the Genocide Convention of 1948, through the four Geneva Conventions and their Protocols on humanitarian law and the two International Covenants on human rights. The post–Cold War era has seen the Vienna Conference on Human Rights of 1993, the establishment of International Criminal Tribunals for former

---

[5] Emanuel Adler makes the same point about "communities of practice". Emanuel Adler, *Communitarian International Relations: The Epistemic Foundations of International Relations* 22 (2005).

Yugoslavia and Rwanda (and mixed national-international tribunals in East Timor, Sierra Leone, and Cambodia), and the International Criminal Court. These were accompanied by important regional developments, including the Helsinki Final Act (1975), the Copenhagen criteria for accession to the European Union (1993), the Santiago Commitment to Democracy and the Renewal of the Inter-American system (1991), and the Inter-American Democratic Charter (2001), as well as the commitments to democracy adopted by Mercosur and other subregional groups in Latin America. In 1998, the OAU decided not to allow governments who come to power through unconstitutional means to participate in its summit-level meetings.[6] Then in 2002 the African Union adopted its new Constitutive Act, which stated that one of the Union's objectives was to promote democracy, human rights and good governance, and it granted the Union the right to intervene to end war crimes, genocide and crimes against humanity.[7] Meanwhile, the International Commission on Intervention and State Sovereignty (ICISS), an independent blue-ribbon panel, coined the term "responsibility to protect" in response to challenges laid down by the UN Secretary-General in speeches and his report to the Millennium Assembly in September 2000.[8] The concept was affirmed by the SG's High Level Panel on Threats, Challenges and Change (HLP),[9] in his own report to the 2005 World Summit[10] and by member states at the summit itself.[11] It was also affirmed in a Security Council resolution a year after the World Summit.[12]

To these legislative and declaratory developments can be added the pattern of practice in the SC since 1991, particularly in the area of humanitarian intervention. The five

---

[6] John Ikenberry sees in these and other developments the emergence of a "single world standard... that acknowledges rights that people are expected to enjoy and that states and the international community are expected to observe and protect." John Ikenberry, "The Costs of Victory: American Power and the Use of Force in the Contemporary Order," in *Kosovo and the Challenge of Humanitarian Intervention* 85, 90–91 (A. Schnabel and R. Thakur eds., 2000). Underpinning all of these normative developments is a belief in the value of multilateralism, defined by John Ruggie as an institutional form that coordinates relations among three or more states on the basis of generalized principles of conduct. John Ruggie, "Multilateralism at Century's End," in *Constructing the World Polity: Essays on International Institutionalization* 102, 109 (1998).

[7] Constitutive Act of the African Union 2002, Articles 3 and 4.

[8] International Commission on Intervention and State Sovereignty (ICISS), *The Responsibility to Protect*, December 2001, available at www.iciss.ca/pdf/Commission-Report.pdf. The co-chairmen of the ICISS said in launching the report that it was a response to the SG's challenge. See Gareth Evans and Mohamed Sahnoun, "Intervention and State Sovereignty: Breaking New Ground", 7 *Global Governance* 119 (2001).. The Secretary-General's Report to the Millennium Assembly is *We the Peoples: The Role of the United Nations in the Twenty-First century*, September 2000. Available at http://www.un.org/millennium/sg/report/ .

[9] Report of the Secretary-General's High Level Panel on Threats Challenges and Change, *A More Secure World: Our Shared Responsibility*, December 2004, para. 203. Available at http://www.un.org/secureworld. hereinafter "HLP Report"

[10] Report of the Secretary-General, "In Larger Freedom: Towards Development, Security and Human Rights for All", March 2005, paras. 125-126. Available at http://www.un.org/largerfreedom/ .

[11] Resolution adopted by the General Assembly, 2005 World Summit Outcome, UN GA Res 60/1 (2005), paras. 138–39.

[12] UN SC Res 1674 (2006), para. 4.

Permanent Members of the SC have been dealing with each other on an almost daily basis for the last 20 years, in effect, debating the shape of the post–Cold war world in the context of particular crises and on occasion thematic issues (such as the protection of civilians in armed conflict). From northern Iraq, through Bosnia, Somalia, Haiti, Rwanda, Sierra Leone, Kosovo, East Timor, the Democratic Republic of the Congo, Liberia, Sudan and Afghanistan, collectively they have found a way of authorizing—or endorsing after the fact—operations that would have been unthinkable during the Cold War.

The response to events of September 11, 2001, initially reinforced this trend toward converging views about the rules of international life. A resolution strongly condemning the terrorist attacks and endorsing the U.S. position that a military response in self-defense was justified, was followed by an unprecedented resolution that outlaws a long list of activities relating to terrorism.[13] The breakdown over Iraq in early 2003 was a setback for this post–Cold War trend, although there is evidence even in those failed deliberations of a fairly robust normative framework, which structured debates and affected the course of events—including the aftermath (discussed in Chapters 5 and 6). More tellingly, divisions over Myanmar and Zimbabwe—with China and Russia vetoing resolutions (in January 2007 and July 2008 respectively) that would have authorized tough action against the two regimes—mark a step away from SC consensus on a connection between security and human rights norms. Russia's reaction to the Ahtissari plan and Kosovo's declaration of independence in early 2008, and its invasion of Georgia in August 2008, signal a further rupture in East-West relations. Yet that did not prevent the SC from reaffirming the responsibility to protect in a resolution adopted at the end of 2009.[14]

Despite the ups and downs in SC unity, the terms of debate on intervention have changed. The degree of interaction since the end of the Cold War, even if it has not always led to consensus on particular cases, has had an impact on how the P5 view their rights and responsibilities in the field of peace and security. In a sense, the P5 have become an exclusive club with a common history, set of experiences, and shared understandings about the meaning of the UN Charter. Paraphrasing John Rawls and Jurgen Habermas, practice within the Council has contributed to "overlapping lifeworlds," if not a common lifeworld, among its members.[15] The deep ideological divide of the Cold War has been replaced by a more fluid dynamic, in which standard forms of argument used to appraise and ultimately accept or reject competing claims, a legal discourse that is fundamentally

---

[13] UN SC Res 1368 (2001) and UN SC Res 1373 (2001).

[14] UN SC Res 1894 (2009).

[15] Thomas Franck describes global fairness discourse as "the reasoned pursuit of. . . John Rawls' 'idea of an overlapping consensus.'" Thomas Franck, *Fairness in International Law and Institutions* 10–19 (1995). Corneliu Bjiola has described the Security Council as an "institutional lifeworld". Corneliu Bjiola, "Legitimatizing the Use of Force in International Politics: A Communicative Action Perspective," 11 *European Journal of International Relations* 266, 279 (2005).

about the limitations imposed by the Charter, and the relative weight to be assigned to the United Nations' overarching purposes.

Additionally, there are elements of SC practice to suggest that the notion of equal status in and access to the discourse is not entirely fanciful. The SC can be conceived as a four-tier deliberative setting. The top tier is the five permanent members of the Council, who have equal voting power and engage in deliberations on relatively equal terms. Differences in material power have a profound impact on the ability of each of the P5 to influence deliberations, but to the extent that political struggle among them takes place through reasoned exchange, it is more evenly matched.

The second tier is the SC as a whole. Nonpermanent members are formally equal in the sense that sovereign equality is a basic principle of the Charter, and each has one vote. Their votes weigh much less heavily, however, because they lack veto power. The voting power of members at this tier resides largely in the fact that any member of the P5 that wants to pass a resolution must solicit their support, sometimes competing with other P5 members soliciting votes for a differently worded resolution. The competition is often crass, as it is in any law-making body, but is typically characterized by appeals to reason, principles, and collective interests. Moreover, UN Charter Article 24 stipulates that the SC acts on behalf of the entire UN membership. Thus, even the smallest members count equally as representatives of the international community and—at least notionally—are expected to speak for all in the collective interest. Whether sincere or strategic, many of these nonpermanent members do "speak in the common interest," whose arguments must be met by responses "in the common interest." They contribute to the deliberative process by setting the parameters of the more equal debates among the P5. While the debates occur against a backdrop of bargaining and with a view to voting (and in full consciousness of which SC members wield the most material and bargaining power), outcomes that cannot somehow be justified in principled terms are harder to push through. If for no other reason, this is because Council members have domestic and regional constituencies to whom they feel they must justify their votes. Domestic public opinion, in democratic societies at least, makes it hard for diplomats to vote for resolutions that seem to contravene international norms, even if their interests point in that direction. A case in point is the reluctance of Chile and Mexico to vote for the famous second resolution on Iraq in March 2003 (discussed in Chapter 6).

The third tier is the rest of UN membership, those who do not have votes in the SC. In multiparty democracies, majority party claims are "examined, challenged, tested, criticized and rearticulated" by the opposition.[16] There is no functional equivalent of a parliamentary opposition in the SC, but nonmembers do have opportunities to wield influence. They can speak in public meetings and, although they do not participate in informal

---

[16] Seyla Benhabib ed., "Towards a Deliberative Model of Democratic Legitimacy" in *Democracy and Difference: Contesting the Boundaries of the Political* 67–94 (1996).

consultations or expert meetings prior to the informal consultations among ambassadors (where most of the real business of the Council is now done), they are often invited to "private meetings," where official records are kept, but the public and media are excluded. In so-called Arria formula gatherings, visiting dignitaries of nonmembers or representatives of nonstate parties to a dispute address the Council in an informal and confidential setting. Troop contributors to peace operations meet with the Council President regularly, and a working group on peacekeeping operations has been established to institutionalize consultations. The president of the SC often briefs interested nonmembers, following closed meetings of the Council. A tentative forecast of the work of the Council is now posted on the Web page of the presidency so nonmembers can marshal their efforts if they want to weigh in on an issue. Draft resolutions are sometimes circulated to the entire UN membership when introduced in informal consultations. More often than in the recent past, open debates are held before the day of a vote to give others a chance to gain insight into what members of the Council are thinking and to state their positions.[17] There are still many complaints about SC working methods, and reform of those methods is a perpetual subject of discussion. But it is inaccurate to state that nonmembers of the Council do not have opportunities to shape Council action.

The fourth tier is the constellation of engaged representatives of nongovernmental organizations, organs of international public opinion, and other citizens who have a stake in and keep a close watch on what is going on in the SC. One need not invoke a mythical "international community" to make the case that the members of the Council feel compelled to appeal to networks of actors and citizens beyond governmental chambers. This network is part of the broader interpretive community whose judgment—real or anticipated—matters to governmental decision makers. The SC is not a sealed chamber, deaf to voices and immune to pressure from beyond its walls. Most of the effort at persuasion (as opposed to after-the-fact justification) takes place behind closed doors where one would suppose reason and legal arguments count for less. But the effort at persuasion is influenced by the subsequent need to justify. If a Council member says in a private meeting, "we will push this to a vote," then other members must consider whether their positions and explanations will pass muster with the outside world. Debates in private are animated by arguments that will be used later to justify positions in public. In fact, informal consultations of the SC are not treated by participants as completely

---

[17] For excellent summaries of the changes in post–Cold War Security Council working methods, see Security Council Reports, *Special Research Report No. 1: Security Council Working Methods-A Work in Progress?* March 30, 2010 available at http://www.securitycouncilreport.org/site/c.glKWLeMTIsG/b.5906427/k.91B7/Special_Research_Report_No_1brSecurity_Council_Working_MethodsA_Work_in_Progressbr30_March_2010.htm; Security Council Reports, *Special Research Report: Security Council Transparency, Legitimacy and Effectiveness,* October 18, 2007 (No.3), available at http://www.securitycouncilreport.org/site/c.glKWLeMTIsG/b.3506555/. The organization also has regular updates on SC working methods, available at http://www.securitycouncilreport.org/site/.

private. With 15 representatives, plus aides and Secretariat staff present, rarely is a word uttered that the speaker would not want to be known publicly. Since there are no official records of the meeting, the utterances can always be denied—not an insignificant point—but the glare of publicity does find its way into consultations of the SC, if only through the cracks in the windows.

III. KOSOVO

The NATO intervention in Kosovo provoked sharp debate on a fairly well-defined though far-reaching issue: namely, the legality of humanitarian intervention without explicit SC authorization.[18] The weight of official and scholarly opinion was against the legality of intervention, and yet NATO went ahead anyway, which might be read as suggesting that legal considerations were either ignored or irrelevant. Yet legal arguments were pervasive in deliberations in and around the SC. Was the legal discourse mere window dressing, or does it suggest that deliberation and appeals to impartial values matter even if they do not impose a decisive constraint on action?

Various legal justifications for the use of force in Kosovo were put forward, each of which was met with compelling counterarguments. The arguments for legality can roughly be grouped into three. First is self-defense: the argument being that the regional instability caused by Belgrade's repression of Kosovo threatened its neighbors, which was tantamount to an "armed attack" within the meaning of Article 51 of the Charter, justifying collective self-defense in response. The second is a customary law doctrine of humanitarian intervention, based on state practice during the Cold War years (including interventions by India in East Pakistan, Vietnam in Cambodia, and Tanzania in Uganda), more recent SC practice, and human rights and humanitarian law norms. For this argument to succeed, one has to read the prohibition against the use of force in UN Charter Article 2(4) narrowly as not applying to humanitarian intervention on the grounds that it does not impinge on a state's territorial integrity or political independence. The third argument sees authority based on existing SC resolutions (especially resolutions 1160, 1199, and 1203 of 1998), which made demands on the Serbs under Chapter VII and threatened "further action." The claim would be that failure to comply with those demands lawfully triggered the action, reinforced by resolution 1244 establishing UNMIK and KFOR, which could be seen as implicit, retroactive approval of the intervention.[19]

---

[18] This discussion of the Kosovo intervention draws on Ian Johnstone, "Security Council Deliberations: The Power of the Better Argument," 14 *European Journal of International Law* 437 (2003).

[19] All of these arguments appear in some form in the comments by Louis Henkin, Ruth Wedgewood, Jonathan Charney, Christine Chinkin, Richard Falk, Thomas Franck, and W. Michael Riesman in "Editorial

The counterarguments can be stated succinctly. First, stretching "armed attack" to include this situation would drain all meaning from the term and open the floodgates to claims that any threat to peace and security justifies the use of force in self-defense. It would collapse the distinction between the threshold for unilateral action (Article 51, "armed attack") and for SC-authorized action (Article 39, "threat to the peace"). Second, Cold War and post–Cold War practice are insufficient to support the development of customary law. In all three Cold War cases cited as precedents for humanitarian intervention, the intervening states claimed self-defense. Moreover, to argue that humanitarian intervention is not "against territorial integrity or political independence" within the meaning of Article 2(4) opens a massive loophole in the Charter. This line of argument was largely rejected during the Cold War, and there is even less rationale for accepting it in the post–Cold War era; now that the SC is no longer paralyzed, Charter rules on the use of force should be construed narrowly in favor of the SC as the international body responsible for decisions about the maintenance of peace and security. Third, to interpret existing SC resolutions as authorizing force would fly in the face of statements made by Russia and China, who explained in their votes on those resolutions that they did not authorize force. It would inhibit future attempts to adopt Chapter VII resolutions threatening action out of fear that they would be interpreted as an implicit authorization to use force. Moreover, even if one accepts the dubious proposition that retroactive approval can render an action "legal" that was initially "illegal,"[20] resolution 1244 did not condone NATO's intervention in March. Unlike in Liberia and Sierra Leone, when the SC welcomed ECOWAS' interventions in 1994 and 1997 respectively, resolution 1244 was forward looking. Russia was prepared to treat NATO's action as a fait accompli and to help deal with the aftermath of the intervention, but not to approve it after the fact.

The weight of scholarly and official opinion is that the intervention was illegal. In my view, the best way of characterizing the situation from a legal perspective is that humanitarian necessity was treated as an excuse for violating the law. This was close to the position taken by the UK and officially presented by Belgium in the ICJ proceedings initiated by Belgrade.[21] The idea in a nutshell is that humanitarian intervention is not an exception to the prohibition against the use of force, but violations of the law will be excused in extreme cases of humanitarian need. In other words, the world will turn a blind eye to the violation and, in effect, pardon those responsible. The fact that a draft resolution introduced by Russia on March 26 failed by a vote of 12-3 suggests that some members of the Council

---

Comments: NATO's Kosovo Intervention," 94 *American Journal of International Law* 83 (1999). See also "Symposium: The International Legal Fallout from Kosovo" 12 *European Journal of International Law* 1 (2001).

[20] Thomas Franck, *Recourse to Force: State Action Against Threats and Armed Attacks* 155–62 (2002). See contra, Christine Gray, *International Law and the Use of Force* 417–18 (3rd ed., 2008).

[21] See Ian Johnstone, "The Plea of Necessity In International Legal Discourse: Humanitarian Intervention and Counter-Terrorism" 43 *Columbia Journal of Transnational Law* 337 (2005) for this argument and for references to the UK and Belgian positions.

were prepared to excuse the intervention, even though they were deeply troubled by the lack of explicit authorization (Brazil, Malaysia, and Gabon). The failure of the GA to condemn NATO is also indicative. It is possible that a supportive vote in the GA under the Uniting for Peace resolution would have passed by the required two-thirds majority but was not resorted to because of the precedent it would have established (the United States, United Kingdom, and France—all participants in the intervention—did not want to see the Uniting for Peace device revived because it is a way of getting around the veto power they possess). If so, then the decision not to go to the GA suggests a willingness to turn a blind eye matched by an unwillingness to announce that is what is going on.

In any case, in this chapter, I am less interested in the substance of the debates than in the power of the interpretive community to shape SC deliberations and action. Five features of the deliberations are highly suggestive. First, the range of legal arguments made in the SC is significant. In the debates of March 24 (the day the airstrikes began) and March 26 (the date of the failed resolution to condemn the bombing), every Permanent Member of the SC (and most others) invoked legal norms and principles. Legal arguments on both sides were pressed with varying degrees of vigor, with some speakers (like the UK, the Netherlands, Russia, and China) passing direct judgment on the legality or illegality of the intervention while others (like the United States, Canada, Argentina, and Slovenia) commented more generally on the legal context in which it took place.[22]

Second, the heavy weather (real and anticipated) that greeted efforts to justify the intervention on legal grounds caused some NATO governments to refrain from pushing the strongest versions of the legal claim. This is certainly true of the United States, which consistently asserted the legality of its position but ultimately relied on a laundry list of factors and a general claim of legitimacy, rather than a single legal justification.[23] One important—perhaps overriding—reason is that the United States was concerned about the precedent that could be set by acceptance of a customary law doctrine of humanitarian intervention. NATO allies, like the UK and the Netherlands, were more explicit about the legal basis for the claim, but they did not push it with the same vigor at the end of discussions as they had at the start, and many turned to emphasizing the exceptional nature of

---

[22] For records of the debates, see United Nations (1999) S/PV.3988, Meeting Records, New York: Security Council, March 24, 1999; and United Nations (1999) S/PV.3989, Meeting Records, New York: Security Council, March 26, 1999.

[23] Thus, in the Security Council debates of March 24 and 26, 1999, the U.S. representative referred to the earlier resolutions in vague terms and simply asserted that "we believe that action by NATO is justified and necessary to stop the violence and prevent an even greater humanitarian disaster." Ambassador Peter Burleigh, S/PV.3988, *supra* note 22, at 5. See also S/PV.3989, *supra* note 22, at 4–5. On that same day, the U.S. Mission to the UN circulated a list of ten factors supporting NATO action in Kosovo without specifying the precise legal justification. "Factors Supporting NATO Action in Kosovo," confidential document on file with author.

the intervention.[24] Thus opinions in NATO ranged from countries that had real doubts about the legality of the action, to those who had no such doubts but were reluctant to push the legal case because of the precedent it might establish, to those who neither had doubts nor were concerned about pushing the claim. The net result was a collective decision (or nondecision) to emphasize the legitimacy of the action, without denying its legality, while putting forward a range of factors—both legal and nonlegal—to justify it.[25]

Third, the positions of non-NATO states were varied and nuanced. Russia and China were deeply opposed, not because they feared "humanitarian intervention" directed against them (given the extreme unlikelihood of that) but because they were disturbed by the notion of a norm- or value-driven intervention, which could shake the foundations of non-Western regimes elsewhere and alter the global balance of power.[26] The reaction of the Non-aligned Movement (NAM) was mixed when the intervention happened and then coalesced into opposition later.[27] This suggests a willingness on the part of some to turn a blind eye at the moment of crisis but an unwillingness to endorse humanitarian intervention without SC authorization as a matter of principle. The Islamic world was not unambiguously supportive of NATO as one might have expected, given that the intervention was on behalf of Kosovo's Muslim population.[28] Not even Bosnia or Albania were explicit about the legality of the intervention in their statements in the SC (as nonmembers).[29] In the Arab world, there was sympathy for the suffering of fellow Muslims and some stated concern about human rights, but they also feared that NATO interference if unchecked would extend to their part of the world, to combat

---

[24] For thorough analyses of debates within NATO and other countries, see various chapters in Albrecht Schnabel, and Ramesh Thakur eds., *Kosovo and the Challenge of Humanitarian Intervention: Selective Indignation, Collective Action and International Citizenship* (2000).

[25] As the Acting Legal Adviser to the U.S. State Department later explained, NATO came up with a "pragmatic basis for moving forward without establishing new doctrines or precedents that might trouble individual NATO members or later haunt the alliance if misused by others." Michael Matheson, "Justification for the NATO Air Campaign in Kosovo," *Proceedings of the 94th Annual Conference of the American Society of International Law* 301 (2000).

[26] Vladimir Baranovsky, "Humanitarian Intervention: Russian Perspectives," in Pugwash Study Group Occasional Papers, 2 *Intervention, Sovereignty and International Security* 12, 17–18 (2001); Zhang Yunling, "China: Whither the World Order after Kosovo?" in Schnabel and Thakur eds., *supra* note 24.

[27] At the South Summit in April 2000, the Group of 77 (comprised at the time of approximately 130 countries) "rejected the so-called right of humanitarian intervention." Declaration of the Group of 77, South Summit in Havana, April 10-14, 2000, para. 54. Available at http://www.nam.gov.za/document/southdecl.htm.

[28] Ibrahim Karawan, "The Muslim World: Uneasy Ambivalence," in Schnabel and Thakur, eds., *supra* note 24, at 215–16.

[29] Statement of the representative of Bosnia to the Security Council. United Nations (1999) S/PV.3988, Meeting Records, New York: Security Council, March 24, 1999, p.19. Statement of the representative of Albania to the Security Council, S/PV.3988, March 24, 1999, p.18.

terrorism for example.[30] This ambivalence is telling. If the legal discourse were meaningless, Islamic leaders would have had fewer qualms about giving in to natural (and politically beneficial) sympathy for the Kosovar Albanians by offering their whole-hearted support to the intervention. They would have no reason to fear that doing so would make intervention against them any more likely unless they believed the precedent would have legal significance. (I return to this point below.)

Fourth, the debates within NATO suggest that the legal discourse over Kosovo may have had an impact on the enunciation of NATO's new strategic concept. As the Washington Summit of April 1999 to celebrate NATOs 50th Anniversary approached, there were debates and differences of opinion among NATO countries over whether the alliance could intervene out-of-area (i.e., not in self-defense) without an SC authorization. Before then, it had been assumed that NATO would only act in such cases in support of and under the authority of the UN.[31] The United States (supported by the United Kingdom), however, was pushing for a revision of this doctrine, a position that was resisted by a number of NATO countries, including France and Germany. While all NATO countries supported the Kosovo action in the end, they were divided on the justification, and the experience was sufficiently disturbing to many that, surprisingly, the new strategic concept reinforced the role of the UN.[32]

Fifth, a broader circle of actors who do not represent governments weighed in on the legal issues. Prominent among them was Secretary-General Kofi Annan. He contributed to the discourse before the intervention by speaking often and eloquently about the Serb campaign against the Kosovars, never calling directly for forcible intervention but suggesting that the use of force might ultimately be necessary.[33] On the day the NATO bombing started, the Secretary-General issued a carefully worded statement regretting the failure of diplomacy and stating that "there are times when the use of force may be legitimate in the pursuit of peace" but adding that "the Council should be involved in any decision to resort to force." International legal scholars also weighed in, mainly after the

---

[30] Karawan, *supra* note 28, citing by way of example an article in the semi-official Egyptian publication Al-Ahram.

[31] Nicole Butler, "NATO: From Collective Defense to Peace Enforcement," in Schnabel and Thakur, eds., *supra* note 24, at 276.

[32] Paragraph 31 of the Alliance's Strategic Concept reads: "NATO recalls its offer, made in Brussels in 1994, to support on a case-by-case basis in accordance with its own procedures, peacekeeping and other operations under the authority of the UN Security Council or responsibility of the OSCE. . . In this context, NATO recalls its subsequent decisions with respect to crisis response operations in the Balkans." North Atlantic Treaty Organization (1999) "The Alliance's Strategic Concept," NAC-S(99)65, NATO Press Release, Washington D.C.: NATO, April 24, 1999.

[33] See, e.g., "Secretary-General calls for unconditional respect for human rights of Kosovo citizens, in statement to North Atlantic Treaty Organization," SG/SM/6878, January 28, 1999.

fact, and while opinions were varied, they leaned in the direction of illegality.[34] In reviewing the scholarly comment, José Alvarez notes that even commentators who supported the objectives of the intervention found NATO's action to be inconsistent with the Charter, and he points to a significant degree of uniformity among them about the range of tools they could use in interpreting it.[35] At the risk of overstating the case, one can infer from the relative weight of opinion against legality that this was the judgment the U.S. government anticipated facing.[36] Legal advisers would have been conscious of the difficulty in making a case likely to differ substantially from the conclusions that legal scholars would draw after the fact.

IV. HUMANITARIAN INTERVENTION AND THE INTERPRETIVE COMMUNITY

Four conclusions can be drawn from the above description of the deliberations. First, the variegated nature of the legal argumentation is circumstantial evidence of a functioning interpretive community associated with SC practice. Legal arguments are advanced in anticipation of the judgment of that community. Its impact will depend in part on the degree of unity within it. Clearly, the international community was not unified on the norm of humanitarian intervention at the time of the Kosovo crisis, which is why arguments in the Council ranged from clear statements of legality or illegality to more tentative statements about the legal context in which the intervention took place. But the mere fact that legal arguments were advanced by all members of the SC, including the most powerful, suggests that the normative framework provided by the Charter and other instruments is sufficiently robust to warrant an effort to justify positions on legal grounds. And because there is an interpretive community to "guard" that normative framework, the law is not infinitely malleable. If it were, either legal arguments would not have been made at all, or they all would have been straightforward claims of legality or illegality rather than the more nuanced claims that were heard since there would be no need to worry about the test of credibility (who would administer that test?).

Second, concerns about precedent are only intelligible if something like an interpretive community is at work. As noted above, many states that supported the action either

---

[34] In a series of editorial comments by seven leading legal scholars (all but one American) in the *American Journal of International Law* of October 1999, only one concludes unequivocally that the intervention was lawful (Michael Riesman) and one other found a measure of legitimacy (Ruth Wedgewood). See comments by Henkin, Louis; Wedgewood, Ruth; Charney, Jonathan; Chinkin, Christine; Falk, Richard; Franck, Thomas; and Riesman, W. Michael. "Editorial Comments: NATO's Kosovo Intervention," 93 *American Journal of International Law* 83 (1999).

[35] Josè Alvarez "Constitutional Interpretation in International Organizations," in *The Legitimacy of International Organizations*, 134 and 136 (J. Coicaud and V. Heiskanen, eds.,, 2001).

[36] For a recent analysis of the evolution of US policy, see Matthew Waxman, *Intervention to Stop Genocide and Mass Atrocities: International Norms and United States Policy* (2009).

refrained from pushing the claim of legality or did so with less vigor than might be expected. The United States, Germany, Brazil, various Islamic countries, and eventually the NAM, as a whole, were concerned about the implications of endorsing a doctrine of humanitarian intervention. One can imagine that the Islamic countries were worried about such humanitarian intervention being directed against them (and the United States about Israel), but the Kosovo "precedent" would not make that any more likely unless one assumes some mechanism for issuing credible judgments that it really is a precedent—some way of evaluating whether like cases are being treated alike. In a decentralized legal system, that mechanism can only be the interpretive community: it is what gives the whole notion of precedent its bite.

Third, concerns about plausibility and the reputational costs associated with advancing implausible arguments are further evidence of rational discourse within an interpretive community. Ultimately, it is the interpretive community, and not just those at whom the arguments are directed, that determines plausibility. The interpretive community, in effect, says about far-fetched claims: "your arguments are not only patently self-serving; they are wrong." In the Kosovo case, reputational concerns cut both ways: on one hand, some states may have been reluctant to put forward implausible legal arguments for fear they would be seen as far-fetched and hypocritical; on the other hand, once it was clear the intervention would go forward, no NATO country wanted to publicly cast doubt on the legality of the action because all have a stake in maintaining a reputation for good faith compliance with the law. Either way, the interpretive community has done its work because it is the entity that extracts reputational costs.

Fourth, while the legal discourse did not affect the decision to intervene, it did affect subsequent developments. The debate over the legality of the action caused such unease among NATO countries that many felt it was important to highlight the exceptional nature of the event rather than set a new policy. NATO enunciated a new strategic concept within a few weeks of the start of the bombing campaign, which reaffirmed the role of the SC in authorizing interventions and implicitly treated the Kosovo case as an exception. Similarly, the felt need to return to the SC for a long-term solution ("whereas NATO made war, it still needed the UN to help secure the peace"[37]) is revealing. Legal boundaries may be pushed by norm entrepreneurs, but to be generally accepted internationally, those pushing the limits must work to some extent within what are regarded as the legitimate venues for discourse. U.S. leadership was followed, and the norm of humanitarian intervention may have received a temporary boost (as I argue below), but the event also provoked a reaction on the broader legal and institutional questions it raised, including among NATO allies. Returning to the United Nations via resolution 1244 alleviated the morning-after regrets by diluting the threat to legal order that the NATO intervention was seen as presenting. It reinforced the

---

[37] Schnabel and Thakur, *supra* note 24, at 14.

sense that institutions are an important check on the unilateral exercise of power in the name of collective values.[38]

V. NORM ENTREPRENEURSHIP AND THE RESPONSIBILITY TO PROTECT

While the NATO intervention in Kosovo was branded illegal though excusable by the interpretive community, it also set in motion a process that led to the World Summit endorsement of the responsibility to protect (R2P) in 2005. Kofi Annan was a key figure in this process, a "norm entrepreneur." [39] Timely speeches and tireless advocacy gave impetus to the R2P project and kept it alive when intergovernmental interest was waning. He tapped into a growing normative movement, precipitated by humanitarian tragedies that he himself had witnessed and been involved in as head of the Department of Peacekeeping Operations before becoming SG. The norm is rooted in three reports issued on the failures in Rwanda and Srebrenica, two by the UN and one by the OAU. The SG commissioned the two UN reports, one by an independent group and the other internal. The Srebrenica report of 1999 found that the problems UN peacekeepers faced in Bosnia—and the fall of the safe area in Srebrenica—were due not just to inadequate means and mandate but to the whole ideology of peacekeeping.[40] The UN's Independent Inquiry on Rwanda and the OAU's Report of the Panel of Eminent Persons on Rwanda drew similar conclusions.[41]

Meanwhile, the UN Secretary-General was a lively participant in the debates leading to and following the Kosovo intervention. In June 1998, he characterized events in Kosovo as reminiscent of the "ghastly scenario" that took place in Bosnia[42] and six months later told the North Atlantic Council that "the bloody wars of the last decade have left us no illusions about. . . the need to use force, when all other means have failed. . ." These and

---

[38] John Ikenberry, "The Costs of Victory", *supra* note 6. at 96.

[39] This part draws on Ian Johnstone, "The Secretary-General as Norm Entrepreneur," in, *Secretary or General? : The UN Secretary-General in World Politics* (Simon Chesterman ed., 2007). On the influential role of the Secretary-General, see also Gareth Evans, *The Responsibility to Protect: Ending Mass Atrocity Crimes Once and for All* 38-50 (2008).

[40] Report of the Secretary-General pursuant to General Assembly resolution 53/35: *The Fall of Srebrenica*, November 15, 1999, UN GA Res 54/549 (1999) para. 505.

[41] See the reports of United Nations and the Organization of African Unity on the Rwanda genocide. Letter dated 15 December 1999 from the Secretary General addressed to the President of the Security Council transmitting the report of the independent inquiry into the actions of the United Nations during the 1994 genocide in Rwanda. December 16, 1999, UN Doc S/1999/1257; Organization of African Unity, *Report of the International Panel of Eminent Personalities to Investigate the 1994 Genocide in Rwanda and the surrounding events*, July 7, 2000. Available at: http://www.oau-oua.org/Document/ipep/ipep.htm

[42] "Secretary-General reflects on 'Intervention,' in 35th Annual Ditchley Foundation Lecture," SG/SM/6613/Rev.1*, June 26, 1998.

other statements were relied on by NATO Secretary-General Solana[43] and British Secretary of State for Defense George Robertson (Solana's successor), who said later that they provided "the moral imperative" from which "flowed the legal justification" for the air war.[44]

Throughout the period of the NATO bombing campaign, the SG strove to ensure two elements remained in the discourse: the imperative to act in the face of massive human rights violations and the fundamental role of the SC as the preeminent body responsible for international peace and security. On the day the bombing started, the SG issued the following carefully crafted statement:

> It is indeed tragic that diplomacy has failed, but there are times when the use of force may be legitimate in the pursuit of peace. . . But as Secretary-General I have many times pointed out, not just in relation to Kosovo, that under the Charter the Security Council has primary responsibility for maintaining international peace and security—and this is explicitly acknowledged in the North Atlantic Treaty. Therefore the Council should be involved in any decision to resort to force.[45]

He spoke in similar terms at the Human Rights Commission on April 7 and again on May 18 in a speech on intervention at the Centennial of the Hague Peace Conference.[46] Both sides of the equation—the need to confront human rights violations and the authority of the SC—were noted and used by governments in their deliberations within and outside the SC.[47]

The SG also contributed to the more general discourse on humanitarian intervention at the start of the 1999 GA session where, in the most famous speech he ever made, he reflected on the SC's inaction in Rwanda and its lack of unity over Kosovo and concluded "the core challenge to the Security Council and the UN as a whole in the next century is to forge unity behind the principle that massive and systematic violations of human rights—wherever they take place—cannot be allowed to stand."[48] His purpose was to

---

[43] NATO Press Release [99] 11, March 28, 1999.

[44] Statement made by Lord Robertson on June 29, 1999, cited by Nicola Butler "NATO: from Collective Defence to Peace Enforcement," in Schnabel and Thakur eds, *supra* note 24, at 281.

[45] Secretary-General's Statement on NATO Military Action Against Yugoslavia, UN Press Release SG/SM/6938 of 24 March 1999.

[46] "The Effectiveness of the International Rule of Law in Maintaining International Peace and Security," SG/SM/6997, May 18, 1999.

[47] For example, the North Atlantic Council issued a statement on April 23 that "NATO's military action against the FRY supports the political aims of the international community, *which were reaffirmed in recent statements by the UN Secretary-General*." NATO Press Release S-1(99)62 - 23 April 1999. Available at: http://www.nato.int/docu/pr/1999/p99-062e.htm .

[48] "Presentation of the Secretary-General's Annual Report to the United Nations General Assembly" (September 20, 1999), SG/SM/7136, GA/9596.

launch a debate on the issue of humanitarian intervention (he often drew an analogy to the "talking stick"), a debate that was joined initially through reactions in the GA itself and then later outside UN circles. Two blue-ribbon panels were established, the Independent International Commission on Kosovo and the International Commission on Intervention and State Sovereignty.[49] The latter was in direct response to what the co-chairmen called "the Secretary-General's challenge."[50] Both commissions brought together respected figures from around the world, connected to officialdom but independent. They were, in a sense, institutionalized expressions of the interpretive community in that the members were chosen precisely because they are recognized experts and distinguished figures whose views on these matters deserve a hearing.

The ICISS elaborated the concept of a responsibility to protect, which the High Level Panel on Threats, Challenges and Change (HLP) later described as an "emerging norm."[51] The SG endorsed it in his own report to the World Summit in 2005, and the principle was affirmed in the World Summit Outcome document, though only after a rancorous and inconclusive debate about the scope of the responsibility and on precisely whom it fell.[52] The Panel argued that when governments were unable or unwilling to fulfill the responsibility to protect, it fell on the SC and recommended the adoption of a set of guidelines or criteria to be taken into account in deciding whether and how to exercise it.[53] An early draft of the document that came out of the 2005 World Summit included a paragraph on the responsibility of the SC to act under Chapter VII when necessary.[54] The United States objected to this language on the grounds that it implied a legal obligation.[55] Responding

---

[49] Independent International Commission on Kosovo, "The Kosovo Report: Conflict, International Response, Lessons Learned" 12 *International Journal of Refugee Law* 696–99 (2000) and *Addendum to the Kosovo Report* (2001); International Commission on Intervention and State Sovereignty, *The Responsibility to Protect* (December 2001).

[50] Evans and Sahnoun, *supra* note 8.

[51] HLP report, *supra* note 9.

[52] For good accounts of the debates leading to the adoption of the responsibility to protect language at the World Summit, see Evans, *supra* note 39 at 43-50; Alex Bellamy, "Whither the Responsibility to Protect? Humanitarian Intervention and the 2005 World Summit", 20 *Ethics and International Affairs* 151 (2006).

[53] HLP report, *supra* note 9 at paras. 203 and 207. The SG, in his report "In Larger Freedom" endorsed this approach. Report of the Secretary-General, "In larger freedom: towards development, security and human rights for all," A/59/2005, March 21, 2005. [hereinafter, "In Larger Freedom"].

[54] World Summit Draft Outcome document, A/59/HLPM/CRP.1/Rev.2, August 5, 2005, para. 118. Available at www.reformtheun.org.

[55] As Ambassador Bolton put it in a letter to the President of the General Assembly: "we agree that the host state has a responsibility to protect its population from such atrocities, and we agree in a more general and moral sense that the international community has a responsibility to act when the host state allows such atrocities. But the responsibility of the other countries in the international community is not of the same character as the responsibility of the host, and thus we want to avoid formulations that suggest that the other countries are inheriting the same responsibilities that the host has. . . [T]he obligation/responsibility discussed in the text is not of a legal character. . . We do not accept that either the United Nations as a whole, or the Security Council, or individual states, have an obligation to intervene under international law." Letter of Ambassador John

to the United States and other objections,[56] the final outcome document simply states that the international community is "prepared to take collective action, in a timely and decisive manner, through the SC, in accordance with the UN Charter, including Chapter VII, on a case by case basis."[57] There is no appeal to adopt guidelines or criteria for humanitarian intervention, although the declaration "stresses the need for the GA to continue consideration of the responsibility to protect. . . bearing in mind the principles of the Charter of the United Nations and international law." Despite the watered-down language, this was the first time a UN meeting had formally endorsed the concept.

A legal question that the World Summit Outcome document does not fully answer concerns the Genocide Convention. Article I of the Convention imposes an obligation on all contracting parties "to prevent and punish" genocide; Article VIII stipulates that any UN organ may take such action as it considers appropriate for the prevention and punishment of genocide. Does this impose a duty to engage in humanitarian intervention to end genocide? That would be a highly implausible reading of the Convention, not only because state practice does not support it, as evidenced by the studious indifference to genocides in Rwanda and elsewhere, but also because it would come into conflict with the prohibition against the use of force in Article 2(4) of the UN Charter. The better reading of the Convention, especially in light of state practice, is that it imposes a duty to prevent or end genocide in a manner that is consistent with the UN Charter. That then begs the question whether the Permanent Members of the SC, who are all parties to the Genocide Convention, have a special duty. If a state or group of states is prepared to intervene to stop genocide, do the P5 (and other SC members at the time) have a duty to authorize the intervention, or at least not to stand in the way, by exercising a veto? Louise Arbour, former High Commissioner for Human Rights, Prosecutor of the ICTY, and Justice of the Supreme Court of Canada makes that argument, based on her reading of the ICJ decision in the *Genocide case (Bosnia v. Serbia)*.[58] This is an interesting but controversial argument because it implies that the P5 can be held responsible for genocides they fail to stop: precisely the scenario that World Summit outcome language sought to avoid. To suggest there is a "duty to protect," even in respect of genocide, would require an expansive interpretation of the Genocide Convention and of the UN Charter itself, an interpretation that flies in the face of the carefully worded World Summit statement. On the other hand, the fact that Ambassador Bolton was adamant about redrafting the

---

Bolton, Permanent Representative of the United States to the UN, August 30, 2005. Available at www.reformtheun.org.

[56] U.S. amendments are marked on the August 5 draft, in a document dated 08/17/05 with the words "OD US Version #2" handwritten at the top. Available at www.reformthun.org.

[57] 2005 World Summit Outcome, *supra* note 11, at para. 139.

[58] Louis Arbour, "The Responsibility to Protect as a duty of care in international law and practice," 34 *Review of International Studies* 445, 453 (2008).

language is circumstantial evidence that words do matter.[59] After all, the World Summit document is a nonbinding declaration (the GA cannot make law). Yet, clearly, the United States and other states were worried that this nonbinding statement could be treated as an authoritative interpretation of the UN Charter and come back to haunt them.

VI. R2P SINCE THE WORLD SUMMIT 2005

Since the World Summit, the post of Special Adviser to the Secretary-General has been created for the purpose of defining and refining the R2P concept, as well as building consensus in support of it.[60] As noted, the SC reaffirmed R2P in resolution 1674 (2006) and again in resolution 1894 (2009). A new NGO called the Global Centre for the Responsibility to Protect was established in New York in February 2008 to advance the R2P agenda.[61] R2P continues to be the focus of lively debate in and around the UN. In March 2007, a report by a UN High Level mission criticized the Government of Sudan for its role in continuing the conflict in Darfur and called upon the international community to act, invoking R2P. The norm found its way into debates of the SC on Darfur, and it is reaffirmed in the resolution that called for an expansion of the United Nations Misssion in Sudan to Darfur.[62] Following the crackdown on the Burmese monks in Myanmar in 2007, the High Commissioner for Human Rights said to the Human Rights Council:

> At their 2005 Summit the World leaders agreed that the international community has a responsibility to protect civilians against serious international crimes. The exercise of such responsibility requires that preventive, reactive and rebuilding measures be put in place to avert and confront crises, as well as to prepare the ground for justice, the rule of law and respect for human rights to take hold. When the situation in Myanmar was first considered by the Security Council in January this year, several members expressed the view that the Human Rights Council was

---

[59] For John Bolton's own account of his years at the United Nations, see John Bolton, *Surrender is not an Option: Defending America a the UN and Abroad* (2007).

[60] Dr. Edward Luck was appointed the first Special Adviser, SG/A/1120, BIO 3963, February 21, 2008.

[61] CUNY Newswire, "New Global Centre for R2P Opens," Feb. 20 2008, available at www.cuny.edu. forum/?P=2126.

[62] UN SC Res 1706 (2006). See "The UN Security Council and the Darfur Crisis: A Country-by-Country Analysis," which looks at statements by SC members before, during and after the adoption of resolution 1706. Available at http://www.africaaction.org/resources/docs/SCAnalysis0610.pdf . On earlier debates in the SC on Darfur, see Alex Bellamy, "Responsibility to Protect or Trojan Horse? The Crisis in Darfur and Humanitarian Intervention After Iraq," 19 *Ethics and International Affairs,* 31–54 (2005).

the proper forum to deal with the human rights concerns, as they then existed. There can be no doubt about the need for action in this Council now.

At an open debate of the SC on protection of civilians in November 2007, 26 ambassadors referred to the responsibility to protect, either to promote the norm or limit its scope; none rejected it.[63] At that stage, the norm was not hard law by any stretch, but a consensus on its meaning and practical application seemed to be emerging, suggesting that it could solidify as a legal principle.

Since then, R2P has fallen on hard times. When Burmese authorities were slow to accept offers of humanitarian assistance after Cyclone Nargis in May 2008, French Foreign Minister Bernard Kouchner invoked the concept again,[64] sparking a lively debate in print among many of the originators of the concept and those seeking to promote it, including Lloyd Axworthy, Gareth Evans, and Ramesh Thakur, as well as senior UN officials Edward Luck and John Holmes.[65] The debate ended with Kouchner backing away from his position, in effect confirming that the norm applies only to the most egregious crimes, not to natural disasters and the like. (Conceivably, the obstructionism of the Government of Myanmar could have risen to the level of a crime against humanity, but that was not deemed to be the case with Cyclone Nargis). Then, just as the dust had settled on that debate, Russia invoked R2P to justify its invasion of Georgia in August 2008, taking a page out of the book on the U.S.-led invasion of Iraq in 2003 (for which humanitarian intervention was a tertiary justification).[66] Russia's claim was given short shrift, but it did stir up concerns about misapplication of the norm, adding to the sense that it was too expansive, overly focused on military action, and too easily abused.

SG Ban Ki-Moon then stepped in, first by making a speech in Berlin in July 2008 and then by issuing a report in January 2009 on "implementation of the responsibility to protect."[67] In the speech and the report, he argued that R2P was "more anchored in

---

[63] United Nations (2007) S/PV.5781, Meeting Records, New York: Security Council, November 20, 2007 and United Nations (2007) S/PV.5781 Meeting Records, New York: Security Council (resumption 1) November 20, 2007.

[64] See Darren Schuettler, "France Suggests Helping Myanmar Without Government Backing," Reuters, May 7, 2008, at http://www.responsibilitytoprotect.org/index.php/government_statements/1627?theme=alt1

[65] For a good summary of what was said and references to the statements, see "Crisis in Burma," at http://www.responsibilitytoprotect.org/index.php/pages/1182. See also Evans, *supra* note 39 at 64-89; Serena Sharma, "Review Essay: Toward a Global Responsibility to Protect: Setbacks on the Path to Implementation," 16 *Global Governance* 121, 128–29 (2010).

[66] For a dismissive analysis of the attempt to apply R2P in Iraq, see Evans, *supra* note 39 at 69–71. On Georgia, see Global Center for the Responsibility to Protect. "The Georgia-Russia Crisis and the Responsibility to Protect: Background Note," August 19, 2008, http://www.globalr2p.org/pdf/related/GeorgiaRussia.pdf. See also Alex Bellamy, *Responsibility to Protect: The Global Effort to End Mass Atrocities* (2009).

[67] Report of the Secretary-General, *Implementing the responsibility to protect*, A/63/677 January 12, 2009. Available at: http://www.un.org/preventgenocide/adviser/pdf/SG%20Report%20R2P.pdf

current international law" than the related and more-controversial concepts of humanitarian intervention and human security. He went on to define its three pillars as follows: the legal obligations of States to protect their populations from genocide, war crimes, ethnic cleansing and crimes against humanity; the commitment of the international community to assist States in meeting these obligations, through public diplomacy, human rights training and education, development assistance in targeted areas, security sector reform and capacity-building for rule of law, for example; and "timely and decisive response," which includes action under Chapter VI as well as Chapter VII of the UN Charter, ranging from fact finding and consent-based peacekeeping to threats of international criminal prosecution, arms embargoes and—as a last resort—coercive military intervention. The emphasis in the Report is that the concept is narrow but the response deep. In other words, it applies only to the crimes agreed on by the world leaders in 2005: genocide, war crimes, crimes against humanity, and ethnic cleansing, not HIV/AIDS, climate change, or response to natural disasters, which would undermine the 2005 consensus and stretch the concept beyond recognition or operational utility. The response is deep in that it entails not only coercive action but a whole range of non-coercive measures as well.

The report then became the subject of a debate in the GA, which was actually more tempered than an informal dialogue that preceded it, spearheaded by the Nicaraguan president of the GA, an avowed critic of R2P.[68] A total of 94 speakers delivered statements, two-thirds of whom spoke positively about the report.[69] Moreover, the NAM, which had firmly rejected the notion of humanitarian intervention in the year 2000, made a statement that was considerably softer than its earlier statements on R2P.[70] The net result is that the consensus reached in 2005 remained intact, but no plan of action emerged to carry the R2P agenda forward.

VII. "RESPONSIBILITY TO PROTECT" AND THE INTERPRETIVE COMMUNITY

What conclusions can be drawn from the story of R2P? First, that emerging norms can crystallize as hard law through discursive interaction, but only if accompanied by state practice. R2P has not crystallized. No military intervention on R2P grounds has ever been undertaken, with or without SC authorization. Rhetorical support for the norm is

---

[68] Sharma, *supra* note 65.
[69] See two comprehensive assessments of the debates, one by the Global Center on R2P, http://globalr2p.org/media/pdf/GCR2P_General_Assembly_Debate_Assessment.pdf, and the other by the International Coalition for R2P, http://www.responsibilitytoprotect.org/ICRtoP%20Report-General_Assembly_Debate_on_the_Responsibility_to_Protect%20FINAL%209_22_09.pdf.
[70] Jutta Brunnée and Stephen Toope, *Legitimacy and Legality in International Law: An Interactional Account* 334–35 (2010).

broad but typically heard in GA debates on the abstract principle or SC debates when thematic issues are being discussed, like the protection of civilians. In the context of particular cases, such as Darfur, support is more equivocal, and action has been limited. So while a reference to R2P appears in resolution 1706, that resolution could not be implemented because the Government of Sudan would not allow a UN mission in Darfur. Instead, a hybrid UN-AU mission was established (UNAMID) by resolution 1769 (2007), which contains no reference to the concept. Moreover, even as a "paper norm,"[71] the scope of R2P is limited. The World Summit affirmed the right of the SC to do what most UN Member States felt it already had the authority to do, namely: to intervene on a case-by-case basis to stop mass atrocities deemed to be a threat to international peace and security. That affirmation is not inconsequential, laying to rest any lingering doubts about SC-authorized humanitarian intervention, but it is not what the most enthusiastic proponents of R2P were striving for when the concept was first introduced. The SG's 2009 implementation report and the subsequent GA debate added little, because most of what the report characterizes as R2P are activities that the UN had been engaged in under a different label, from preventive diplomacy and human rights monitoring to robust peacekeeping. Arguably, the World Summit and subsequent developments set back the case for *unilateral or regional* coercive humanitarian intervention—the sharp edge of R2P. Agreement among 192 states that it is permissible with SC authorization implies it is not permissible without. The consensus could have an impact on interpretation of the Constitutive Act of the AU, which establishes "the right of the Union to intervene in a Member State pursuant to a decision of the Assembly in respect of grave circumstances, namely: war crimes, genocide and crimes against humanity."[72] It is silent on whether such intervention would require UN Security Council authorization, as is the Protocol establishing the AU Peace and Security Council.[73] One could read the silence as the AU asserting a right to intervene on its own, but a better reading is that the Constitutive Act ought to be interpreted in light of the UN Charter requiring SC authorization. This interpretation is reinforced by the World Summit Outcome document, signed onto by all African states, as well as the wider UN membership. So while R2P has not crystallized as hard law permitting unilateral intervention, the discursive interaction around it has impacted interpretation of the UN Charter and other legal instruments.

Second, an important feature of the debate on R2P is whether criteria for its application should be adopted. When Secretary-General Kofi Annan made his famous September 1999 speech to the UN General Assembly, the reaction was mixed but leaning

---

[71] Michael Glennon distinguishes what he calls "paper rules" from "working rules". Michael Glennon, *The Fog of Law: Pragmatism, Security and International Law* 21, 27 and 58 (2010).

[72] Constitutive Act of the AU, Article 4(h), http://www.africa-union.org/root/au/Aboutau/Constitutive_Act_en.htm.

[73] Protocol establishing the AU Peace and Security Council. http://www.africa-union.org/root/AU/Documents/Treaties/Text/Protocol_peace%20and%20security.pdf.

toward negative. Most Member States who commented on it were either mildly or strongly opposed to the notion of humanitarian intervention. The main objection was not so much to the principle but related to fears of selective application. This prompted calls for criteria—from Egypt, for example—but that got nowhere in the GA. Outside the GA, however, both the Independent International Commission on Kosovo and International Commission on Intervention and State Sovereignty came up with a set of what are essentially just war principles. The High Level Panel on Threats, Challenges and Change endorsed the R2P criteria and recommended that they be embodied in declaratory resolutions of the SC and GA.[74] They are framed as "considerations the SC should take into account," rather than triggering criteria that would "produce agreed conclusions with push-button predictability." Instead, the guidelines are a set of questions the SC should ask itself each time the issue of intervention arises. To the disappointment of many R2P advocates, the World Summit did not endorse criteria.[75] The appeal for criteria resonates with the thesis of this book: the purpose is to induce SC members to justify their positions, for and against intervention on the basis of agreed standards, and to give others (nonmembers and nonstate actors) an opportunity to judge the Council against those standards and to weigh in on the debates, through formal or informal channels. From the point of view of deliberative legitimacy, they would lead to more accountability and better decision making, maximizing the likelihood of consensus—hopefully stimulating action when it should happen and constraining action when it should not.[76] The P5 in particular do not want to have their hands tied in this way. They want to preserve their discretion to act on a case-by-case basis, after hard bargaining within the Council, without getting entangled in the sticky process of explaining and defending their action or inaction to the world. Deliberation on the basis of agreed criteria can create pressures that states want to avoid; powerful states know that, which is why they want to limit opportunities for that discourse. The resistance to criteria in other words is circumstantial evidence that justificatory discourse matters.

Third, the "interpretive community" has made its presence felt in the R2P debate. It largely rejected misapplication of the concept: in Iraq, Georgia, and Cyclone Nargis. The last is an especially telling illustration of the interpretive community in action. There was a crisis precipitated by a natural disaster and exacerbated by the Government of Myanmar. The foreign minister of France, one of the earliest proponents of humanitarian intervention as head of Médecins Sans Frontières, and a supporter of R2P both before and after he joined the government (thus someone who straddled both the middle and inner circles of the interpretive community) claimed R2P applied. Other influential voices weighed in

---

[74] HLP, *supra* note 9 at para. 208.

[75] Gareth Evans, co-chair of the ICISS report, is among them. Evans, *supra* note 39, at 48.

[76] Brunnée and Toope go a step further by arguing that criteria would enhance the legal status of the norm, by subjecting case-by- case decisions to overarching criteria. Brunnée and Toope, *supra* note 70 at 335.

on the debate, commenting not only on the wisdom of nonconsensual intervention but also the meaning of the norm. The debate was conducted in a highly public manner (in op-eds for example) as well as in the corridors of power at the UN and in capitals. Ultimately, it was settled in favor of a narrow interpretation of the norm. This was affirmed by the SG in his report on implementation of R2P and by the GA in how it reacted to that report. The GA is not a judicial or quasi-judicial body authorized to render authoritative interpretations of the law, but as a venue for deliberation and discourse, it is a place where interpretive disputes play out and on occasion get settled, perhaps not once and for all, but at least until better arguments are introduced to justify a different approach.

Fourth, both Secretaries-General Kofi Annan and Ban Ki Moon played key roles as norm entrepreneurs and participants in a complex deliberative process, involving a multitude of actors. The SG is not a normative free agent, but rather enmeshed in and constrained by the political and institutional context in which he operates and must tap into normative processes he does not control. Yet, that embededness is also a source of influence. If the UN is an "organizational platform" (see Chapter 3), then the SG has a privileged place on that platform. He is consulted by governments and his words carry weight. He is at the center of what Ramesh Thakur calls a "communications network," in which he speaks not only to governments but also civil society representatives and business leaders.[77] As a norm entrepreneur, the SG is likely to succeed best when he taps into emerging understandings and expectations, rather than trying to generate new norms on his own. He is most effective when he makes the case for normative change by building on prevailing interpretations of international law, advancing values embodied in the UN Charter in light of changing circumstances, within the constraints of what the political traffic will bear. The SG has considerable leverage precisely because he is a key member of the interpretive community associated with the UN, and he operates in a highly structured institutional setting. The Charter and Charter-based law provide the normative framework within which questions of peace and security are debated. This framework evolves through a combination of practice and argumentation about that practice, in which the SG plays a critical though by no means decisive role.

Fifth, the R2P debate illustrates the power and limitations of nonstate actors in debates on security issues. Human rights is the handle that gave NGOs a voice in the humanitarian intervention/R2P debates. The connection between human rights and security (embodied in the concept of human security) has changed the political dynamics at the UN and other international organizations like the AU, EU, and NATO. The relative "power shift" from central governments to NGOs, the business community, and other

---

[77] Ramesh Thakur, *The United Nations, Peace and Security: From Collective Security to the Responsibility to Protect* (2006).

sources of global influence means that the constituencies of IOs have broadened.[78] These new actors are increasingly important participants and partners in deliberations. The interpretive community associated with UN law on the use of force is larger than the handful of diplomats seated at the table and their political masters at home. The political figures must appeal to networks of interested officials, experts, and citizens, who, among other things, sit in judgment of legal claims. How weighty the voices of these nongovernmental actors are on security matters is an empirical question. The groundswell of support for R2P across civil society, not only in the North but also parts of the South (especially sub-Saharan Africa), has not led to crystallization of the norm. But the debate is not over. The term has found its way into international discourse; even if governments tire of it, a powerful constituency of nongovernmental actors will keep the fires burning.

Sixth, while non-consent-based intervention in the name of R2P has not occurred, the norm has had some practical effect. In Chapter 7, I discuss the connection between it and the "protection of civilian" mandates in peace operations. The connection is politically controversial, precisely because R2P is controversial, but I argue that the protection of civilians is a concrete manifestation of the norm—giving it life and content. Alternatively, if peacekeepers are not given the mandate and resources to protect civilians dying before their eyes in the context of an armed conflict, what hope is there for the crystallization of the broader principle that all states and international organizations have a legal "responsibility to protect"?

VIII. CONCLUSION

The intervention in Kosovo in 1999 was a defining moment in the post–Cold War order. The legality of the military action was questionable from the start and, despite the unanimous adoption of resolution 1244, the aftermath has been difficult—culminating in Kosovo's unilateral declaration of independence in 2008, recognized by many states but bitterly opposed by Belgrade and Russia. It would be an overstatement to say that international legal considerations were decisive at any moment. But precisely because there was so much at stake, the fact that the law counted at all is telling. The legal argumentation in and around the UN Security Council, as well as NATO, was consequential. It was consequential because something like an interpretive community was at work.

---

[78] Early statements of this proposition are Jessica T. Matthews, "Power Shift," 76 *Foreign Affairs* (1997); Martha Finnemore and Kathryn Sikkink, "International Norm Dynamics and Political Change," 52 *International Organization* 887 (1998). More recent analyses are in Jen Steffeck and Patrizia Nanz, "Emergent Patterns of Civil Society Participation in Global and European Governance," in *Civil Society Participation in European and Global Governance: A Cure for the Democratic Deficit* 3 (J. Steffeck, C. Kissling and P. Nanz eds., 2007); Magdelana Bexell, Jonas Tallberg and Andres Ullin, "Democracy in Global Governance: The Promises and Pitfalls of Transnational Actors," 16 *Global Governance* 81, 85–89 (2010).

The judgment—real and anticipated—of the interpretive community had an impact on how each state sought to justify the action and on the desire of all concerned to return to the SC.

The Kosovo also stimulated a debate on humanitarian intervention that continues to this day. It led to the endorsement of R2P at the World Summit of 2005 and ongoing discursive interaction both in the abstract and in connection with crises in Darfur, Myanmar, Zimbabwe, Georgia, and elsewhere. One can see evidence of an interpretive community at work, even identify the key players in this community, like the two UN Secretaries-General and their senior advisers, the foreign minister of France, the former Foreign Minister of Canada, the president of the GA, and the co-chair of the commission that coined the term R2P and launched the debate. One can see also see the outlines of a transnational public sphere, where deliberations on the meaning and application of the concept of human security occur. The outline is apparent as much for what has not happened, as from the debates themselves. Resistance to criteria for R2P comes partly from states that are opposed to the concept, but also from powerful states that support it but do not want the particulars of its application debated in the transnational public sphere. Ironically, the failure to adopt criteria for intervention is evidence that deliberation is understood as having constraining power even by the most powerful states.

5

COUNTER-TERRORISM

I. INTRODUCTION

THE LEGAL AND institutional framework for counter-terrorism has evolved in recent years, accelerated by the terrorist attacks on September 11, 2001. Combined with concerns about weapons of mass destruction falling into the hands of nonstate actors, terrorism has become a security priority for great and emerging powers. The depth of concern is not shared throughout the developing world, but counter-terrorism has risen on the agenda of many international organizations, including the UN. This chapter considers that evolution through an examination of three phenomena: the contrasting international reactions to self-defense as a justification for U.S.-led military action in Afghanistan and Iraq, as well as the drone strikes in Pakistan, the quasi-legislative acts by the SC in adopting resolutions 1373 and 1540, and the quasi-judicial nature of the Taliban-Al Qaeda sanctions regime.

The interventions in Afghanistan and Iraq prompted lively debate in official and non-official circles on the concept of self-defense as embodied in Article 51 of the UN Charter. Those debates, and the consequences for the United States in terms of support for the interventions, demonstrate that the interpretive community can stretch the interpretation of a concept like 'armed attack' without heading so far down a slippery slope that it becomes meaningless as a legal construct. The line between permissible and impermissible self-defense is still elusive, but we can now say with relative legal certainty that it falls somewhere between Afghanistan and Iraq. The drone strikes raise different questions, but the burgeoning justificatory discourse on their legality demonstrates that the US is still determined to make the best legal case it can for its forcible actions. The quasi-legislative and quasi-judicial resolutions demonstrate the legitimating effect of deliberation when it comes to new forms of law making. They sparked controversy because the SC is not designed for these sorts of functions. Yet by building support for them through responsive deliberative politics, the regimes created by the resolutions remain intact. Together these various counter-terrorism activities illustrate the power of legal discourse and deliberation in shaping, though not determining, the behavior of states in meeting new threats to national and international security.

II. SELF-DEFENSE

A. From Afghanistan to Iraq

The differing reactions to military action in Afghanistan and Iraq suggest that the law of self-defense is flexible enough to permit the use of force against terrorism, but not so open-ended that it drains the threshold concept of "armed attack" of all meaning. In the *Nicaragua* case, the International Court of Justice (ICJ) ruled that "the sending by or on behalf of a state of armed bands, groups, irregulars or mercenaries" could amount to an armed attack within the meaning of Article 51 of the UN Charter.[1] The high threshold set by the Court has been questioned, including by some of the dissenting judges in the *Nicaragua* case and later by the International Criminal Tribunal for former Yugoslavia in the *Tadic* case. Nevertheless, there is little doubt that self-defense is permissible against a state that is substantially involved in the organization of terrorist groups operating in another state, depending on a factual assessment of the "scale and effects."[2]

A more difficult legal issue concerns the use of force against terrorists when their actions cannot be attributed to a state. Both the International Law Commission (ILC, in 1980) and the International Court of Justice (in 1986) took the position that self-defense can be exercised only against a state, not against nonstate actors.[3] The ILC was explicit about this in its 1980 commentary on the Draft Articles on State Responsibility, concluding that self-defense is invokable only against a state that itself had wrongfully used force.[4] The ICJ and ILC "cut the umbilical cord" between extraterritorial action against armed

---

[1] *Nicaragua v. U.S.*, 1986 I.C.J, at para. 195.

[2] Oscar Schachter, "The Use of Force Against Terrorists in Another Country," 19 *Israel Yearbook on Human Rights* 209, 218 (1989).

[3] The ICJ did not address this specifically in its *Nicaragua* decision, but Oscar Schachter concludes that it is a fair inference. Schachter, *id.* at 216. See also, John-Alex Romano, Note "Combating Terrorism and Weapons of Mass Destruction: Reviving the Doctrine of a State of Necessity," 87 *Georgetown Law Journal* 1203 (1999).

[4] ILC 32nd Report, Commentaries, Article 34, para. 2. In 2001, the ILC was silent on the issue. ILC 52nd Report, Commentary, Article 21.

bands and the principle of self-defense, and according to Oscar Schachter, there was no indication at the time that governments had or would take a different position.[5] As a result, he argued in 1989 that the legal limits of self-defense precluded the use of force against terrorists on the territory of another state when the government was not substantially involved in attacks carried out by the terrorists, or when the *threat* of terrorism had not materialized as an armed attack within the meaning of Article 51.[6]

This line of reasoning has been overtaken by events, to the point where it is now a reasonable inference that self-defense can be invoked against nonstate actors. A number of scholars note that the language of the Charter does not preclude such an inference and, in fact, invites it by not limiting self-defense to "armed attack *by a Member state*", which would parallel the prohibition against the use of force in Article 2(4).[7] Moreover, in contrast to the firm position of the ILC in 1980 that self-defense could be invoked only against a state, it was silent on the issue in 2001.[8] More important, state practice on the law of self-defense has evolved following the September 11 terrorist attacks on the World Trade Center and the Pentagon, and the U.S. reaction to those attacks. The international reaction suggests that most states have accepted that terrorism by a nonstate actor can constitute an "armed attack" within the meaning of Article 51 and that military action against those terrorists is justifiable self-defense. The following evidence may be adduced in support of that conclusion:

- Security Council resolutions 1368 and 1373 both contain preambular paragraphs reaffirming "the inherent right of individual and collective self-defense," signaling the Council's judgment that the events of September 11 constituted an armed attack.
- Both NATO and the OAS adopted statements indicating that the acts were armed attacks that could be met by a proportional military response.[9] The Gulf

---

[5] Schachter, *supra* note 2, at 229; Oscar Schachter, *International Law in Theory and Practice* 172 (1991).
[6] Schachter, "The Use of Force," *id.* at 225–29.
[7] Sean Murphy, "Terrorism and the Concept of 'Armed Attack' in Article 51 of the UN Charter" 43 *Harvard International Law Journal* 41, 50 (2002). Thomas Franck, "Terrorism and the Right of Self-Defense," 95 *American Journal of International Law* 839, 840 (2001); Christine Gray, *The Use of Force in International Law* 199 (3rd edition, 2008). A recent contribution to scholarship on the use of force against terrorists is Lindsay Moir, *Reappraising the Resort to Force: International Law, Jus Ad Bellum and the War on Terror* (2010).
[8] ILC 52nd Report, Commentary, Article 21.
[9] NATO Press Release No. 124, Statement by the North Atlantic Council (Sept. 12, 2001); Terrorist Threat to the Americas, Res. 1 Twenty-fourth Meeting of Consultation of Ministers of Foreign Affairs Acting as Organ of Consultation in Application of the Inter-American Treaty of Reciprocal Assistance, OEA/Ser.F/II.4/RC.24/RES.1/01 (September 21, 2001).

Cooperation Council did not go that far but expressed a "willingness to participate in any joint action that has clearly defined objectives."[10]

- In its letter of October 7 to the president of the SC, the day the military action in Afghanistan began, the United States claimed it had authority to act in self-defense against Al-Qaeda and the Taliban.[11] International reaction to the U.S. letter and the military action in Afghanistan was either supportive or muted. For example, after a meeting on the day the strikes began, the president of the SC said to the press that the unanimous support expressed in earlier resolutions "is absolutely maintained."[12]
- The UK participated in the airstrikes, and many states provided the United States with access to airspace and facilities. At least 15 countries participated in Operation Enduring Freedom from the start, and many more joined the coalition as the war progressed. Russia, China, and a number of Arab states did not participate but announced support for the U.S. campaign. The Organization of the Islamic Conference (OIC), League of Arab States (LAS), and Asia-Pacific Economic Cooperation (APEC) forum did not express support for the U.S. military action but pointedly refrained from condemning it.[13]
- The Security Council authorized a UN civilian mission (UNAMA) and a non-UN military peace operation, the International Security Assistance Force (ISAF) to help with the reconstruction effort in Afghanistan. Forty-eight countries were contributing troops and police personnel to ISAF at the end of 2010, and the total number of participants since 2001 is well over 50.[14] A great many other states are providing financial, political, and diplomatic support.

Antonio Cassese concluded shortly after the United States action justified as self-defense: "it would seem that in a matter of a few days, practically all states. . . have come to assimilate a terrorist attack by a terrorist organization to an armed aggression by a state, entitling the victim state to resort to individual self-defence."[15] He questions

---

[10] Quoted in Sean Murphy, "Terrorist Attacks on the World Trade Center and Pentagon," 96 *American Journal of International Law* 244, 245 (2002).

[11] Letter by the Permanent Representative of the U.S. to the President of the Security Council, UN S/2001/946, Oct. 7, 2001.

[12] Quoted in Murphy, "Terrorist Attacks," *supra* note 10, at 246.

[13] Sean Murphy, "Terrorism and the Concept of Armed Attack in Article 51 of the UN Charter," 43 *Harvard International Law Journal* 42, 48–49 (2002). For a compatible review and analysis of the reaction to the U.S.-led action in Afghanistan, see Stephen Ratner, "Jus Ad Bellum and Jus in Bello after September 11," 96 *American Journal of International Law* 909 (2002).

[14] International Security Assistance Force Placemat archive, available at http://www.isaf.nato.int/en/isaf-placemat-archives.html

[15] Antonio Cassese, "Terrorism is also Disrupting Some Crucial Legal Categories of International Law," 12 *European Journal of International Law* 993, 996–97 (2001).

whether "instant custom" can develop in this way,[16] but it is hard to dispute that September 11 and its aftermath signified a shift of the law of self-defense in that direction.

This shift does not represent a complete break from the past: there is some prior practice of military action against terrorists, justified on the grounds of self-defense. U.S. cruise missile attacks on a pharmaceutical plant in Sudan were justified as self-defense in relation to the Al-Qaeda sponsored bombings of U.S. embassies in Kenya and Tanzania in August 1998.[17] The reaction of other governments to the U.S. action was surprisingly muted, including among Arab states.[18] Even if the factual basis for the strikes was questionable (there are doubts, for example, that the targeted plant in Sudan really was a chemical weapons factory[19]), few questioned the legal principle at the time. It did come up later in the ICJ Advisory Opinion on *The legal consequences of the construction of a wall in the Occupied Palestinian Territory*,[20] where the Court stated: "Article 51 recognizes the inherent right of self-defense in the case of armed attack *by one state against another state*."[21] However, the Court qualifies that categorical position in the very next sentence by distinguishing the Israel/Palestine situation from Afghanistan on the grounds that in the former case, the attacks originated from within Israeli-occupied territory. Further casting doubt on the significance of the brief statement on self-defense, the majority refers to SC resolutions 1368 and 1373, suggesting that it approves the Council's interpretation of Article 51.

Given the abbreviated and rather cryptic nature of its references to self-defense in the *Wall* opinion, it was clear that was not going to be the final word. Indeed, a year later in the *DRC-Uganda* case, the ICJ majority was far more equivocal, and Judges Simma and Kooijmans expressly accepted self-defense against nonstate actors, joining Judge Buergenthal who had said the same in *the Wall* opinion.[22] Thus, while the events of

---

[16] For a review of the development of "traditional and modern" approaches to customary law, see Anthea Elizabeth Roberts, "Traditional and Modern Approaches to Customary International Law: A Reconciliation," 95 *American Journal of International Law* 757 (2001). See also Michael Byers *Custom, Power and the Power of Rules: International Relations and Customary International Law* (1999).

[17] Letter to the President of the Security Council, UN S/1998/780, August 21, 1998.

[18] Thomas Franck, *Recourse to Force: State Action Against Threats and Armed Attacks* 95 (2002); Murphy, *supra* note 13, at 48–49; Gray, *International Law, supra* note 7, at 118. See generally Campbell, "Defending Against Terrorism: A Legal Analysis of the Decision to Strike Sudan and Afghanistan," 74 *Tulane Law Review* 1067 (2000); R. Wedgewood, "Responding to Terrorism: The Strikes Against Bin Laden," 24 *Yale Journal of International Law* 559 (1999).

[19] Gray, *supra* note 7, at 118, fn. 129.

[20] *The Legal Consequences of the Construction of a Wall in the Occupied Palestinian Territory*, International Court of Justice, July 9, 2004.

[21] *Id.*, para. 139 (Emphasis added).

[22] *Armed Activities on the Territory of the Congo (DRC-Uganda Case)*, 2005 ICJ Rep 201. A good analysis of the series of IJC opinions on this is Christian Tams, "The Use of Force Against Terrorists," 20 *European Journal of International Law* 359, 384–85 (2009). See also Sean Murphy, "Self-Defense and the Israeli Wall Opinion–A Ipse Dixit from the Court?" 99 *American Journal of International Law* 62 (2005); Christian Tams, "Light

September 11 may have rendered the relevant conditions "fuzzy" (in Cassese's words), they have not rendered the law incoherent—or at least no more incoherent than it already was.[23] The law of self-defense has evolved but remains reasonably robust, even in the foggy realm of counter-terrorism. This is illustrated by the largely negative reaction to the U.S. attempt to justify military action in Iraq as part of the ongoing war on terrorism.

The United States claimed a right to invade Iraq in 2003 on two distinct grounds: self-defense against terrorism and enforcement of SC resolutions to rid Iraq of weapons of mass destruction (Saddam Hussein's human rights abuses were a third possibility, but that was never the primary justification for military action, invoked mainly after the fact when evidence of links to Al-Qaeda and weapons of mass destruction proved to be slim). In his February 5, 2003, briefing to the SC, Secretary Powell sought to present forensic evidence to support the case on both counts. He clearly failed on the first terrorism-based claim. While there was substantial international support for the legality of military action in Afghanistan, the argument could not be stretched to Iraq 17 months later. The debate was waged intensely in and around the UN in the months between September 2002 and March 2003, and in the end, the "interpretive community" was not persuaded that the links between Iraq and the events of September 11 were sufficiently tight to justify military action on that basis. The argument that military action against Saddam Hussein was needed to forestall future acts of terrorism by Al-Qaeda was not persuasive. When that became obvious, the Bush Administration largely gave up trying to make its case in those terms—at least to international audiences. There is no better evidence of this shift than the letter of March 20 from the United States to the president of the SC, setting out the legal justification for the war.[24] The letter did not say a word about terrorism or preemption and contains only a cryptic reference at the end to "defense of the U.S. and the international community," which in the context is better read as a claim that the United States was taking enforcement action to defend SC resolutions. The legal case was based entirely on the enforcement of existing SC resolutions relating to Iraq's weapons of mass destruction.[25]

Treatment of a Complex Problem: The Law of Self-Defense in the 'Wall Case,'" 16 *European Journal of International Law* 963 (2005).

[23] Michael Glennon argues that the law of self-defense became incoherent long before September 11. Michael Glennon, "Military Action Against Terrorists Under International Law: The Fog of Law: Self-Defense, Inherence and Incoherence in Article 51 of the UN Charter," 25 *Harvard Journal of Law and Public Policy* 539, 543–44 (2002). On the desuetude of Charter rules on the use of force generally, see Chapters 4 and 6 of Michael Glennon, *The Fog of Law: Pragmatism, Security and International Law* (2010).

[24] UN Doc S/2003/351, March 21, 2003. See also Letter of the Permanent Representative of the United Kingdom to the to the President of the SC, UN Doc S/2003/350, March 21, 2003.

[25] For a good assessment of the merits of the U.S. legal claim-based on existing SC resolutions, see Sean Murphy, "Assessing the Legality of Invading Iraq," 92 *Georgetown Law Journal* 173 (2004) See also Christopher Greenwood, "International Law and Preemptive Use of Force: Afghanistan, Al-Qaida and Iraq," 4 *San Diego Law Journal* 7 (2003).

B. Doctrine of Preemption

The contrasting reactions to the Afghanistan and Iraq cases demonstrate that the law of self-defense has evolved to accommodate military action against terrorists and their bases without necessarily heading down the slippery slope that would completely negate the constraining force of Article 51. Even the controversial doctrine of preemption can be accommodated by evolving self-defense norms, although the manner in which it was presented in the U.S. National Security Strategy of 2002 goes well beyond existing law. Anticipatory self-defense was the legal basis for the doctrine:

> For centuries, international law recognized that nations need not suffer an attack before they can lawfully take action to defend themselves against forces that present an imminent danger of attack. Legal scholars and international jurists often conditioned the legitimacy of preemption on the existence of an imminent threat... We must adapt the concept of imminent threat to the capabilities and objectives of today's adversaries... The United States has long maintained the option of preemptive actions to counter a threat to our national security. The greater the threat, the greater the risk of inaction—and the more compelling the case for taking anticipatory action to defend ourselves, even if uncertainty remains as to the time and place of the enemy's attack. To forestall or prevent such hostile acts by our adversaries, the United States will, if necessary, act preemptively.[26]

What this contemplated was not preemption of a truly imminent attack based on clear and convincing evidence, but rather military action to prevent some future but not well-specified threat from materializing. That stretches the concept of "armed attack" so far beyond its original moorings that it becomes virtually meaningless.[27] To the extent that the concept informed the debates over intervention in Iraq, it was soundly rejected.

---

[26] The National Security Strategy of the United States of America, (Sept. 17, 2002). The strategy was essentially reaffirmed in the 2006 US National Security Strategy.

[27] The literature on the legality of the doctrine of preemption is large. See, for example, the various contributions to Lori Fischler Damrosch and Bernard Oxman eds., "Agora: Future Implications of the Iraq Conflict," 97 *American Journal of International Law* 553 (2003); William H. Taft, Legal Adviser, Department of State, *The Legal Basis for Pre-emption*, (Nov. 18, 2002), available at <http://www.cfr.og/publication.php?id=5250>; Mary Ellen O'Connell, "The Myth of Pre-emptive Self-Defense," in the *Report of the ASIL Task Force on Terrorism* 7 (2002); Abraham Sofaer, "On the Necessity of Pre-emption," 14 *European Journal of International Law* 209 (2003); Michael Bothe, "Terrorism and the Legality of Pre-emptive Force," 14 *European Journal of International Law* 227 (2003); Anthony Clark Arend, "International Law and the Preemptive Use of Military Force," *Washington Quarterly* 89 (Spring 2003); Greenwood, *supra* note 25; Vaughan Lowe, "The Iraq Crisis: What Now?" 52 *International & Comparative Law Quarterly* 859 (2008); Jordan Paust, "Use of Armed Force against Terrorists in Afghanistan, Iraq, and Beyond," 35 *Cornell International Law Journal* 533 (2002); Michael Byers, "Pre-emptive Self-defense: Hegemony, Equality and Strategies of Legal Change," 11 *Journal of Political Philosophy* 171 (2003); M. Sapiro, "The Shifting Sands of Preemptive Self-Defense," 97 *American Journal of*

It was also rejected by the High Level Panel (HLP) on Threats, Challenges and Change in 2004. The HLP concludes that a state can act preemptively against an imminent threat, weighing in firmly on one side of the dispute over whether a state must wait until it is actually attacked by weapons of mass destruction (WMD) before it can act in self-defense.[28] But the panel went on to state that if the threat is not truly imminent or proximate, it cannot act in self-defense.[29] In other words, it can act preemptively but not preventatively. In the latter circumstances, its only recourse is to put the matter to the SC. If the SC does not act, then there will be time to pursue other strategies and "to visit again the military option." This view is consistent with that expressed by Lord Goldsmith, UK attorney general legal adviser, first in a letter to Secretary of State for Defense Geoffrey Hoon in March 2002, stating: "I see considerable difficulties in being satisfied that military action would be justified on the basis of self-defence. In particular, I am not aware of the existence of material indicating the existence of an *imminent* threat."[30] Then, on March 7, 2003, he wrote: "The USA has been arguing for recognition of a broad doctrine to use force to pre-empt danger in the future. . . this is not a doctrine which, in my opinion, exists or is recognised in international law" [31]

In his last years in office, Secretary of State Powell sought to play down the revolutionary nature of the doctrine of preemption. In a *Foreign Affairs* article, he stated that observers have "exaggerated both the scope of preemption in foreign policy and the centrality of preemption in U.S. strategy as a whole"; the novelty of the doctrine "lies less in its substance than its explicitness."[32] The doctrine remained on the books throughout the Bush

---

International Law 599 (2003); D. Brown, "Use of Force Against Terrorism After September 11: State Responsibility, Self-Defense and Other Responses," 11 *Cardozo Journal of International and Comparative Law* 1 (2003); A. Buchanan and R.O Keohane, "The Preventive Use of Force: A Cosmopolitan Institutional Perspective," 18 *Ethics and International Affairs* 1 (2004).

[28] Though in a minority, Michael Glennon among others claims the plain language of Article 51 and the travaux preparatoires for the UN Charter are clear that anticipatory self-defense is illegal (or at least was until the rules on the use of force fell into desuetude). Glennon, *The Fog of Law, supra* note 23,116–18.

[29] Report of the Secretary-General's High Level Panel on Threats Challenges and Change, *A More Secure World: Our Shared Responsibility*, paras. 188-90, December 2004. Available at http://www.un.org/secureworld.

[30] http://www.iraqinquiry.org.uk/media/42845/goldsmith-hoon-letter.pdf

[31] Attorney General Goldsmith's Secret Memorandum to Prime Minister Blair, March 7, 2003, para. 3. Available at http://www.ico.gov.uk/upload/documents/library/freedom_of_information/notices/annex_a_-_attorney_general's_advice_070303.pdf.

[32] Colin Powell, "A Strategy of Partnerships," 83 *Foreign Affairs* 22, 24–25 (2004). Similarly, Secretary Albright has argued that the doctrine set out in the National Security Strategy 2002 is not new, that the administration's mistake was to arouse global controversy by elevating what has always been a residual option into a highly publicized doctrine. "Whether tracking the language of Article 51 or not, the Bush Administration's preemption doctrine will prove a departure for past practice only if it is implemented in a manner that is aggressive, indifferent to precedent, and careless of information used to justify military action. Calibrated and effective actions taken against real enemies posing an imminent danger should not overturn the international legal apple cart." Albright, "Think Again: the United Nations," *Foreign Policy*, www.foreignpolicy.com/articles/2003/09/01/think_again_the_united_nations.

years but was not discussed much by the administration. President Obama's new National Security Strategy (NSS), adopted in May 2010, makes no mention of it. Reading between the lines, that strategy reverts to more traditional understandings of the law of self-defense. About the use of force, the NSS states:

> When force is necessary, we will continue to do so in a way that reflects our values and strengthens our legitimacy, and we will seek broad international support, working with such institutions as NATO and the UN Security Council. The United States must reserve the right to act unilaterally if necessary to defend our nation and our interests, yet we will also seek to adhere to standards that govern the use of force. Doing so strengthens those who act in line with international standards, while isolating and weakening those who do not.[33]

An alternative legal argument for action against terrorists without SC authorization is the "defense of necessity," discussed in Chapter 4, in relation to humanitarian intervention. While it makes some sense in that context as a "safety valve" for unilateral action when the SC is paralyzed, it makes less sense in the context of counter-terrorism, where the self-defense paradigm still has some traction. Applied to terrorism, the logic of the necessity defense is as follows: if a state is unable or unwilling to control the activities of groups based on its territory, when such activities create a grave and imminent peril to an essential interest of another state, then a violation of the first state's territorial integrity to eliminate the danger is excusable.[34] The *Caroline* incident, in which British soldiers crossed the U.S. border and seized a steamboat being used by U.S. sympathizers to support Canadian rebels, is seen as a "necessity" case rather than self-defense because, in the diplomatic notes exchanged between the United States and Britain, neither side suggested that the wrongfulness of Britain's conduct could only be precluded if the British destruction of the ship was taken in response to international wrongs committed by the U.S. government.[35]

Yet, if as argued above, the concept of self-defense can accommodate military action against terrorists and their sponsors, then the necessity excuse is not required and may simply add to the legal uncertainty. The ILC states that the peril must be "grave and imminent" rather than "merely apprehended or contingent," and force must be the only means of eliminating that peril.[36] The interests being protected must outweigh all other considerations, "not merely from the point of view of the acting State but on a reasonable

---

[33] U.S. National Security Strategy, May 2010, p. 21
[34] Article 25 of the International Law Commission (ILC) Articles on State Responsibility.
[35] ILC 32nd Report, Commentaries, Article 33, para. 24, fn. 155.
[36] ILC 53rd Report, Commentary, Article 25, para. 15.

assessment of the competing interests, whether these are individual or collective."[37] These are rather vague admonitions, but it seems clear that if self-defense could not justify U.S. action in Iraq in 2003, necessity would not excuse those actions either.

C. Drone Strikes in Pakistan

The latest test case for the law of self-defense is the targeted killing of insurgents and suspected terrorists by unarmed aerial vehicles, or drones. US strikes began under the Bush Administration and made the headlines when a CIA-fired missile killed a suspected Al-Qaeda leader, who was alleged to have planned the attack on the USS Cole in Yemen in 2002. Although the Yemeni government consented, a UN Special Rapporteur called it a case of extrajudicial killing and therefore illegal. When discussed in the Human Rights Commission, the United States took the position—without elaborating—that the strikes were "lawful under the laws of armed conflict and that the Commission and its special procedures had no mandate to address the matter."[38]

The drone policy continued through the Bush years and accelerated under President Obama, especially against Al-Qaeda and the Taliban in Pakistan. Reportedly, the Pakistani government has acquiesced to the strikes but has never explicitly consented for fear of a domestic backlash.[39] Without consent of the host government or SC authorization, the only possible legal justification for the strikes is self-defense, in which case they would still have to comply with the laws of armed conflict and human rights standards. The Bush Administration never made the legal case, other than the brief riposte in the Human Rights Commission noted above.

In his presidential campaign, Obama announced that he would take the fight against Al-Qaeda to Pakistan, including through drone strikes. He made good on his promise: in 2009, there were 51 reported strikes in Pakistan, compared with 45 during the entire Bush Administration. In 2010, the number rose to 106 by the end of November.[40] Initially, the administration offered no legal justification, although President Obama made an oblique reference to the strikes in a speech at West Point. Formal justification was left to State Department Legal Adviser Harold Koh who—more than two years into Obama's first term—set out the administration's legal position in a speech to the American Society

---

[37] *Id.* at para. 17.

[38] Michael Dennis, "Human Rights in 2002: The Annual Sessions of the UN Commission on Human Rights and the Economic and Social Council," 97 *American Journal of International Law* 364, 367 (2003).

[39] Shane Harris, "Are Drone Strikes Murder," *National Journal* 21, 25 (January 9, 2010),. Available at http://www.nationaljournal.com/njmagazine/cs_20100109_2393.php.

[40] The New American Foundation, "The Year of the Drone: An Analysis of US Drone Strikes in Pakistan 2004-2010, available at http://counterterrorism.newamerica.net; Peter Bergen and Katherine Tiedemann, "The Year of the Drone: An Analysis of US Drone Strikes in Pakistan, 2004–2010," Counterterrorism Strategy Initiative Policy Paper, New American Foundation, February 24, 2010.

of International Law.[41] The Obama administration not only ratcheted up the intensity of the drone strikes, it also ratcheted up the legal justifications, albeit belatedly.

The justificatory process is telling. The pressure to present a legal case came from two critics in particular: Philip Alston, UN Special Rapporteur on extrajudicial, summary, or arbitrary executions; and Kenneth Anderson, professor of international law at the American University Washington College of Law. The two occupy different positions in the "interpretive community," and their views on the legality of the strikes differ (Alston doubts they are legal, Anderson insists they are). Where they agree is that the United States should publicly justify them, according to Alston, because the law requires "transparency and accountability"[42]; according to Anderson, it is in order to counter an "international soft law campaign" against the strikes.[43] Others chimed in on the substance of the debate, including Mary Ellen O'Connell, Sean Murphy, Jordan Paust, and Nils Melzer.[44] Articles appeared in influential magazines, like *The New Yorker, Harpers, The Weekly Standard, The New Republic,* and *The National Journal.*[45] The ACLU weighed in as did the ICRC, indirectly, by issuing guidance on who is "a direct participant" in conflict and therefore a legitimate target. Other influential voices were the head of the International Law Branch of the U.S. Judge Advocate's General Office,[46] two former high-ranking British intelligence officers,[47] and the ICC prosecutor. The latter reportedly "chuckled" when asked whether he would investigate the drone strikes and said, "we have

---

[41] Harold Koh, "The Obama Administration and International Law," Annual Meeting of the ASIL, March 25, 2010, available at http://www.state.gov/s/l/releases/remarks/139119.htm.

[42] Philip Alston, "Report of the Special Rapporteur on extrajudicial, summary or arbitrary executions: Addendum," UN Doc. A/HRC/1424/Add.6 (May 28, 2010).

[43] Kenneth Anderson, "Predators Over Pakistan," *The Weekly Standard,* March 8, 2010, 26 (Washington College of Law Research Paper no. 2010-06). See also Anderson, "Targeted Killing in US Counterterrorism Strategy and Law," Working Paper of the Series on Counterterrorism Strategy and American Statutory Law, a joint project of the Brookings Institution, Georgetown University Law Center and the Hoover Institution, May 11, 2009. Available at http://papers.ssrn.com/sol3/papers.cfm?abstract_id=1415070.

[44] Mary Ellen O'Connell, "Unlawful Killing with Combat Drones: A Case Study of Pakistan, 2004-2009," University of Notre Dame Law School Legal Studies Research Paper No. 09-43 (November 2009). Sean Murphy, "The International Legality of U.S. Military Cross-Border Operations from Afghanistan into Pakistan," 84 *International Law Studies* 18 (2009); Nils Melzer, *Targeted Killing in International Law* (2008); Jordan Paust, "Self-Defense Targetings of Non-State Actors and Permissibility of US Use of Drones in Pakistan," 19 *Journal of Transnational Law and Policy* (2010).

[45] Jane Mayer, "The Predator War, What are the Risks of the CIA's Covert Drone Program?" *The New Yorker,* October 26, 2009, 36; Scott Horton, "Rules for Drone Wars: Six Questions for Philip Alston," *Harper's Magazine,* June 2010; Kenneth Anderson. "Predators Over Pakistan," *The Weekly Standard,* March 8, 2010, 26–34; Bergen and Tiedemann, *supra* note 40; Harris, *supra* note 39.

[46] Chris Jenks, "Law from Above: Unmanned Aerial Systems, Use of Force and the Law of Armed Conflict," 85 *North Dakota Law Review* 650 (2009).

[47] Steven Simon and Jonathan Stevenson, "Afghanistan: How Much is Enough?," 51 *Survival* 47–67 (2009).

people around the world concerned about this. . . whatever the gravest war crimes are that have been committed, we have to check."[48]

Meanwhile, the Obama administration is replete with lawyers who profess commitment to international law, including the president and secretary of state, as well as Harold Koh, Ann Marie Slaughter, Michael Posner, and Sarah Cleveland. Originally, Koh avoided commenting on the issue, for example, in an informal televised discussion with his predecessor John Bellinger.[49] Then, in his ASIL speech, he stated categorically that "lethal operations conducted with the use of unmanned armed vehicles comply with all applicable law, including the laws of war." The United States was in an "ongoing armed conflict with al-Qaeda, the Taliban, and associated forces in response to 9/11 and may use force consistent with its inherent right to self-defense. In targeting decisions, the principles of distinction and proportionality are respected." Koh then went on to address four of the objections raised against U.S. targeting killing. While not a "detailed legal opinion," as he acknowledged, the ASIL speech was a serious attempt at legal justification.

Following the speech, debate on the blogs caught fire. Anderson responded (favorably) as did Alston (less favorably). The latter called the speech an "important starting point," but it failed to address the questions about overreach and did not mention that the strikes were conducted by the CIA.[50] Both human rights and international humanitarian law impose requirements of transparency, accountability, and disclosure[51]; the CIA, which operates in virtual secrecy, fails the test. The most striking thing about Alston's report issued shortly before the Koh speech, and in an interview he gave to *Harper's* magazine just after, is that they are, in essence, appeals for explicit legal justification. Almost all of his recommendations pertain to the need for states to identify the rules of international law they are operating under, the bases for decisions to kill, the procedural safeguards in place to ensure they comply with the law, the number of citizens killed collaterally, and the measures in place to provide "prompt, thorough, effective independent and public investigations of international law."[52] All are presented as legal requirements, not simply as good policy.

Coming at it from a different angle, Anderson appeals for an "aggressive defense" against the critics of the policy, who are moving to create around drone warfare "a narrative of American wickedness and cowardice and CIA perfidy."[53] He refers to an international soft law campaign conducted by the "legal-media-academic-NGO-international organization-global opinion complex." Similarly, Shane Harris recalls how debates that

---

[48] Quoted in Harris, *supra* note 39, at 24
[49] Anderson, "Predators," *supra* note 43, at 27.
[50] Horton, *supra* note 45.
[51] Alston, "Report of the Special Rapporteur," *supra* note 42, paras 88-90.
[52] *Id.* para. 93.
[53] Anderson, "Predators," *supra* note 43, at 27.

started in the "rarefied circles of scholars and activists" eventually changed U.S. law on detention and interrogation.[54] As Benjamin Wittes put it:

> What starts as academic papers becomes the position of human rights groups and international NGOs. And then, over time, they make their way first into foreign legal opinions, and eventually into U.S. legal opinions, either migrating generally through academic authority or through institutions.[55]

This is a fascinating account of the power of legal discourse starting in the broader, outer circle of the interpretive community, gathering steam, and penetrating the corridors of power, leading to a change in policy. In a ringing realist appeal for public justification, of the drone strikes, Anderson states:

> Other states, the United Nations, international tribunals, NGOs and academics can cavil and disagree with what the United States thinks is the law. But no Great Power's consistently reiterated views of international law, particularly in the field of international security, can be dismissed out of hand. It is true of the United States and it is also true of China. It is not a matter of 'might makes right'. It is, rather, a mechanism that keeps international law grounded in reality. . . It remains tethered to the real world both as law and practice, conditioned by how states see and act on the law. . . . The Obama administration has an obligation to itself and its successors to preserve their legal powers of national security. The United States must use these legal powers or lose them.[56]

In other words, the U.S. government needs to defend its practices, or it will lose its legal right to engage in those practices, compromising its ability to win support for its policies both nationally and internationally. Legal justification matters.

III. SECURITY COUNCIL LEGISLATION: RESOLUTIONS 1373 AND 1540[57]

When the end of the superpower rivalry freed the SC from the relative paralysis of the Cold War, it began to assume expansive new functions. The extensive obligations on Iraq in the aftermath of the 1991 Gulf War, the creation of criminal tribunals in former

---

[54] Harris, *supra* note 39.

[55] Benjamin Wittes, *Law and the Long War: The Future of Justice in the Age of Terror* (2008).

[56] Anderson, "Predators," *supra* note 43, at 30. For a similar argument about the impact of the practice of great powers on legal rules, see Glennon, *The Fog of Law*, Chapter 4, *supra* note 23.

[57] This section draws on and updates Ian Johnstone, "Security Council legislation and adjudication: bringing down the deliberative deficit" 102 *American Journal of International Law* 275 (2008).

Yugoslavia and Rwanda, and the establishment of international transitional administrations in Kosovo and East Timor, for example, far exceeded what the founders of the UN envisioned. The Council also began to play a more significant role in shaping international law through its declarative, interpretive, and enforcement functions.[58] Yet all of these innovations either respond to a particular crisis or do not impose binding obligations and therefore are not truly "legislative." Resolutions 1373 and 1540 are different. By establishing new rules of international law rather than issuing commands to deal with a discrete conflict, they create obligations of a sort usually found only in treaties.[59] These acts create law for all states in a general issue area, without setting any time limit or conditions for terminating the obligations.[60] They were possible in the post-9/11 climate because that shocking event provoked a widespread belief that traditional ways of making international law were not up to the challenge of countering terrorism and the risk of the proliferation of WMD to nonstate actors. However, they have been controversial, seen by some as examples of "hegemonic law" in action: the United States using its overwhelming influence in the SC to redefine the role of the institution and rewrite the rules of international law.[61] While there is truth to that characterization of the resolutions, my argument is that democratic deliberation can legitimize outcomes that serve collective interests, even when initiated by a hegemon.

---

[58] Steven Ratner, "The Security Council and International Law," in *The UN Security Council: From the Cold War to the 21st Century* 591–605 (David Malone ed., 2004),.

[59] Many commentators have pointed to the unprecedented nature of the resolutions, some though not all describing them as legislation. See Paul Szasz, "The Security Council starts legislating," 96 *American Journal of International Law* 901, 902 (2002); José Alvarez, "Hegemonic International Law Revisited," 97 *American Journal of International Law* 873 (2003); Jane Stromseth, "The Security Council's Counter-Terrorism Role: Continuity and Innovation," *ASIL Proceedings 2003*, 41 at 41; Matthew Happhold "Security Council resolution 1373 and the Constitution of the UN," 16 *Leiden Journal of International Law* 593–610 (2003); Eric Rosand, "Security Council Resolution 1373, the Counter-Terrorism Committee, and the Fight Against Terrorism," 97 *American Journal of International Law* 333 (2003); Curtis Ward, "Building Capacity to Combat International Terrorism: The Role of the United Nations Security Council," 8 *Journal of Conflict and Security Law* 298 (2003), Nicholas Rostow, "Before and After: The Changed UN Response to Terrorism since September 11," 35 *Cornell Journal of International Law* 475, 482 (2002); Cortright, Millar, Gerber and Lopez, "An Action Agenda for Enhancing the UN Program on Counter-Terrorism," Fourth Freedom Forum and Joan Kroc Institute for International Peace Studies and University of Notre Dame (2004) at 3. For a comprehensive treatment of the lawmaking powers of the Security Council, see José Alvarez, *International Organizations as Law-Makers* 189–217 (2005).

[60] As José Alvarez states: "the generalizable legal effects of the Council's work are not incidental to its efforts to enforce... They are express attempts to make global law." *Id, International Organizations* at 198.

[61] José Alvarez, "Hegemonic International Law Revisited," 97 *American Journal of International Law* 873, 875 (2003); Alvarez, *International Organizations, supra* note 59, at 202 Alvarez invokes Detlev Vagts concept of hegemonic law, who in turn refers to three German scholars, Heinrich Triepel, Carl Schmitt, and Grewe. Detlev Vagts, "Hegemonic International Law," 95 *American Journal of International Law* 843 (2001).

A. Negotiation and Implementation of Resolution 1373

Resolution 1373 was adopted 17 days after 9/11. A Chapter VII resolution, it obliges all states to suppress financing and other forms of support for terrorist groups. The SC created a Counter-terrorism Committee (CTC), composed of all its members, to oversee the resolution by reviewing state reports on implementation and arranging for technical assistance to upgrade national legislative and executive machinery.[62]

A U.S. initiative, the unanimous passage of resolution 1373 was very smooth. All SC ambassadors, including representatives of the P5, had received instructions from their capitals to cooperate with the United States in the post-9/11 climate.[63] The resolution was presented as both a response to 9/11 and as the logical next step in the Council's counter-terrorism efforts, which included three sanctions regimes (against Libya in 1992, Sudan in 1996, and the Taliban in 1999)[64] and a thematic 1999 resolution declaring terrorism to be a threat to the peace.[65] No delegation objected to the SC "legislating," and it is doubtful any member states even saw it in those terms.[66] While generic in its language, the resolution came in the wake of a clear and devastatingly real manifestation of the type of threat it was aimed at preventing.[67] As such, it could be seen as a natural extension of the SC's traditional crisis management role. In a Ministerial meeting of the Council on November 12, 2001, all 15 foreign ministers expressed their support for resolution 1373 and willingness to cooperate with the CTC.[68] U.S. Secretary of State Colin Powell called it "a mandate to change fundamentally how the international community responds to terrorism." No minister dissented.

The early stages of implementation of resolution 1373 also proceeded smoothly, due largely to the deft diplomacy of the first chairman of the CTC, Ambassador Jeremy Greenstock of the UK. Greenstock stressed the nonthreatening character of the CTC, claiming it was designed to engage states in an open-ended dialogue and to build national capacity in areas like legislative drafting, investigation, and border control. He described

---

[62] Eric Rosand, "Security Council Resolution 1373, the Counter-terrorism committee and the fight against terrorism" 97 *American Journal of International Law* 333, 334 (2003). See also Alistair Millar and Eric Rosand, *Allied Against Terrorism: What's Needed to Strengthen Worldwide Commitment* (2006).

[63] Interview with Carolyn Wilson, Permanent Mission of the United States to the United Nations, July 19, 2004. In addition to this general sense of grievance, there was also a desire on the part of some delegations–especially the French–to avoid marginalization of the UN by the US. Interview with Ambassador Kishore Mahubani, Permanent Representative of Singapore to the United Nations, July 21, 2004.

[64] UN SC Res 748 (1992); UN SC Res 1054 and 1070 (1996); UN SC Res 1267 (1999).

[65] UN SC Res 1269, (1999). Danilo Turk, "Law and Policy: Security Council's Ability to Innovate," *American Society of International Law Proceedings* 51, 53 (2003).

[66] Interviews with Wilson and Mahubani, *supra* note 63. See also Paul Szasz, "The Security Council starts legislating," 96 *American Journal of International Law* 901, 905 (2002).

[67] Interview with Ambassador Akram, Permanent Representative of Pakistan to the United Nations, July 21, 2004.

[68] United Nations (2001) S/PV.4413, Meeting Records, New York: Security Council, November 12, 2001.

the Committee as a "switchboard," brokering deals between states who needed technical assistance and those who could provide it.[69] In the fall of 2003, one of the CTC experts did an informal analysis of the overall picture of compliance with 1373.[70] The expert rated the compliance of 30 countries as good; 60 more as being in transition, moving gradually into compliance; 70 as "willing but unable"; and 20 as materially able to comply but unwilling.[71]

Despite the steady record of reporting, the dialogic approach of the CTC began to run out of steam in late 2003. Based on a report on implementation problems written by the new Spanish chairman, the Committee proposed (and the SC approved in resolution 1535) a set of reforms designed to enable the Committee to play a more proactive compliance monitoring role, to make more site visits, and to facilitate technical assistance to states that needed it most.[72] The most innovative structural reform was a new Counter-Terrorism Executive Directorate (CTED)—a body of 20 experts—created in March 2004 but not declared operational until the end of 2005.

The proposal for a new CTED generated controversy, reflected in a row over whether it should report directly to the CTC or through the Secretary-General. The controversy stemmed from a concern that the Directorate could undermine the Secretariat and authority of the Secretary-General by creating a new structure accountable to the SC only (and, by implication, its most powerful members).[73] The end result was a compromise in which the CTED would operate under the "policy guidance" of the CTC, but the Executive Director would be appointed by and report through the Secretary-General,

---

[69] Report by Chair of the Counter-Terrorism Committee on the problems encountered in the implementation of UN SC Res 1373 (2001), UN S/2004/70, January 26, 2004, at 8.

[70] Curtis Ward, CTC independent expert, describes the responses of states as "overwhelming and unprecedented." C. Ward, "Building Capacity to Combat International Terrorism: The Role of the UN Security Council." 8 *Journal of Conflict and Security Law* 289, 299 (2003).

[71] David Cortright et al., "An Action Agenda for Enhancing the United Nations Program on Counter-Terrorism," 7 (2004), available at http://www.fourthfreedom.org/Applications/cms.php?page_id=183.

[72] UN SC Res 1535 (2004) The Committee's proposals are contained in UN S/2004/124, February 19, 2004.

[73] The United States and UK pushed hardest for direct reporting of the CTED to the CTC. Evidence of the depth of concern about that approach is the number of states who stressed in an open meeting several weeks prior to the adoption of resolution 1535 that the CTED should be part of the Secretariat and not in any way undermine it. United Nations (2004) S/PV.4921, Meeting Records, New York: Security Council, March 4, 2004. Statements of Spain (as Chair of the Committee); p. 4, Benin, p. 5; UK, p. 9; Germany (referring to the views expressed by the Secretariat in a letter of March 3, 2004), p. 15; Pakistan, p. 17; Ireland (on behalf of the EU), p. 19. S/PV.4921 (Resumption 1), March 4, 2004. Statements of Argentina (on behalf of the Rio Group), p. 4; South Africa, p. 8; and Indonesia, p. 11. That the concerns persisted until the end of 2006 is reflected in the felt need of the Security Council to clarify reporting lines between the CTED, Secretariat and CTC. UN S/PRST/2006/56, December 20, 2006.

and its staff members would be subject to Article 100 of the UN Charter, the cornerstone of an independent international civil service.[74]

While the CTC continues to be controversial, the level of cooperation with it is impressive, and its workload continues to expand. Most countries have established legal frameworks for the expeditious freezing of assets; administrative infrastructure (such as financial intelligence units) is being strengthened in many countries; banks and other financial institutions are increasingly aware of the new regulations; and prosecutions are ocurring.[75] In 2006, the CTED began doing "preliminary implementation assessments" of all states; by May 2010, these had been received from every state and had been analyzed by the directorate, which was moving on to stock taking and capacity building for those who were lagging in implementation.[76] In September 2005, the CTC was given the added responsibility of monitoring implementation of a Council resolution on incitement to terrorism.[77]

B. Resolution 1373 and Deliberative Legitimacy

Deliberative principles informed the implementation of resolution 1373, if not its adoption. There were few active participants in the negotiations on drafting the resolution (indeed, there was not much negotiation at all), but the sense of urgency and the post-9/11 political climate made quick adoption both possible and tolerable.[78] Participation in the debates and discussions on *implementation*, on the other hand, has been extensive. The first opportunity came with the Ministerial meeting of November 2001, six weeks after the resolution was adopted, signifying an effort on the part of Council members to publicize its involvement in the fight against terrorism and to give a high-profile launch to the CTC. All 15 foreign ministers spoke in support of the resolution. Nonmembers were not invited to speak at that meeting, but its highly public nature presented a perfect opportunity for states who wanted to mobilize opposition to do so. None did.

---

[74] Article 100 reads in part "In the performance of their duties the Secretary-General and the staff shall not seek or receive instructions from any government... Each Member of the United Nations undertakes to respect the exclusively international character of the responsibilities of the Secretary-General and the staff."

[75] See Thomas Biersteker, "The UN's Counter-Terrorism Efforts: Lessons for UNSCR 1540," in *Global Non-Proliferation and Counter-Terrorism* 29–34 (O. Bosch and P. van Ham eds., 2007); United Nations Counter-Terrorism Committee, *Survey of the Implementation of Security Council Resolution 1373 (2001) by Member States*, 3 December 2009, S/2009/620; James Cockayne, Alistair Millar and Jason Ipe, *An Opportunity for Renewal: Rebuilding the UN Counterterrorism Program* (2010).

[76] Briefing by the Chairman of the CTC to the Security Council on May 10, 2010, available at http://www.un.org/en/sc/ctc/pdf/CTC_chair_may_2010.pdf

[77] UN SC Res 1624 (2005).

[78] Nicholas Rostow, Legal Adviser in the US Mission to the UN at the time, states that it might not have been possible reach agreement on the resolution even a few weeks later. Nicholas Rostow, "Before and After: The Changed UN Response to Terrorism since 9/11," 35 *Cornell International Law Journal* 475, 482 fn. 40 (2002).

As the CTC went about its work, the Chairman made a conscious effort to operate on the basis of transparency and dialogue.[79] Resolution 1373 was not likely to be enforced coercively, and so effective implementation would require buy-in by the wider UN membership. Guidelines on the work of the CTC were published, and regular briefings to member states and the media were conducted. The late 2003 revitalization was the subject of intense and fairly inclusive debate. A package of measures agreed within the Committee was published as an official document in January 2004, giving the entire UN membership a chance to review, consider, and comment on them informally. A formal, open meeting of the Council was held on March 4, at which 36 states offered opinions on the proposals. In that meeting, many of the Council members stressed that the Committee would continue to operate on the basis of "transparency, cooperation and even-handedness." Many of the non-Council members expressed appreciation for the open debate and for the transparent way in which consultations had been conducted. The statement of Ireland, speaking for the EU, is illustrative:

> The European Union attaches real importance to these periodic open debates of the Security Council in which we review the work and progress of the CTC. . . . Such a transparent debate will contribute to a key goal of the reform: that is, to maintain and, hopefully, to strengthen the CTC's general acceptance by—and perceived legitimacy with—all members of the United Nations family.[80]

Somewhat less enthusiastically, the Ambassador of South Africa said about the opportunity to participate in the debate on reform of the CTC:

> We meet today at a time when the Security Council has already completed its review of the strategic direction, structure and procedures of the Counter-Terrorism Committee and has even commenced negotiations on a new resolution. We would hope that it is not too late for the views of the wider UN membership to be taken into consideration and that we can accurately express our views in the few short minutes allocated to us.[81]

Concerns that the "revitalization" of the CTC might alter the working methods of the Committee were ultimately dispelled.[82] In a review published in September 2010, the

---

[79] Ward says transparency was "the hallmark of [the CTC's] operations—its modus operandi if you will." Ward, *supra* note 70, at 298. See also Rosand, *supra* note 62, at 335–36; Rostow, *id.* at 482–83.
[80] S/PV.4921 *supra* note 73, at 19. See also statement of India, p. 20; Switzerland, p. 21; South Korea, p. 30; Argentina (on behalf of the Rio Group), S/PV.4921 (Resumption 1), p. 3.
[81] S/.PV.4921 (Resumption 1), *supra* note 73, atp. 7.
[82] For expressions of that anxiety, see S/PV.4921, the Philippines, pp. 13–14; India, p. 21; Egypt, Resumption 1, p. 2.

Centre on Global Counterterrorism found a consensus among the many diplomats and others it interviewed that the committee have made significant progress in developing a more transparent, inclusive, and collegial decision-making style.[83] The preliminary assessments of member states' implementation of their obligations under Resolution 1373 served, in the words of the representative of the Russian Federation, "as basic documents for regular dialogue with States and as an objective, non-discriminatory and systemic foundation for monitoring the counter-terrorism efforts of States."[84] Moreover, that views other than those of the most powerful Council members were taken into account in the revitalization process is reflected in the CTC's greater attentiveness to human rights since then.[85]

Thus, the knowledge that implementation of resolution 1373 was a long-term, potentially highly intrusive exercise generated a good deal of concern about the Council acting as a legislature. The Council and CTC responded by engaging in unusually wide consultations and transparent working methods, even at the expense of some efficiency. This nod to deliberative principles assuaged the worst fears of some of the UN membership, and implementation improved in direct proportion to the Committee's ability to address legitimacy concerns. With a comprehensive review of the CTED's work scheduled for the end of 2010, the UN membership will have another chance to engage in intensive debate on this unusual legislative act by the Security Council.[86]

C. Negotiation and Implementation of Resolution 1540

Resolution 1540 is both a counter-terrorism and non-proliferation resolution that aims at preventing WMD from falling into the hands of terrorists. Adopted under Chapter VII, it demands that all states refrain from supporting efforts by nonstate actors to acquire such weapons and to adopt appropriate legislation and enforcement

---

[83] Cockayne et al, *supra* note 75, at 10. See also, Eric Rosand, "From Adoption to Action: The UN's Role in Implementing its Global Counter-terrorism Strategy." Center on Global Counter-terrorism Cooperation, Policy Brief April 2009.

[84] United Nations (2010), S/PV.6310, Meeting Records, New York: Security Council, 11 May 2010, p. 16.

[85] The Committee had initially taken the position that it was not a human rights body and that human rights considerations should be dealt with elsewhere in the UN system. In the revitalization debate, Brazil, Germany, Chile, Ireland for the EU, Liechtentstein, Argentina for the Rio Group, Mexico, Costa Rica and Canada all expressed concerns about the impact of counter-terrorism measures on human rights. See S/PV.4921 and S/PV/4921 (Resumption 1), March 4, 2004. The UN Secretary-General first expressed his concern that action against terrorism should not undermine human rights to the Security Council in January 2002. United Nations (2002) S/PV.4453, Meeting Records, New York: Security Council, January 18, 2002, p. 3. In May 2006, the CTC gave "policy guidance" to the CTED on how to ensure human rights are respected in the implementation of resolution 1373. S/2006/989 (December 18, 2006). Endorsed by the Security Council in S/PRST/2006/56 (December 20, 2006). For a recent assessment of the CTC's evolving practice with respect of human rights, see Cockayne et al, *supra* note 75.

[86] UN SC Res 1805 (2008).

measures to prevent that. It established a committee to oversee implementation of the resolution–the so-called 1540 Committee—which lacks a CTED-type structure, but it can call on appropriate expertise to assist in its work. Implementation occurs through a system of state reporting to the 1540 Committee on measures taken. These are reviewed by the Committee and its group of experts, who engage in constructive dialogue and try to broker technical assistance to help states come into compliance.

The seeds for the resolution were planted by the UK when it circulated a non-paper among EU countries in early 2003 proposing the idea of a "counter-proliferation committee," modeled on the CTC.[87] U.S. President Bush picked up the idea in a speech to the UN General Assembly on September 24, 2003, when he called for the SC to adopt a new anti-proliferation resolution, which would require "all members of the UN to criminalize the proliferation of weapons of mass destruction, to enact stringent export controls consistent with international standards and to secure any and all sensitive materials within their own borders."[88]

Consultations among the P5 began in October 2003 and proceeded exclusively among them for five months. By the end of that period, four of the five had reached agreement on a draft. (China did not oppose it but took the position that it would continue to negotiate.[89]) The consultations extended to other members of the Council in March 2004, and on April 22, the draft resolution was discussed at length. Meanwhile, the co-sponsors became active in briefing regional groups (the Non-Aligned Movement, Arab Group, Latin American group, and the African group), and in trying to "de-fang" opponents by providing answers to questions and rumors that had been building up during the period of more closed negotiations.[90] After the open meeting, the resolution was revised once more and then adopted by unanimous vote on April 29.

Negotiation of resolution 1540 was more contentious than 1373, for several reasons.[91] First, the political climate had changed in the years between 9/11 and early 2004, not least because of the Iraq war. Second, it came on the heels of the U.S.-led Proliferation

---

[87] Merav Datan, "Security Council resolution 1540: WMD and Non-state Trafficking," 79 *Disarmament Diplomacy* (April/May2005).

[88] Bush's speech is reproduced in full in *New York Times*, Sept. 24, 2003, p. A10. He repeated it again in Feb. 2004 in a speech at the National Defense University, *New York Times*, Feb. 12, 2004.

[89] Interview with Sohail Mahmood, Permanent Mission of Pakistan to the UN, July 21, 2004.

[90] Interview with Nicholas Rostow, U.S. Mission to the UN, July 19, 2004. One theory circulating was that resolution 1540 was a backdoor way of circumventing the IAEA process to bring states like Iran into line. Interview with Harsh Shringla, Permanent Mission of India, July 21, 2004.

[91] My analysis of the contentious nature of 1540 is based on concerns expressed in the Security Council meetings in late April by Pakistan, India, Brazil, Algeria, South Africa, Indonesia, Iran, Egypt, Mexico, and Cuba. United Nations (2004) S/PV.4950, Meeting Records, New York: Security Council, April 22, 2004; United Nations (2004) S/PV.4956, Meeting Records, New York: Security Council, April 28, 2004. It is also based on personal interviews with diplomats from the United States, Spain, Brazil, India, and Pakistan, between July 19 and July 21, 2004 all of whom were involved in the negotiations.

Security Initiative, which generated suspicion that 1540 was designed primarily to universalize and make mandatory the interdiction principles that only a limited number of states had agreed to at that time. Third, while resolution 1373 takes elements of international law and extends it to all UN members, 1540 "fills gaps" in existing law. In that sense, its "legislative" character was more unsettling. Fourth, resolution 1540 encroaches more deeply on existing treaties and the institutions established to monitor them than resolution 1373. Finally, many states feared that adopting the resolution under Chapter VII could trigger military enforcement action.

Pakistan in particular was adamant that resolution 1540 exceeded the competence of the SC.[92] The threat of terrorists acquiring WMD was real, but there had never been a concrete manifestation of that threat, unlike the subject matter of resolution 1373. To Pakistan, 1540 looked like "abstract legislation," disconnected from the Council's crisis management role. Moreover, the SC was not the best "repository of authority" on WMD, where disarmament by the declared nuclear powers, who also happen to be the five permanent members of the Security Council, was not likely to see much headway. Brazil, South Africa, Egypt, India, Germany, and other European countries were less adamant, but they also took pains to stress that SC action should complement and strengthen rather than undermine the existing non-proliferation regimes.

Ultimately, the resolution was adopted unanimously because those who had doubts about the propriety of this kind of SC action could claim it temporarily filled a gap in the law to address an urgent threat, pending adoption of a multilateral treaty (Pakistan, New Zealand, India, Iran, Kuwait, China, and Nigeria). Many also commented on the explicit assurance in the resolution that it would "not conflict with or alter the rights and obligations" of parties to existing conventions or with the responsibilities of the IAEA and OPCW (Ireland on behalf of EU, Australia, Jordan, Lichtenstein, Spain, and Brazil). The fact that it was explicitly connected to terrorism also made the resolution more acceptable: as an anti-terrorism rather than non-proliferation measure, it was easier to rationalize the minimal references in it to disarmament.[93]

Although many of the concerns of member states were taken into account in the final version of resolution 1540, "in the end, lots of delegations still had some misgivings about

---

[92] The following account of Pakistan's position is from my interview with Ambassador Akram on July 20, 2004, a non-paper circulated by Pakistan to the entire UN membership in late March 2004, and the statements of Pakistan in SC meetings on April 22 and 28, 2004.

[93] Interviews with Davide Carrideo, Permanent Mission of Spain, July 20, 2004 and Luis Guilhermo, Permanent Mission of Brazil, July 21, 2004. Brazil, in particular, wanted to avoid the term "non-proliferation" in connection with 1540, as that applied to states, and instead to introduce new concepts like "non-access, non-transfer and non-availability" to non-state actors. S/PV.4950, p. 4. On the connection between 1540 and the broader counter-terrorism agenda of the Security Council, see Peter van Ham and Olivia Bosch, "Global Non-Proliferation and Counter-Terrorism: The Role of Resolution 1540 and Its Implications," in O. Bosch and P. van Ham eds, *Global Non-Proliferation and Counter-terrorism* (2007) at 7–9, 24, 29–34.

the text," according to Germany's Permanent Representative to the UN.[94] Pakistan worked hard to dilute the mandate of the 1540 committee, successfully stalling any substantive action until it rotated off the Council at the end of 2004.[95] The Committee's work accelerated in 2005, but by September 2006, 59 states had still not submitted their first national reports, and of the 132 who had, only 84 had provided additional information as requested by the Committee.[96] Things did not improve much and by October 2009, a close follower of the resolution and its committee said it was not getting the support or cooperation it needed.[97] Only eight experts had been assigned to its work, due to combined resistance of the United States (which under the Bush administration was not enthusiastic about creating new positions for international civil servants) and the NAM, which was never enthusiastic about the 1540 Committee. The mandate of the experts was quite limited, they were not able to do much capacity building or threat analysis, and the interaction with NGOs and other expert groups has been minimal.[98] On the other hand, the Committee and resolution received a strong boost from the SC summit chaired by President Obama in September 2009.[99] A comprehensive review held at the end of that month gave all states the chance to weigh in on the functioning of the regime, and the

---

[94] Colum Lynch, "Weapons Transfers Targeted: UN Security Council resolutions seeks criminalization," *The Washington Post*, April 29, 2004, p. A21. Similarly, Ambassador Baali of Algeria told the *New York Sun*, Pakistan and other members were concerned about the resolution, but "unless you are one of the five veto powers, it is very difficult to remain outside the consensus." Benny Avni, "WMD Proliferation resolution passes," *New York Sun*, April 29, 2004, p. 7.

[95] Millar and Rosand, *supra* note 62, at 18.

[96] United Nations (2006) S/PV.5538, Meeting Records, New York: Security Council, September 28, 2006, p.7.

[97] Eric Rosand, *Global Implementation of SC Resolution 1540: An Enhanced UN Response Needed*, Center for Global Counterterrorism Cooperation, Policy Brief October 2009.

[98] *Id.*

[99] UN SC Res 1887 (2009) adopted at the conclusion of that Summit contains many provisions that address the risk of nuclear terrorism and nuclear trafficking, including two that refer to resolution 1540 directly:

> 22. *Welcomes* the March 2009 recommendations of the Security Council committee established pursuant to resolution 1540 (2004) to make more effective use of existing funding mechanisms, including the consideration of the establishment of a voluntary fund, and *affirms* its commitment to promote full implementation of resolution 1540 (2004) by Member States by ensuring effective and sustainable support for the activities of the 1540 Committee;
>
> 23. *Reaffirms* the need for full implementation of resolution 1540 (2004) by Member States and, with an aim of preventing access to, or assistance and financing for, weapons of mass destruction, related materials and their means of delivery by non-State actors, as defined in the resolution, *calls upon* Member States to cooperate actively with the Committee established pursuant to that resolution and the IAEA, including rendering assistance, at their request, for their implementation of resolution 1540 (2004) provisions, and in this context *welcomes* the forthcoming comprehensive review of the status of implementation of resolution 1540 (2004) with a view to increasing its effectiveness, and *calls upon* all States to participate actively in this review;

chairman of the 1540 Committee produced a report in early 2010 that gave the impression of continued support for the resolution, despite its controversial nature.[100]

D. Resolution 1540 and Deliberative Legitimacy

While there is general sympathy with the need for the P5 to consult among themselves first on certain issues, the far-reaching implications of what was seen as a generic "non-proliferation" resolution under Chapter VII caused considerable anxiety. Thus negotiation of resolution 1540 was initially more contentious and ultimately more open and inclusive than 1373. A measure of the importance attached to the deliberative process is the number of states that referred to the process in the open meeting on April 22, 2004, requested by Canada, Mexico, New Zealand, South Africa, Sweden, and Switzerland. Fifty-one states spoke at the meeting, totaling over one quarter of the UN membership. More than half commented on the scope and timing of the consultations to that point, and almost as many expressed appreciation for the open meeting as an opportunity to participate in the negotiations on the draft.

The language of deliberative democracy permeated the debates. For example, the Permanent Representative of the Philippines stated:

> My delegation appreciates the timeliness of this open debate and the value of listening to the views of the general membership, who would be implementing the resolution. *Those who are bound should be heard. This is an essential element of a transparent and democratic process*, and is the best way to proceed on a resolution that demands legislative actions and executive measures from the 191 members of the U.N.[101][my emphasis]

New Zealand's ambassador said support for the draft resolution "requires the Council to dispel any impression of negotiations behind closed doors or that a small group of states is drafting laws for the broader membership without the opportunity for all Member States to express their views."[102] And the Permanent Representative of Malaysia struck a chord in this statement on behalf of the NAM:

> The Non-Aligned Movement sincerely hopes that the sponsors and other Council members will continue to take into consideration the views and concerns expressed

---

[100] Letter dated 29 January 2010 from the Chairman of the Security Council Committee established pursuant to resolution 1540 (2004) addressed to the President of the Security Council, 1 February 2010, S/2010/52.

[101] United Nations (2004) S.PV/4950, Meeting Records, New York: Security Council, April 22, 2004, p. 2. See also statements of Brazil, p. 3; China, p. 6; France, p. 8; Angola, pp. 9–10; UK, p. 11; Benin, p. 13; Romania, p. 14; United States, p. 18; Peru, p. 20; South Africa, p. 22; Ireland for the EU, pp. 25–26; Sweden, p. 27; Switzerland, p. 28; Indonesia, p. 32. S/PV.4950, Resumption 1: Egypt, p. 2; Mexico, p.4; Nigeria, pp. 15–16. S/PV.4956, France, p. 2; US, p. 5.

[102] *Id.* at 20.

by NAM member countries. . . . After all. . . governments, national legislatures and, for that matter the private sector in all Member countries are expected to cooperate and take appropriate measures, including the enactment of new legislation and the streamlining and amendment of existing legislation where applicable.[103]

When the application of resolution 1540 was extended for two years by resolution 1673 and a new program of work was devised, similar views were expressed.[104]

There was also organized nongovernmental input into the negotiating process, especially after March 24, 2004, when a draft resolution surfaced.[105] A group of NGOs called for an open meeting of the Council, sent a memorandum to the SC setting out its position as well as draft language for the resolution, issued a media advisory, and made regular statements to the press. Merav Datan describes the negotiations as "formally closed but informally and intentionally porous," out of awareness that the issue required "as much impact by global civil society as the SC negotiating process can tolerate."[106]

As with the revitalization of the CTC, changes were made to the draft of 1540 as a result of the broad consultations: references to disarmament obligations and the integrity of existing treaty regimes were added; a reference to "interdiction" was removed (discussed in Chapter 6); the sovereign rights of nonparties to non-proliferation treaties were affirmed; language on the usefulness of peaceful dialogue was strengthened; and the proposal to create a monitoring committee was introduced, with suitable reassurances about its role provided in the explanation of votes.[107] The changes were sufficient to induce even the staunchest critic to vote for the resolution (Pakistan), and a number of other states expressed satisfaction that their concerns had been taken into account (Brazil, Germany, Algeria, and the Philippines).

More than resolution 1373, implementation of resolution 1540 has had its ups and downs. But the United States and other permanent members of the SC have not given up on building support for it, as reflected in resolution 1887. They understand that its utility is primarily as a platform for cooperation rather than sanctioning mechanism, and that it is best cast as a counter-terrorism rather than non-proliferation initiative to keep the skeptics on board. The comprehensive review held at the end of September 2009 gave all states the chance to weigh in on the functioning of the regime—a significant attempt at

---

[103] *Id*, (Resumption 1), at 4.

[104] See generally Olivia Bosch and Peter Van Ham, "UNSCR 1540: Its Future and Contribution to Global Non-Proliferation and Counter-Terrorism," in Bosch and Ham, *supra* note 75, at 207–26.

[105] Datan, *supra* note 87.

[106] *Id*.

[107] Datan goes too far when she claims that a "counter-proliferation and PSI-type initiative. . .was transformed into a cooperative, iterative and interactive effort to address non-state access to NBC [nuclear, biological and chemical] weapons and affirm state non-proliferation and disarmament obligations," but her point about the organized input into the drafting process is well-taken. Datan, *id*.

legitimation through inclusive deliberation. Thus, despite its shaky start, resolution 1540 still had life in 2010 as an experiment by the SC in managing noncoercive efforts to address the risk of WMD terrorism.

IV. THE SECURITY COUNCIL AS QUASI-JUDICIAL BODY

As well as legislating, the SC has begun to act in a more overtly quasi-judicial manner in recent years most notably through the imposition of targeted sanctions that directly affect the rights of individuals. The first time the Council did this was in 1994, against the military junta in Haiti (resolution 917). Since then, a total of ten sanctions committees have been created with a mandate to list individuals and entities who are the target of sanctions: Sierra Leone (resolution 1132), the Taliban/Al Qaeda (resolution 1267), Iraq (resolution 1518), Liberia (resolution 1521), the Democratic Republic of the Congo (resolution 1533), Côte d'Ivoire (resolution 1572), Lebanon/Syria (resolution 1636), Sudan (resolution 1591), North Korea (resolution 1718), and Iran (resolution 1737).

A. The 1267 Targeted Sanctions Regime

The most controversial of these is the Taliban/Al Qaeda sanctions regime, imposed after the bombing of U.S. embassies in Kenya and Tanzania, for which Osama Bin Laden was held responsible. Resolution 1267 (1999) demanded that the Taliban end its support for terrorism and extradite bin Laden. It also set up a committee to monitor an asset freeze and travel ban on the Taliban. The sanctions were expanded by resolution 1333 (2000) to include an arms embargo, diplomatic restrictions, a broadened aviation ban, and an asset freeze on Al Qaeda and associated individuals. In that resolution, the Council called on the 1267 committee to keep a list of individuals associated with the Taliban, Al-Qaeda, or Osama Bin Laden, all of whom would be subject to the financial and travel sanctions. After the September 11 terrorist attacks and overthrow of the Taliban in 2001, the SC lifted the broader aviation sanctions but maintained the targeted travel and financial sanctions, as well as the arms embargo on the Taliban and Al-Qaeda.[108]

The 1267 committee has placed more than 500 names on its consolidated list. Most were designated by the United States shortly after 9/11, either alone or in conjunction with allies. A no-objection procedure is used: a name is submitted by any member state, international or regional organization, and unless there is an objection or hold placed, all states must freeze the assets of the person and ban his or her travel. According to a U.S. diplomat, in the early stages, the listing was based largely on political trust, with the

---

[108] UN SC resolution 1390 (2001).

committee having no formal guidelines or evidentiary standards for states to follow in proposing names.[109] Nor was there any provision for removing names from the list.

All of the "listing" committees have given rise to due process concerns, ranging from the adequacy of the presentation of the case against an individual prior to listing, to the time period for making decisions, the lack of notification, the process of requesting exemptions, and the way delisting petitions are handled.[110] The criticisms have been sharpest in the context of the 1267 regime because its scope is the widest; it is directly focused on nonstate actors; and it is preventative in character, imposing restraints on people and corporations not for what they have done in the past but for what they may do in the future. In response to the criticisms, a number of procedural changes have been made over the years, most recently in December 2009.[111] These are worth describing in some detail because both the process that led to the incremental changes and the changes themselves are illustrative of deliberative politics at work.

In August 2002, the Committee announced "delisting" procedures for the first time and, in November, adopted written guidelines both for listing and delisting. In December 2002, the SC carved out a set of humanitarian exemptions to the financial ban, allowing the release of funds to meet basic needs and for other "extraordinary expenses."[112] Resolution 1526 (2004) calls on states that propose names to include information about the individual's connection with Bin Laden, Al-Qaeda, or the Taliban. Resolution 1617 (2005) decides that states must provide the committee with a detailed "statement of the case describing the basis of the proposal." The resolution also clarified what activities would constitute "association" with Al-Qaeda and the Taliban.

---

[109] Millar and Rosand, *supra* note 62, at 20.

[110] Bardo Fassbender, *Targeted Sanctions and Due Process*, Study Commissioned by the UN Office of Legal Affairs, at 29–30 (2006); Thomas Watson Institute of International Studies, *Strengthening Targeted Sanctions Through Fair and Clear Procedures* (2006); Iain Cameron, "The European Convention on Human Rights, Due Process and United Nations Security Council Counter-terrorism Sanctions," Report commissioned by the Council of Europe, February 6, 2006; Alvarez, *International Organizations, supra* note 59, at 176, Peter Guthrie, "Security Council Sanctions and the Protection of Individual Rights," 60 *New York University Survey of American Law* 491, 503–06 (2004); Erika de Wet and Andre Noellkaemper eds, *Review of the Security Council by Member States* (2003). For an interesting application of administrative law standards of procedural fairness to global governance, see Benedict Kingsbury, Nico Krisch and Richard Stewart, "The Emergence of Global Administrative Law," 68 *Duke University School of Law* 15, 32, 34, 38, and 39 (Summer/Autumn 2005); David Dyzenhaus, "The Rule of (Administrative) Law in International Law," 68 *Law and Contemporary Problems* 127, 140–52 (Summer/Autumn 2005).

[111] For a good summary of the changes made to the end of 2008, see Thomas Watson Institute, *Addressing Challenges to Targeted Sanctions: An Update of the Watson Report* (October 2009), Appendix C [Hereinafter "Addressing Challenges"]. Since then, the Security Council has adopted Resolution 1904 (December 17, 2009), a 15-page resolution that, among other things, creates an Office of the Ombudsperson to carry out a range of tasks.

[112] UN SC Res 1452 (2002).

The Secretary-General's HLP on Threats, Challenges and Change recommended further reform, and the 2005 World Summit called for "fair and clear procedures" for listing and delisting individuals by all sanctions committees. In 2006, the UN Office of Legal Affairs commissioned a study by Professor Bardo Fassbender on due process concerns.[113] A number of governments commissioned a study by the Thomas Watson Institute at Brown University, also published in March 2006.[114] The 1267 committee all but ignored these academic studies, but the Secretary-General and his legal counsel drew on them in a letter sent to the president of the Security Council in mid-2006. Although not issued as an official document, legal counsel Nicolas Michel read the contents of the letter into the record at a public meeting.[115] In it, the SG set out what he thought were the minimum standards required to ensure fair procedures for listing and delisting: the right of targeted individuals to be informed of measures taken against them and why; the right of such individuals to make written submissions and to be represented by counsel; the right to review by an impartial, independent mechanism able to provide a remedy; and periodic review of the lists by the SC itself. These constitute a much fuller set of procedural rights than the Council as a whole was prepared to guarantee.

After some delay, the Committee and Council acted on the recommendations, as well as those put forward earlier in the year by the Sanctions Monitoring Team.[116] Revised procedures were approved by the committee in November, and endorsed by the SC in resolution 1735 at the end of December 2006.[117] The most important changes relate to the listing of names: a fuller statement of the case is required, including specific information and supporting documentation to show that the individual belongs on the list; designating states are requested to identify which parts of the statement can be publicly released; additional information is to be submitted as it becomes available; the country of residence or nationality of the target must be notified of the listing decision within two weeks; and those states are to endeavor to notify the individual of the decision and case against him or her.

Resolution 1735 does not add much to the delisting procedures, but a few days before it was adopted, the SC established a "focal point" to deal with delisting petitions for all sanctions regimes that target individuals.[118] The focal point would receive the petitions and forward them to the governments concerned for possible consideration by the

---

[113] *Security Council Report*, "Targeted Sanctions: Listing/De-Listing and Due Process" January 10, 2007, p. 19. Available at http://www.securitycouncilreport.org/site/c.glKWLeMTIsG/b.2294423/k.3920/January_2007 BRTargeted_Sanctions_ListingDeListing_and_Due_Process.htm.

[114] Thomas Bierkester and Sue Eckert, *Strengthening Targeted Sanctions Through Clear and Fair Procedures* (2006) [Hereinafter Watson Report].

[115] United Nations (2006) SPV 5474, Meeting Records, New York: Security Council, June 22, 2006, pp. 7–8.

[116] UN S/2006/154, March 10, 2006.

[117] UN SC Res 1735 (2006).

[118] *Id.*

Committee. Individuals can send petitions directly to the focal point—a significant step—but that is no guarantee the Committee will consider the request. Some government must take up the cause.

Further reforms were enacted with resolution 1822, adopted in June 2008. This ten-page resolution specifies the type of information states must provide for release to the public and as notification to the affected individual or entity: so-called narrative summaries of the case. It also calls for this information to be posted on the 1267 Web site. Most importantly, the Council launched a review of all the names on the list by June 2010 and then on an annual basis, thereafter, to ensure every name is reviewed at least every three years. This was seen as progress, but not enough by the critics who continued to complain about the lack of a transparent, deliberative process in the 1267 Committee on delisting requests and the lack of an effective remedy if a wrong decision is made. There is no independent review of SC decisions; the only review that takes place is in the 1267 Committee itself.[119]

This was partially remedied by resolution 1904 at the end of December 2009, a mammoth 15-page resolution that reaffirms or restates many of the existing obligations and enacts further procedural reforms. The most important is the creation of an Ombudsperson's Office, to be led by an "eminent individual of high moral character, impartiality and integrity with high qualifications and experience in relevant fields."[120] The Ombudsperson took over the "focal point" functions with respect to the Al-Qaeda-Taliban sanctions committee (but not the other listing committees). The office is also tasked with information gathering on any delisting petitions, dialogue with the petitioner, submission of a report to the Committee laying out the principal arguments concerning the delisting request, and responding to Committee questions as it considers the petition and report. The Ombudsperson does not make the delisting decision nor make recommendations on whether an individual should be delisted and so there is still no truly independent review of Council decisions.

B. Resolution 1267, Due Process, and Deliberative Legitimacy

Despite general support for the SC's counter-terrorism initiatives, the 1267 regime has been under siege since its inception, and it remains contested. At least 50 states have expressed concerns.[121] A Council of Europe report in 2006 stated that the process was contrary to the European Convention on Human Rights because it provides no protection against arbitrary decisions and has no mechanism for reviewing the accuracy

---

[119] Addressing Challenges, *supra* note 111, at 22–23.
[120] UN SC Res 1904 (2009), para. 20.
[121] Watson Report, *supra* note 114, at 6 and fn.9. See also the open Security Council debate on "Strengthening international law: the rule of law and maintenance of international peace and security," S/.PV 5474, June 22, 2006.

of allegations made.[122] The Committee's decisions have been challenged indirectly in many regional and national courts.[123] Three Swedish citizens of Somali descent objected to their being listed, and one (Mr. Kadi) brought action in the European Court of First Instance (CFI) challenging the EU regulations that put him on the list pursuant to the SC's action.[124] This was combined with a similar case brought by the Barakaat Foundation, also put on the list. Both Mr. Kadi and the Barakaat Foundation complained that they were being deprived of fundamental rights (to property, a hearing, and the right of judicial review), and therefore the EU regulations enacted to implement the SC resolution should be struck down. The CFI ruled that it could not engage in judicial review of SC decisions, but it could check "indirectly the lawfulness of the resolutions of the Security Council in question with regard to jus cogens" since these are non-derogable, meaning not even the SC can override them. In other words, under Article 103 of the UN Charter, SC resolutions prevail over EU law, unless those rights constitute *jus cogens* norms. The CFI assumes that the human rights norms at issue were *jus cogens* obligations but concludes that the SC's actions did not violate them—basically because in exercising its reponsbility to maintain peace and security, the SC could not be expected to grant a hearing or judicial remedy when it freezes the assets of those associated with terrorism.

On appeal, the European Court of Justice (ECJ) disagreed with the CFI and struck down the EC regulation. The ECJ ruled that it was not passing judgment on the SC resolution, but only on the regulation. It did not have the power to review SC decisions, not even their compatibility with *jus cogens* norms, but it could review the compatibility of the EC regulations with the fundamental human rights embodied in the EC's legal order. It took a strict (and highly controversial) "dualist approach" to the international legal system: the EU is an autonomous legal order, and obligations imposed by international agreements (such as the UN Charter) cannot have the effect of undermining constitutional principles in the EU system. It got around the fact that the wording of the SC resolution and EC regulation are identical by saying that "the UN Charter left a free choice among the various possible models for transposition of those resolutions into their domestic legal order." The implication is that judicial review of the EU would not be tantamount to judicial review of the SC.

---

[122] Cameron, *supra* note 110. David Crawford, "UN program generates blacklist," *The Wall Street Journal*, October 2, 2006, p. 9.

[123] As of October 2009, more than 30 legal challenges had been pursued in courts worldwide: in Belgium, Canada, Italy, the Netherlands, Pakistan, Switzerland, Turkey, the United Kingdom, the United States, and European Regional Courts. Addressing Challenges, *supra* note 111., Appendix B. See also Guthrie, *supra* note 110, at 518; Dyzenhaus, *supra* note 110; de Wet and Knoellkamper eds, *supra* note 110.

[124] Ahmed Ali Yusuf and Al Barakaat International Foundation v. Council and Commission, Case T-306/01 September 21, 2005. A similar case brought at the same time involved a Saudi citizen, Abdullay Kadi v. Council and Commission, Case T315/01, September 21, 2005. See also *R.* Aden v. Council of Eur. Union, 2002 E.C.R. II-02387.

The substantive reasons for striking down the regulations were that they violated rights to a defense, effective legal remedy, effective judicial protection, and to property—all of which are guaranteed in EU "constitutional" law. The EC was given three months to remedy the defect, putting it in the difficult position of trying to comply with the SC resolution without running afoul of EU fundamental rights. The EC Commission conveyed to Kadi and Barakaat general summaries of the reasons for their listing, listened to and considered their responses, and then promptly relisted them. Kadi and Barakaat then went to the CFI to challenge the new procedures of the EU, a case that remained pending at the time of writing. Meanwhile, in November 2008, the Council of Ministers adopted a new regulation that requires the EU to tell individuals why they have been listed and to give them an opportunity to respond. It has also proposed to amend the procedure for listing, requiring a statement of reasons and giving the Commission more leeway to make the final decision on listing within the EU context.

While all this was going on in the European and other courts, the UN Security Council was reforming the 1267 procedures. Permanent Members of the Council have been careful not to state publicly that the reforms are a direct response to the legal challenges because it behooves them to insist on the primacy of binding Council decisions over other areas of international and regional law (under Article 103 of the UN Charter). The UK and France, of course, are in the most delicate position: as members of the Council, they adopted the resolutions and are meant to oversee their implementation; as members of the EU they are bound by the ECJ opinion that struck down the regulations. On the whole, the UK and France have held firm about the prerogatives of the SC, but the bind created by the ECJ decision is not a comfortable one for them.

Even though the SC has never officially stated it was responding to these court challenges, a fair inference is that it was. One piece of evidence is paragraph 15 in resolution 1904, which "encourages member states and relevant international organizations to inform the Committee of any relevant court decisions and proceedings so that the Committee can consider them when it reviews a corresponding listing or updates a narrative summary of reasons for listing." Beyond that, many of the procedural reforms have responded to the criticisms leveled by the ECJ in *Kadi*, as well as other judicial and quasi-judicial opinions.[125] Unsurprisingly, the SC has not established a mechanism for truly independent review of its decisions—the major outstanding complaint of critics. The Office of the Ombudsperson, which could be characterized as serving an "advisory role," is a step in that direction, but it remains to be seen whether that will satisfy the European and other courts.

---

[125] For a summary of these opinions, see Larissa van den Herik and Nico Schrijver "Delisting Challenges in the Context of UN Targeted Sanctions Regimes: A Legal Perspective," Appendix A of *Addressing Challenges, supra* note 111; David Cortright and Erica de Wet, "Human Rights Standards for Targeted Sanctions," Fourth Freedom Organization Policy Brief SSRP 1001-January 1, 2010, available at http://www.fourthfreedom.org/pdf/10_01_HR_STANDARDS_FINAL_WEB.pdf.

The larger point for the purposes of this book is that many of the procedural protections the courts and other critics have been insisting on correspond to deliberative principles.[126] No one expects the SC to abandon the listing regimes altogether, as they serve an important preventative function. On the other hand, no one expects the Council to provide full due process rights either, which would be unrealistic and counterproductive. More consultation on and notification of the case against an individual, more reason-giving and public justification of decisions, and more independent review are all principles that the Council can and has taken on board. Closer to administrative law principles of procedural fairness than criminal due process, they illustrate a point made in Chapter 2, namely, that the line between the democratic deliberation of law-making bodies and the judicial reasoning of law-applying bodies, is blurry.

V. CONCLUSION

There are good instrumental reasons for engaging in legal argumentation and justification. It is hard to prove costs and benefits empirically, but the available evidence lends credence to the basic proposition that governments find it easier—as a matter of politics and policy—to support action that rests on a sound legal foundation than action widely seen as illegal. Discursive interaction is the process through which the rough weighing of these costs and benefits plays out. Moreover, action that can be justified in legal terms is more likely to be seen as legitimate. Thus successful justification reinforces the existing normative order and the actor's reputation in that order.

An interpretation of Article 51 of the UN Charter that sees the intervention in Afghanistan as legal and in Iraq as illegal strengthens the rules on the use of force by adapting them to new circumstances without opening the floodgate to abuse. The 2002 National Security Strategy version of the doctrine of preemption, on the other hand, was widely seen as destructive of the normative order and the reputation of the United States as the architect of that order. It remains to be seen whether the policy of "targeted killings" through drone strikes can be justified to the interpretive community, but the mere fact that the Obama Administration is engaging in the effort is illustrative of an attitude toward international law that differs sharply from that of the Bush Administration. Resolutions 1373 and 1540 are controversial, in part because they are seen as the Council assuming "legislative" functions. Yet, despite the concerns about "hegemonic law" in action, the resolutions still have life because they are filling gaps in fields where existing law is inadequate; and a proactive and innovative Council is welcome, especially if the perceived alternative is U.S. unilateralism.

---

[126] See Ian Johnstone, "Legislation and Adjudication in the UN Security Council," *supra* note 57, at 297–99 and 303–07.

The counter-terrorism action analyzed in this chapter (especially with respect to resolutions 1267, 1373, and 1540) suggests that the Council is a more deliberative body than meets the eye. Discourse there is not entirely dominated by the P5. Nonpermanent members do wield some "discursive" power because the P5 must compete for their support. The competition is often crass, but the elected 10 help set the parameters of the more equal deliberations among the P5. Plus, non-Council members can speak in public meetings and, in the implementation of resolutions 1373 and 1540, were given ample opportunity to have their voices heard. Beyond state representatives, the Council is influenced by the constellation of engaged representatives of nongovernmental organizations, organs of international public opinion, and other citizens who keep a close watch on what is going on in the SC. When the Council legislates, members feel compelled to appeal to networks of citizens and entities beyond governmental chambers because the action is only likely to succeed with the cooperation of key nongovernmental actors (like banks with respect to resolution 1373). At a minimum, that cooperation requires some sense among affected constituencies that their concerns have been taken into account. These features suggest that it is possible for something like a "public sphere" to coalesce around the SC.[127] When it was paralyzed by the Cold War and served mainly as a venue for political one-upmanship by the two superpowers, weaker states had little influence over what was decided there, let alone non-state actors. Yet, as the Council becomes more active in the field of counter-terrorism and other areas that touch on human security, the range of actors who have a stake in its decisions broadens, and agitation for greater influence over those decisions increases.

Similarly, the SC is a place where "interpretive communities" coalesce. The structure and rules of the organization influence the voices that are heard and how loudly. In the SC, the P5 undoubtedly hold the lion's share of discursive power (along with material power), but the community of experts and institutions that pass judgment on positions taken in the Council and Council action is much broader. The lesson of the Taliban/Al Qaeda sanctions regime is that regional and national courts are key elements of that interpretive community. While ruling on cases that purported only to bind their own constituencies, they, in effect, passed judgment on Council action. No court has yet ruled the Council to have acted *ultra vires*, but the decisions of the ECJ have certainly given pause to Council members (especially the European members). Arguably, the ECJ opened a "dialogic exchange" with the Council not unlike the "expressive mode of review" José Alvarez claims the ICJ engaged in through its *Lockerbie* and *Bosnia*

---

[127] On public sphere theory, see Jennifer Mitzen, "Reading Habermas in Anarchy: Multilateral Diplomacy and Global Public Spheres," 99 *American Political Science Review* 401, 404 (2005); James Bohman, "International Regimes and Democratic Governance," 75 *International Affairs* 499, 500, 505 (1999); John Dryzek, "Transnational Democracy," 7 *The Journal of Political Philosophy* 30–51 (1999).; Dennis Thompson, "Democratic Theory and Global Society," 7 *The Journal of Political Philosophy* 111-125 (1999).

Genocide rulings.[128] These courts delivered warnings, in effect, "*cueing* the Council to internalize the limits suggested, and to impose restraints on itself that would prevent violations of the law."[129] The ICJ and ECJ have signaled to the members of the Council that they ought to exercise self-restraint in how they carry out their functions. The main signal delivered by the *Kadi* case, combined with the lesson of resolutions 1373 and 1540, is that while the SC may be a more deliberative body than meets the eye, there is still room for improvement.

A final point that comes out of this study of counter-terrorism is that legal argumentation, while principally directed at interpretation and implementation of the law (compliance), also has a creative, law-making effect. The reaction to the Afghanistan intervention shifted our understanding of what the rules on the use of force permit and prohibit. The limits of "anticipatory" or preemptive self-defense were defined, not with precision, of course, but the judgment of the interpretive community was surprisingly clear in both cases: self-defensive action was permissible against the Taliban regime in Afghanistan but not against the regime of Saddam Hussein in Iraq.

---

[128] José Alvarez, "Judging the Security Council," 90 *American Journal of International Law* 1 (1996). Grainne de Burca argues that the ECJ passed up an opportunity to engage in a dialogue about due process in the *Kadi* case, Grainne de Burca, "The European Court of Justice and the International Legal Order after *Kadi*," 51 *Harvard International Law Journal* 1, 42 (2009). By insisting on the EU as an autonomous legal order, de Burca is correct that the ECJ passed up the opportunity for a direct dialogue with the Council, but the effect of the judgment seems to be indirect dialogue with the two bodies not speaking directly to each other but hearing each other.

[129] Alvarez, *id.* at 30.

6

NUCLEAR NON-PROLIFERATION

I. INTRODUCTION

THE FIELD OF nuclear non-proliferation is in ferment. The existing regime is under considerable stress, facing challenges it was not designed for, like the threat of nuclear terrorism. The ferment is manifest in tension between traditional approaches to non-proliferation and various *ad hoc* initiatives that are less universal and depend less on international institutions. The traditional approach, in brief, is to negotiate a multilateral treaty whose goal is universal adherence, to establish a verification mechanism to monitor compliance with the treaty, and to count on the SC as the ultimate enforcer. This is the regime around the Nuclear Non-Proliferation Treaty (NPT), as well as the Chemical Weapons Convention and the Biological Weapons Convention, although the last lacks a verification agency. Two non-traditional approaches were discussed in Chapter 5: the doctrine of preemption and SC resolution 1540. Another nontraditional mechanism is the Proliferation Security Initiative (PSI): an arrangement whereby states agree to interdict ships suspected of carrying WMD or WMD-related material through their territorial waters. This began in 2003 as a partnership among 11 countries and had expanded to almost 100 participants by September 2010.[1] Similarly, the Global Initiative

---

[1] See the United States Government fact sheet on the Proliferation Security Initiative, Available at http://www.state.gov/t/isn/c27732.htm.

to Combat Nuclear Terrorism, announced by the United States and Russia in July 2006, started as a voluntary arrangement among 13 partners and now numbers 82.[2] While the Obama Administration has revitalized the "grand bargain" that underpins the traditional approach to non-proliferation, it has not abandoned any of the Bush initiatives and, in fact, added a new dimension by hosting the first-ever nuclear security summit in April 2010, attended by some 40 states.

An interesting question is whether these new approaches complement and reinforce existing regimes or whether they undermine them. Arguably, the PSI and resolution 1540 fill gaps that would not be filled quickly enough if traditional approaches to multilateral decision making were pursued. On the other hand, the regimes are based on a carefully calibrated set of bargains and compromises. While useful on their own terms, the new approaches could throw that delicate balance off, leading to collapse of existing non-proliferation norms and institutions.

In this chapter, I consider three sets of issues that have arisen in the context of the recent ferment: interpretive disputes over key provisions in the NPT; weapons inspections and military action against Iraq, based on SC resolutions; and the interdiction of ships suspected of carrying WMD or related material to and from North Korea. The UN Security Council has been a central player in all three areas but not a sole practitioner. My central claim is that both management and enforcement are affected by a diffuse discursive process among a network of actors and institutions struggling to preserve the integrity of a regime that is in jeopardy. While legal considerations may seem tangential in the politics of non-proliferation, I argue that the legal discourse has had a significant impact on how the politics play out.

II. THE NPT: INTERPRETIVE DISPUTES

The NPT is the centerpiece of the nuclear non-proliferation regime. As of November 2010, it had 188 or 189 adherents (depending on whether you count North Korea, discussed below), including all five declared nuclear weapon states: China, France, Russia, the United Kingdom, and the United States. The only UN member states that are not parties are India, Israel, and Pakistan. The NPT has two types of parties: nuclear weapons states (NWS) and non-nuclear weapon states (NNWS). The main obligation on the non-nuclear powers is to not acquire, manfacture, or possess such weapons and to accept a system of IAEA safeguards on all peaceful nuclear activities. The nuclear states, in turn, commit not to transfer nuclear weapons or devices to any recipient, while agreeing to assist in the peaceful development of nuclear energy. To further balance the equation

---

[2] See the United States Government fact sheet on the Global Initiative to Combat Nuclear Terrorism. Available at http://www.state.gov/t/isn/c18406.htm.

between nuclear haves and have-nots, the former undertake to pursue negotiations in good faith toward nuclear disarmament. The NPT parties see it as a "grand bargain" between the two types of states. The holdouts see it as discriminatory because it creates two classes of international citizens.

The IAEA was originally formed in 1957 but came to occupy a central role in non-proliferation efforts in 1970, with the entry into force of the NPT. Broadly, the twin aims of the IAEA are to promote the safe use of nuclear power and to ensure that any nuclear assistance is not used to further a military purpose. The second goal is realized through a system of safeguards administered by the Agency. Article III of the NPT requires non-nuclear weapon states to accept IAEA safeguards to verify that they are fulfilling their NPT obligations. In 1997, a model Additional Protocol (AP) was adopted to tighten the regime after the IAEA's failure to detect Iraq's clandestine program prior to 1991. The AP sets out four new elements of every NPT state party's safeguards agreement, designed to give the IAEA broader access to undeclared sites.[3] By November 2010, 135 states had signed APs, and it was in force for 103 of them.[4]

As an international legal instrument, the NPT is drafted in quite general terms. It leaves open a number of interpretive issues, many of which are currently contested. Below, I summarize the debates over the most important of those issues (and the conditions that prompted them), culminating in the 2010 NPT Review Conference. The disputes over interpretation may look like technicalities that do not get to the heart of the matter, but the legal quibbles do affect even the high politics of non-proliferation.[5]

Article I of the Treaty prohibits nuclear weapons states from providing any "assistance, encouragement or inducement" to non-nuclear states to develop a weapon. This became a source of controversy in 2007 when the United States and India signed an agreement on civilian nuclear cooperation. Among other things, the agreement provides for U.S. assistance to India's civilian nuclear energy program and expands U.S.-Indian cooperation in energy and satellite technology. When the deal was being negotiated and approval sought in the U.S. Congress and the Nuclear Suppliers Group (a group of 45 countries who have agreed to a "trigger list" of nuclear fuel and equipment that would only be exported to NNWS under safeguards), a question arose as to whether it violated Article 1 of the Nuclear NPT. The United States claimed it did not,

---

[3] Specifically, the Additional Protocol calls for an expanded declaration each state must make on nuclear-related activities, covering all parts of the nuclear fuel cycle; "complementary" access to any location referred to in the expanded declaration or that IAEA wants to see in order to determine whether there are undeclared nuclear material and activities; streamlined visa process to allow for short-notice inspections; and environmental sampling during inspection of declared and undeclared sites. Available at http://www.iaea.org/Publications/Documents/Infcircs/1997/infcirc540c.pdf.

[4] International Atomic Energy Agency, Status of Additional Protocols (as of 7 November 2010). Available at http://www.iaea.org/OurWork/SV/Safeguards/sg_protocol.html

[5] I am grateful to Emma Belcher for her research assistance on the disputes over NPT interpretation.

because assistance goes only to civilian programs, which would be separated from India's military programs and placed under IAEA safeguards.[6] The principal counterarguments are, first, that the distinction between civilian and military facilities is artificial as the two programs are deeply intertwined; and second, that assisting India's civilian program by providing nuclear fuel frees up resources for its military program. That allows it to expand its nuclear arsenal more quickly than it could do if it had to choose between the two programs in deciding how to use its limited reserves of uranium. Thus, the cooperation agreement, even if restricted to civilian facilities, "assists," "encourages," and/or "induces" India to expand its military program.

The IAEA ultimately approved the safeguards agreement with India. Director-General Mohammad El-Baradei spoke strongly in favor of the U.S.-India deal, stating that "it would be a milestone, timely for ongoing efforts to consolidate the non-proliferation regime, combat nuclear terrorism and strengthen nuclear safety... The agreement would be a step forward towards universalization of the international safeguards regime."[7] Neither the IAEA board of governors nor its director-general are responsible for monitoring compliance with the NPT, so care should be taken in inferring an interpretation of Article I from their statements. But when the NSG agreed to an exemption from its export guidelines for India, a German spokesman (Germany was chair of the NSG at the time) claimed that the IAEA's support was critical in convincing NSG members to allow India an exemption.[8]

At the 2010 NPT Review Conference, many NPT parties did object to the U.S.-India deal and the related NSG exemption. Few, if any, mentioned Article I, but they claimed the deal contravened a decision of the 1995 Review and Extension Conference that full scope safeguards would be a precondition for all new nuclear supply arrangements.[9] Although most NSG members were unwilling to directly defend the exemption decision, the United States made it clear that it would not revisit the deal with New Delhi. In vague compromise language, the final conference document urges supplier states to ensure that their exports do not "directly or indirectly assist the development of nuclear weapons" and are "in full conformity with the objective and purposes of the Treaty."[10]

---

[6] One of the conclusions of the U.S. government's Nuclear Proliferation Assessment Statement is that "the safeguards and other control mechanisms and the peaceful use assurances in the proposed Agreement are adequate to ensure that any assistance furnished under it will not be used to further any military or nuclear explosive purpose." See http://www.hcfa.house.gov/110/press091108e.pdf, accessed July 23, 2010 [pages 27–29].

[7] IAEA Press Release, "IAEA Director-General Welcomes US and India Nuclear Deal," March 2, 2006. Available at http://www.iaea.org/NewsCenter/PressReleases/2006/prn200605.htm.l

[8] DW-World.de, "Germany Accepts Landmark Nuclear Deal with India", September 9, 2008. Available at http://www.dw-world.de/dw/article/0,2144,3629002,00.html.

[9] William Potter, Patricia Lewis, Gaukhar Mukhatzhanova and Miles Pomper, *The 2010 NPT Review Conference: Deconstructing Consensus,* CNS Special Report, June 17, 2010, p. 16.

[10] 2010 Review Conference of the Parties to the Treaty on the Non-Proliferation of Nuclear Weapons, Final Document, NPT/Conf.2010/50 (Vol I), New York 2010, Action 35, p. 36.

The larger policy issue is not likely to dissipate, given that China has proposed a similar arrangement with Pakistan.[11] Whether or not NPT Article I considerations are revived in that debate, there is little doubt that some states will see this as further erosion of the integrity of the NPT.

Article IV declares the "inalienable right" of all parties to the NPT to develop nuclear energy for "peaceful purposes." It also requires all parties—including the nuclear weapon states—to "facilitate the fullest possible exchange of equipment, materials and scientific and technological information for the peaceful uses of nuclear energy." A question this raises is whether Article IV represents a promise to facilitate all types of civilian nuclear cooperation, or do suppliers have discretion to deny access to sensitive technology deemed to be proliferation prone, such as facilities for enriching uranium and for reprocessing spent fuel to obtain plutonium. A related question is whether proposals to multinationalize the fuel cycle regime erode Article IV rights. Both have come up in the context of Iran. The problem that the Iran case highlights—especially when paired with North Korea—is that NPT parties can go a long way toward building a bomb without breaking any NPT rule and then withdraw from the Treaty. Multinationalization of the fuel cycle would mitigate that problem by restricting the right of NPT members to enrich uranium or reprocess spent fuel.

In February 2004, President Bush proposed that the NSG members should refuse to sell enrichment and reprocessing equipment to any state that does not already have full-scale functioning enrichment and reprocessing plants.[12] Instead, the world's leading nuclear exporters would ensure that states have "reliable access at reasonable costs to fuel for civilian reactors." This is essentially a policy of denial accompanied by a promise to provide nuclear fuel. At the same time, IAEA Director-General Mohammed El-Baradei made a more ambitious proposal. He called for a five-year moratorium on the creation of facilities for uranium enrichment and plutonium separation, during which period, states with such facilities would guarantee an economic supply of nuclear fuel to the others. At the end of the five years, all sensitive fuel cycle facilities would be placed under international control of some kind. The options for international control were spelled out in an "Expert Group" report that he commissioned and presented at the 2005 NPT Review Conference.[13]

Both approaches— those of Bush and El-Baradei—entail a reinterpretation of NPT Article IV by shifting the emphasis from "inalienable right" to "peaceful purposes." The difference between them is that the first sought to impose the reinterpretation, while

---

[11] "The Power of Nightmares: Nuclear Proliferation in South Asia," *The Economist,* June 26, 2010, p. 61

[12] Remarks by President George W. Bush on Weapons of Mass Destruction Proliferation delivered at Fort Lesley J. McNair, February 11, 2004. Available at http://daccess-dds-ny.un.org/doc/UNDOC/GEN/G04/602/83/PDF/G0460283.pdf?OpenElement.

[13] IAEA Expert Group report on "Multilateral Approaches to the Nuclear Fuel Cycle," February 22, 2005. Available at http://www.iaea.org/NewsCenter/News/2005/fuelcycle.html.

the second was a proposal to negotiate it. The problem with an imposed reinterpretation is that many NPT parties would see it as evidence that the NWS and nuclear suppliers were backing away from their side of the NPT bargain. The problem with the El-Baradei approach is that a negotiated reinterpretation would require all states to agree first to the moratorium, then to the international management arrangement, which would be very hard to achieve.

Neither proposal got off the ground, but in 2007 Russia established the International Uranium Enrichment Centre (IUEC).[14] A reserve of low-enriched uranium fuel is to be stored there and made available, under IAEA auspices and control, to IAEA member states. The IAEA board of governors approved this in November 2009, though not unanimously: eight countries were opposed, and three abstained on the grounds that the arrangement could erode Article IV rights.[15]

There is room to argue that the right to enjoy the benefits of peaceful nuclear technology does not necessarily entail the right to possess enrichment or reprocessing facilities.[16] By extension, Article IV(2) of the NPT would not *require* parties to help other states develop *all* elements of the nuclear fuel cycle.[17] But the negotiating history of the NPT and subsequent practice does suggest that countries should be allowed to build all elements of the nuclear fuel cycle, including sensitive—potentially dual use—nuclear facilities, as long as only for peaceful purposes and subjected to safeguards. The Iran issue, then, is not whether states have an inalienable right to develop peaceful nuclear energy (they do), but whether Iran has violated its safeguards agreement (it has) and whether its programs are for "peaceful purposes" (a matter of intention).

At the 2010 NPT Review Conference, NAM states would not support any specific multinational fuel cycle proposal because they perceived the initiatives as challenging their "inalienable rights."[18] In the end, the final document came down on the side of a permissive reading of Article IV. It stated that "nothing in the treaty shall be interpreted as affecting the inalienable right" to develop peaceful nuclear energy, and that "each country's choices and decisions should be respected, without jeopardizing its policies or international cooperation agreements" (para. 31). It called upon all states to "observe the legitimate right of all state parties to full access to the equipment, material and information for peaceful nuclear energy" (para. 34). It took note of the IAEA resolution on the

---

[14] Francois Carel-Billiard and Christine Wing, *Nuclear Energy, Non-Proliferation and Disarmament: Briefing Notes for the 2010 NPT Review Conference* 10-11 (International Peace Institute, April 2010).

[15] *Id.* at 12.

[16] George Perkovic, Jessica Tuchman Matthews and Joseph Cirincione, *Universal Compliance: A Strategy for Nuclear Security* 93 (2007).

[17] Lori Fisler Damrosch, "Codification and Legal Issues," in *The United Nations and Nuclear Orders* 170, 178 (J. Boulden, R. Thakur and T. Weiss eds., 2009). See also, Emma Belcher PhD dissertation on the negotiating history of Article IV (on file with the author).

[18] Potter et al., *supra* note 9.

Russian LEU reserve for use by IAEA members but underlined that this and other *voluntary* multilateral mechanisms for assurances of the nuclear fuel supply should not affect the right of states to develop their own programs (paras. 56 and 57). The consensus at the NPT Review Conference was that multilateral mechanisms should be pursued but in a way that did not undermine Article IV rights.

Article X grants a right to withdraw from the NPT on three months' notice if a state decides that "extraordinary events, related to the subject matter of the Treaty, have jeopardized the supreme interests of its country." A statement to that effect must be sent to all other Parties to the Treaty and to the SC. A legal question thrown up by the North Korea situation is whether that is simply a procedural requirement: is it enough for a party to issue the notification and accompanying statement; or can the depositaries, other parties to the Treaty, and the SC question the right to withdraw?

On March 12, 1993, after a run-in with the IAEA, North Korea announced its decision to withdraw from the NPT. One day before the three-month deadline was to expire, it "suspended the effectuation of its withdrawal." When a new crisis erupted a decade later, the DPRK announced on January 10, 2003, that it was ending the "suspension" of its withdrawal, meaning it would be out of the Treaty the next day. Leaving aside the "suspension" and "unsuspension" issue (which became moot after three months), the language of Article X seems to suggest that it is up to each party to decide for itself whether it is facing "extraordinary events" that would justify withdrawal. Yet in 1993, the United States, United Kingdom, and Russia—the three depositories of the NPT—issued a statement "questioning whether DPRK's stated reasons for withdrawing from the Treaty constitute extraordinary events relating to the subject-matter of the Treaty."[19] Although the three did not elaborate, the negotiating history of the treaty supports their position. The NPT withdrawal clause was modeled on a provision in the 1963 Partial Test Ban Treaty (PTBT), with two important modifications. No reference to the SC appears in the PTBT, nor does it require that the withdrawing party must include in the notice a statement of the extraordinary events it regards as having jeopardized its supreme interests.[20] This suggests, at a minimum, that the SC was meant to consider whether withdrawal from the Treaty constituted a threat to international peace and security, justifying action under Chapter VII. Whether it means that the withdrawal itself can be questioned is less clear. But if the Article X obligation to notify were entirely procedural, then why require reasons for withdrawal? Asking for reasons invites debate. If a state were to announce that poor refereeing in the soccer World Cup jeopardized its supreme interests, would the depositaries and all other NPT states be required to accept that as grounds for NPT withdrawal?

---

[19] The letter of the depositaries was noted in UN SC Res 825 (1993).

[20] George Bunn and John Rhinelander, "The Right to Withdraw from the NPT: Article X is Not Unconditional" 79 *Disarmament Diplomacy* (April/May 2005).

The issue of North Korea's status was disputed at the NPT Review Conferences of 2005 and 2010. Unable to settle the dispute in 2005, the Chair of the RevCon simply removed the DPRK nameplate.[21] This ended discussion but did not resolve whether the DPRK was still a party to the NPT. Since then, Iran has maintained that denying a unilateral right to withdraw would be tantamount to amending Article X.[22] Similarly, the NAM argues that attempts to further specify the terms of withdrawal would go beyond the provisions of the NPT.[23] During the debate at the 2010 Review Conference, Syria, Iran, Egypt, and Libya argued that new language on withdrawal would constitute an unacceptable reinterpretation of the Treaty.[24] Only a few states spoke on the precise question of whether North Korea is still a member of the NPT: Bulgaria (yes), South Korea (DPRK "abused but did not violate Article X"), and Russia (DPRK abused Article X).[25] U.S. Secretary of State Clinton stated:

> [T]his treaty is weakened when a state flouts the rules and develops illicit nuclear weapons capabilities... We should find ways to dissuade states from utilizing the treaty's withdrawal provision to avoid accountability... Now, I am not proposing to amend the treaty to limit the rights of states to withdraw. But we cannot stand by when a state committing treaty violations says it will pull out of the NPT in an attempt to escape penalties and even pursue nuclear weapons.[26]

This suggests that the United States accepts the withdrawal of North Korea as valid but reserves the right of the SC to act on that withdrawal. On the other hand, Gary Samore (White House coordinator for Arms Control and WMD, Proliferation, and Terrorism) said in response to a question on engaging the DPRK at the RevCon: "I think as a technical legal matter we don't recognize that they (North Korea) have withdrawn from the treaty. But as a practical matter, I don't think we can drag them to the meeting

---

[21] Rebecca Johnson, "Day 3 at NPT: P-5 statement and 3 Subsidiary bodies" http://acronyminstitute.wordpress.com/2010/05/05/day-3-interim/.

[22] http://www.reachingcriticalwill.org/legal/npt/revcon2010/papers/WP42.pdf.

[23] Statement by HE Dr. R.M. Marty M. Natalegawa, Minister for Foreign Affairs of the Republic of Indonesia, on behalf of the NAM States Party to the Non-Proliferation of Nuclear Weapons Treaty (NPT) before the 2010 Review Conference of the Parties to the Non-Proliferation of nuclear weapons Treaty. Available at http://www.reachingcriticalwill.org/legal/npt/revcon2010/statements/3May_NAM.pdf, accessed July 25, 2010.

[24] Potter et al., *supra* note 9.

[25] The statements are compiled at http://www.reachingcriticalwill.org/legal/npt/revcon2010/statements.html.

[26] Available at http://www.reachingcriticalwill.org/legal/npt/revcon2010/statements/3May_US.pdf, accessed July 25, 2010.

if they refuse to come."[27] Meanwhile, the DPRK is still on the status list maintained by the depositaries of the treaty, the UN, and the IAEA.[28]

The final document of the 2010 NPT Review Conference repeated the language of Article X in paragraph 118 but then added in paragraph 119 that "numerous States recognize that the right of withdrawal is established in the provisions of the Treaty. There were divergent views regarding its interpretation with respect to other relevant international law. The Conference notes that many States underscore that under international law a withdrawing party is still responsible for violations of the Treaty committed prior to its withdrawal..." And then in paragraph 120, "Without prejudice to the legal consequences of the withdrawal and to the status of compliance by the withdrawing State... the Conference notes that numerous States reaffirm the responsibility entrusted to the Security Council under the Charter of the United Nations."

These inelegantly drafted paragraphs might suggest that the question of whether the DPRK has validly withdrawn is a legal technicality of no real consequence. Yet, the amount of energy invested in debating this question and the implications one way or the other suggests that many states do not see it as inconsequential. Consider the U.S. position. As with the claims about a legal right of humanitarian intervention discussed in Chapter 4, the United States tried to strike a balance because it does not want to get trapped by its own arguments. For political reasons, the United States would benefit from unequivocally rejecting North Korea's right to withdraw; for fear of setting a legal precedent, it is reluctant to do that since the United States itself withdraws from treaties from time to time. The fact that the United States has equivocated is revealing about the power of legal discourse. If legal arguments were inconsequential, then the North Korea precedent would not matter; the United States could simply say, "that was different." Being worried about setting precedents is circumstantial evidence of the existence of an interpretive community that can extract reputational costs from states who behave hypocritically.

Whether a state has validly withdrawn from the NPT under Article X, whether an NPT party can be denied certain technology under Article IV, whether helping a non-NPT member with its civilian nuclear programs violates Article I: these are not inconsequential questions. They have an impact on the negotiation of sanctions on the DPRK and Iran in the SC. They have an impact on decisions about nuclear assistance to states of proliferation concern. And they have an impact on the overall integrity of a regime that has helped keep the number of nuclear weapon states to nine despite dire predictions four decades ago. Legal quibbles matter. The only question is how much.

---

[27] Gary Samore, "International Perspectives on the Nuclear Posture Review," Carnegie Endowment for International Peace, April 10, 2010. Available at http://carnegieendowment.org/files/0422carnegie-samore.pdf.

[28] Damrosch, *supra* note 17 at 181–82.

III. IRAQ: INSPECTIONS AND INVASION

Enforcement of the NPT is the responsibility of the UN Security Council. The Statute of the IAEA says violations of safeguards agreements must be reported to SC. Yet the SC's basic authority stems not from these external sources but from the general powers conferred by the UN Charter (Articles 24, 25, 26, and Chapter VII as whole). Thus, even if a matter is not referred to the SC by some other agent or if it falls outside the treaty regimes, the Council can act. Whether and how it chooses to respond in a particular situation is a matter of discretion, within the constraining force of Article 24(2), which stipulates that it must act in accordance with the purposes and principles of the UN. The Council has only acted on a few occasions: against South Africa many years ago, to condemn the nuclear tests by India and Pakistan, to impose sanctions on North Korea and Iran, and against Iraq.

In Chapter 5, I discussed the legality of military action against Iraq on the basis of self-defense in response to terrorism. An alternative—and more plausible legal justification—is the enforcement of obligations that the SC imposed to control Iraq's WMD. I now turn to an assessment of that claim.

A. *The Weapons Inspection Regime*

Security Council resolution 687 (1991) required Iraq to accept the destruction and long-term monitoring of its nuclear, chemical, biological, and long-range ballistic missile programs. The IAEA was assigned primary responsibility for nuclear programs, at the insistence of the French. Because no comparable body existed for chemical and biological weapons or ballistic missiles, the SC created a new organization, called the UN Special Commission (UNSCOM), to deal with those programs in Iraq. UNSCOM was established as a subsidiary organ of the SC under Article 29 of the Charter. It reported directly to the SC, not the SG, an unusual and ultimately controversial arrangement that made UNSCOM the staff of members of the SC.

Iraq was a member of the NPT in 1990, and the IAEA was operating there, but it had not detected any nuclear weapons program in Iraq. The safeguards agreement in place for NPT parties at the time required them to declare where their nuclear facilities were, and the IAEA would set up a verification system only on those. It also had the power to conduct "special inspections" of undeclared facilities if it believed proscribed activities were underway. But the right to conduct special inspections had not been exercised in Iraq, or anywhere else, until the North Korea situation erupted in 1993.

The inspection regime created by resolution 687, more intrusive than that required by the safeguards agreement, was imposed under Chapter VII but nevertheless could only function with some cooperation from Iraq. The IAEA worked in the country for many years and, by 1998, was close to declaring Iraq clean of nuclear weapons programs. But then, along with UNSCOM, it was kicked out. UNSCOM functioned by receiving information from countries that had intelligence on Iraq and gathered its own through a program of inspections and technical devices, approved by the SC. UNSCOM managed to uncover a chemical weapons complex and biological weapons research program, as well as Iraq's capacity to modify ballistic missiles to give them longer range.[29]

Iraq's cooperation with UNSCOM and the IAEA was always grudging, and there were a number of serious standoffs when the inspectors were denied access to suspect sites. The most serious incident began in November 1997 and started a chain of events that led to the inspectors being kicked out of the country. Direct SC pressure was insufficient to secure their return, prompting a visit by the Secretary-General to Baghdad in February 1998, with the blessing of the SC, but without explicit terms of reference.[30] The Memorandum of Understanding the SG agreed to with Saddam Hussein set out some "special procedures" for inspection of so-called presidential sites. Iraq let the inspectors back in, but more Iraqi obstructionism six months later provoked the United States and the United Kingdom to launch air strikes in December 1998, in what was called Operation Desert Fox. Predictably, the strikes did not cause Saddam Hussein to readmit the inspectors.

Serious splits on how to proceed emerged in the Council, with the United States and the United Kingdom on one side, Russia and China on the other, and France leaning toward the latter. The SG proposed a "comprehensive review" of Iraq's compliance with resolution 687, which was undertaken by three panels, and the SC began to negotiate a new inspections regime. The negotiations continued for eight months, finally ending with the adoption of resolution 1284 in December 1999. That resolution replaced UNSCOM with the United Nations Monitoring, Verification and Inspection Commission (UNMOVIC). The vote was 11 in favor and four abstentions: from China, France, Malaysia, and Russia. UNMOVIC was meant to be sufficiently different from UNSCOM (for example, the inspectors were subject to Article 100 of the Charter, which prohibits them from taking instructions from any government) to induce Saddam Hussein to allow the inspectors back. He was not persuaded, and so between December 1998 and November 2002, there were no weapons inspections at all in Iraq.

The rest of the story is well known. In the summer of 2002, the United States signaled it was ready to take more assertive action. President Bush made a speech to the UN General Assembly on September 12, suggesting that the United States was prepared to act militarily but wanted to build a coalition to do so. He, in effect, challenged members of the SC to enforce its own resolutions against Iraq, or render itself irrelevant. Hard negotiations led to resolution 1441, adopted on November 7, 2002, by a vote of 14-0

---

[29] For a fuller discussion of the inspection regimes, see David Malone, Chapter 3 in *The International Struggle Over Iraq* (2006).

[30] Ian Johnstone, "The Role of the Secretary-General: The Power of Persuasion Based on Law," 9 *Global Governance* 441, 443–44 (2003).

(with Syria absent). Resolution 1441 tightened the inspection regime by demanding that Iraq make a new declaration of all its WMD programs, granting the right to interview officials and scientists outside Iraq, doing away with the special procedures for presidential sites negotiated by the Secretary-General in 1998, and authorizing UNMOVIC and IAEA to declare "exclusion zones" where no ground or aerial movement would be allowed by Iraq.[31] Two weeks later, the IAEA and UNMOVIC were back in the country for the first time in four years. They submitted several reports to the SC, which noted some lack of cooperation and compliance on the part of Iraq but never explicitly declared Iraq to be in "material breach" of its obligations; the heads of the two organizations, Mohamed El-Baradei and Hans Blix, thought it was the job of the SC to make that determination. The United States and the United Kingdom were not satisfied with Iraq's cooperation. They pushed for a new resolution that would explicitly authorize military action but maintained they did not need it: they already had sufficient legal authority. Difficult negotiations (discussed below) did not bear fruit, and so the United States led a coalition to war without a new resolution.

B. *Use of Force, Based on SC Resolutions*

As discussed in Chapter 5, the legal case for military action in Iraq based on self-defense was soundly rejected by the interpretive community. A more plausible argument and the one that was pushed hardest by the United States in the final days before the war, and immediately after, was that the coalition had the authority, based on a combined reading of resolutions 678, 687, and 1441. The legal case is set out in letters by the United States and the United Kingdom to the president of the SC on March 20, 2003,[32] further elaborated by the U.S. legal adviser in an *American Journal of International Law* article.[33] The argument, in a nutshell, is that resolution 687 merely suspended the original right to use force to drive Iraq out of Kuwait and "restore international peace and security" granted by resolution 678, and the right was revived by the declaration in resolution 1441 that Iraq was in "material breach" of its obligations. The counter-argument is that resolution 687 extinguished the grant of authority in resolution 678: the right to use force would require a new explicit authorization, which resolution 1441 did not provide. A great deal has been written on this, and there is no need to review the relative merits of the legal arguments here.[34] My own reading is that the latter argument is more persuasive,

---

[31] UN SC Res 1441 (2002).

[32] Letter of the Permanent Representative of the United States to the President of the Security Council, UN S/2003/351, March 21, 2003; Letter of the Permanent Representative of the United Kingdom to the President of the Security Council, UN S/2003/350, March 21, 2003.

[33] William Taft IV and Todd Buchwald, "Preemption, Iraq and International Law", 97 *American Journal of International Law* 557 (2003).

[34] For good compilations of the arguments on both sides, see Lori Damrosch and Bernard Oxman, eds., "Agora: Future Implications of the Iraq Conflict," 97 *American Journal of International Law* 553 (2003); and

ultimately because resolutions that purport to authorize the use of force ought to be construed narrowly in line with the SC's responsibility for the maintenance of international peace and security as a collective decision-making body.[35] But the case is not open and shut. The language of the resolutions, explanations of votes, and practice since 1991 are sufficiently ambiguous that the legal case was not as far-fetched as the argument based on self-defense. Moreover, it is not fatally undermined by the subsequent failure to find any weapons of mass destruction.[36] Unlike the connection with Al-Qaeda, U.S./UK beliefs about the status of Iraq's WMD programs were not out of line with what others—including UN inspectors believed—in the lead-up to the war.[37] The sharpest differences of opinion were about the urgency and magnitude of the threat and how to deal with it, not whether it existed.

An analysis of the debates and how they were conducted leads to conclusions similar to those on NATO's intervention in Kosovo, discussed in Chapter 4. Legal argumentation, constrained by an interpretive community, is consequential, even for the world's only superpower. Four elements of the debate support that conclusion. First, by means of his speech to the General Assembly on September 12, 2002, President Bush launched an extended and highly public deliberative process from which the United States had something to lose as well as to gain. Explicit SC authority for military action would translate into greater international and domestic support. Even if the decision to go to war had been taken before September 12, 2002, and the time table was set by military, not diplomatic considerations, to suggest that the United States had nothing to lose by going to the UN requires an extraordinarily narrow reading of how the United States defines its interests. To begin with, SC authority mattered to other states whose support the United States felt it needed, including the UK and key strategic allies like Turkey. Moreover, the American electorate cares about international opinion—as polls throughout the period from September 2002 to March 2003 show[38]—and with midterm congressional elections

---

C. Warbrick and D. McGoldrick, "Current Developments: The Use of Force Against Iraq," 52 *International and Criminal Law Quarterly* 811 (2003).

[35] I. Johnstone, "US-UN Relations after Iraq: the end of the world (order) as we know it?," 15 *European Journal of International Law* 813, 831–32 (2004); Ian Johnstone, *Aftermath of the Gulf War* (1994).

[36] The Carnegie Endowment for International Peace concluded that UNSCOM and the IAEA successfully discovered and eliminated most of Iraq's unconventional weapons and production facilities and destroyed most of its chemical and biological weapons agents. Joseph Cirincione, Jessica Tuchman Matthews, George Perkovich and Alexis Orton, *Weapons of Mass Destruction in Iraq: Evidence and Implications* (Carnegie Endowment for International Peace, January 2004). This was confirmed by the Iraq Survey Group, a U.S. team who scoured the country after the invasion. Iraq Survey Group Final Report, September 30, 2004. Available at http://www.globalsecurity.org/wmd/library/report/004/isg-final-report/

[37] Even Hans Blix acknowledges that he believed Iraq was hiding weapons and weapons programs at least until January 2003. Hans Blix, *Disarming Iraq* (2004).

[38] S. Kull, M. Ramsay and C. Lewis, "Misperceptions, the Media and the Iraq War," 118 *Political Science Quarterly* 569 (2003-04).

approaching, the Bush Administration was cognizant of the political cost of publicly seeking but not obtaining international support. Some U.S. officials may regret having made the effort, but that supports the argument that the outcome of those deliberations did indeed matter.

Second, the United States worked hard to secure the unanimous passage of resolution 1441 in November 2002, which included what it saw as critically important language declaring Iraq to be in "material breach" of its obligations. Moreover, the ambiguous commitments in that resolution to "assess" (para. 4) and "consider the situation" (para. 12) should Iraq fail to comply with its obligations are revealing. It called for a second set of deliberations that had real consequences, for both sides. The United States and United Kingdom opened themselves to another round of public persuasion, explanation, criticism, and justification, giving other SC members, the broader UN membership, legal and other experts, and attentive civil society groups the opportunity to pass judgment on its legal stance, even while making it clear that they did not believe the decision to take military required a new vote. France and Russia were prepared to vote for resolution 1441 (indeed, it was thanks to the French that the resolution passed unanimously[39]) knowing the U.S./UK position and thus tacitly accepted it, even if they wanted to reserve the right to read it differently when push came to shove. A second set of Council deliberations meant those who were resisting precipitous military action could tell their domestic constituents that there was no "automaticity" in resolution 1441.

Third, the decision to withdraw the famous second resolution in March 2003 is evidence that legal arguments have consequences. That draft, deemed essential by Prime Minister Blair and supported reluctantly by the United States, was first floated on February 24 and debated outside Council chambers for five weeks. The resolution would have had the Council decide that "Iraq has failed to take the final opportunity afforded to it in resolution 1441 (2002),"[40] which would have been understood by all concerned as the trigger for military action. The draft sparked a frantic scramble for votes, which the United States ultimately lost. In a press conference on March 11, President Bush said he would put the resolution to a vote, "win or lose," [41] presumably because he felt the weight of international and domestic opinion would see matters as the United States did, regardless of the outcome of the vote. Yet, on March 18, the United States decided not to table the draft, knowing it would not get even a majority. Interestingly both Spain (a supporter of the United States) and France (an opponent) urged the Bush Administration to withdraw the draft because both felt that a failed vote would do more diplomatic harm than

---

[39] Gerard Baker, James Blitz, Judy Dempsey, Robert Graham, Quentin Peel and Mark Turner "Blair's Mission Impossible: The Doomed Effort to Win a Second Resolution," *Financial Times*, May 29, 2003, p. 4.

[40] Quoted by Sean Murphy," Assessing the Legality of Invading Iraq", 92 *Georgetown Law Journal* 173 (2004).

[41] David Sanger, "Canvassing the Votes to gain legitimacy," *New York Times*, March 13, 2003, p. A12.

no vote at all.[42] This deliberative move by Spain and France helped to salvage some credibility for the SC and international law. The decision to go to war having been made, it was better to do so on the basis of existing resolutions rather than push the doomed draft to a vote, rendering it all but impossible to claim that the military action was being taken to enforce SC demands. That the United States agreed, despite the desire of some to use the Iraq crisis as an opportunity to permanently damage the Council (what better way than to lose the vote and declare the SC irrelevant!) is evidence that "the better legal argument" mattered to both sides.[43] Richard Haass, director of policy planning in the State Department at the time, said that by avoiding a vote on the second resolution, "[n]ow we can argue that we are acting pursuant to the UN, in 1441. This is a way, I believe, quite honestly, of preserving the UN's potential viability in the future. We've not destroyed it. We've just admitted, though, that it can't do everything when the great powers of the day disagree."[44]

Fourth, the deliberations over Iraq highlight the role of nonpermanent members. The main protagonists were the United States and France, but the debates were conducted in large part with a view to persuading nonpermanent members. After testy public exchanges with French leaders in early 2003, the United States and the United Kingdom largely gave up trying to win France's support directly and instead focused on the nonpermanent members, thinking that if six or seven could be convinced to vote yes, France and Russia would be under pressure to abstain. Even if France or Russia were to vote no, the United States and the United Kingdom could claim majority support and argue that they had been blocked—in Blair's words—by an "unreasonable veto,"[45] giving the military action a veneer of legitimacy. Of the nonpermanent members, Spain and Bulgaria were supportive of the United States from the start, while Germany and Syria were opposed. That left six "swing votes"—Pakistan, Cameroon, Angola, Guinea, Chile, and Mexico—who came under intense pressure. The United States' failure to secure their support suggests that material power is not all that matters. Despite the threats made and incentives offered, the presidents of Chile and Mexico made clear in private meetings with Bush Administration officials that they could not vote with the United States nor had the African members indicated their support.[46] If the United States had hammered away in the deliberations on the issue that had preoccupied the Council since 1991, namely, the need to rid Iraq of its weapons of mass destruction, the result might well have

---

[42] Baker, et al. *supra* note 39.

[43] Among those who anticipated the end of the UN with pleasure were Richard Perle, who at the time of writing the article was Chairman of the Defense Policy Board, an advisory panel to the Pentagon, "Thank God for the death of the UN," *The Guardian*, 21 March, 2003, and Charles Krauthammer, "UN: RIP," *Washington Post*, January 31, 2003.

[44] Quoted in Nicholas Lehman, "How it came to war," *The New Yorker*, March 31, 2003.

[45] Baker et al., *supra* note 39 at 4.

[46] *Id.* at 4. See also James Rubin, "Stumbling into War," 82 *Foreign Affairs* 55 (September–October, 2003).

been different. A number of close observers, such as British ambassador to the UN Sir Jeremy Greenstock, believed that "with a little more patience and diplomacy, the administration could have obtained another resolution that would have focused on the sins of Saddam Hussein rather than allowing France and Russia to turn the problem into one of American power."[47] By speaking at diplomatically inopportune moments about tenuous linkages to terrorism, a doctrine of preemption that was hard to square with existing international law and the desire to transform the entire Middle East, Bush Administration officials made it very difficult for leaders of most of the six swing vote countries to sign onto a war that would look to their constituents like the first step in a U.S. effort to remake the world in a manner that served only United States interests.[48]

Fifth, there were costs associated with not being able to get an explicit authorization for the war. Despite U.S. offers of billions of dollars in new assistance, for example, the Turkish government could not get parliamentary support to allow American troops to move into Iraq from Turkish bases, which complicated U.S. military strategy. When the United States began seeking international help in reconstructing Iraq, both in terms of financial aid and troop contributions, it had to overcome resentment bred of the go-it-alone approach during the war. Efforts to enlist the support of others stalled in July 2003 when India decided not to contribute the 17,000 soldiers it had planned to dispatch, despite the obvious benefits that a closer relationship with the United States would bring. India made this decision because the war in Iraq was extremely unpopular domestically, and military participation in the aftermath would be seen as joining an occupation.[49] The calculation would have been different if the war had been explicitly authorized and, in fact, the Indian government indicated it would participate in peacekeeping in Iraq if there were "an explicit UN mandate for the purpose."[50] Pakistan, Bangladesh, Russia, and Turkey all said the same.[51] Meanwhile, France and Germany indicated that they would contribute more to the reconstruction financially if there were a stronger

---

[47] Joseph Nye, "US Power and Strategy After Iraq," 82 *Foreign Affairs* 60, 63 (July/August, 2003). As late as March, not even France had ruled out signing on to a resolution authorizing force following a 30-day deadline with tough benchmarks, Baker et al, *supra* note 39.

[48] As Fareed Zakaria said about Bush Administration policy more generally, the United States suffers from "a deep and widening mistrust and resentment of American foreign policy around the world. . . What worries people above all is living in a world shaped and dominated by one country—the U.S. And they have come to be deeply suspicious and fearful of us." Fareed Zakaria, "The Arrogant Empire," *Newsweek*, March 24, 2003.

[49] John Kifner, "India decides not to send troops to Iraq now," *New York Times*, July 13, 2003, p. A13.

[50] Quoted in Kifner, *id*.

[51] Pakistan's position was stated by Foreign Minister Khurshid Mahmood Kasuri as quoted by the BBC, "Pakistan troops only under UN," October 13, 2003 available at http://news.bbc.co.uk/2/hi/south_asia/3187946.stm. A Bangladeshi official is quoted as saying, "We will be willing to take part in the peacekeeping in Iraq only after a clear UN mandate," Farid Hossain, "Bangladesh Against Sending Troops to Iraq," *The Guardian*, September 27, 2003, available at http://www.guardian.co.uk/worldlatest/story/0,1280,-3198501,00.html. On the Russian position, see "Putin: Russia won't rule out sending troops to Iraq," in an AP report published in *USA today*, September 20, 2003, available at http://www.usatoday.com/news/world/iraq/2003-09-20-russia-iraq_x.htm.

UN mandate. "The India effect" apparently had an impact on the United States and led to serious talk about a new SC resolution, first in July and then in September 2003 following the attack in Baghdad that took the life of Special Representative of the Secretary-General Sergio Vieira de Mello. This culminated in resolution 1511 of October 16, 2003, authorizing a multinational presence to protect the UN alongside the coalition. As it turns out there were few volunteers even for this dedicated force,[52] but from the U.S. point of view, resolution 1511 is an acknowledgment that while unilateralism may bring fewer pesky entanglements, it is not risk or cost free. The adoption of SC resolutions authorizing the U.S.-led coalition and multinational presence in post-war Iraq reflects an effort to minimize the risks and costs.

Justificatory discourse clearly matters to the weaker states in the SC. It is highly plausible that at least some of the members who did not support the United States would have done so if the legal diplomacy surrounding the deliberations had been conducted more adroitly. By March 2003, states that may have been persuaded to support the United States in the Council could not do so, given the difficulties they would have explaining and justifying that support to their own constituents. Whether they like it or not, the most powerful states feel compelled to engage in this justificatory discourse. Perhaps the United States had decided to go to war prior to September 12, 2002, regardless of what would happen in the SC, but that reinforces the point. If the United States felt unilateral action was no more risky or costly than multilateral action, why engage so strenuously in diplomatic efforts to obtain multilateral support? If the entire diplomatic game between September 2002 and March 2003 was a charade, why bother? Clearly, some in the Bush Administration thought it was worth the effort and worked hard to build a factual and legal case that could be supported by others. There was something to gain (and lose) by the argumentation. Indeed, a price was paid for going to war without clear legal authority. In addition to the relative lack of direct support for the original war and the reconstruction effort, as early as 2003, some knowledgeable observers saw setbacks in efforts to curb terrorism and stem the proliferation of WMD caused by the Iraq adventure.[53]

On Turkey, see Ian Fisher, "Iraqi Leaders Condemn Plan for Troops from Turkey," *New York Times*, October 9, 2003, p. A14.

[52] Partly because the United States was reluctant to dilute its authority in Iraq, offers of military and financial help were slow in coming. Steven Weisman, "U.S. Seeks Help with Iraq costs, but donors want a larger say," *New York Times*, July 14, 2003.

[53] Madeleine Albright, "Bridges, Bombs or Bluster?," 82 *Foreign Affairs* 4 (September–October, 2003); Rubin *supra* note 46 at 64.

IV. INTERDICTION

Iraq is the only case where the Security Council has come close to authorizing military action to counter the spread of weapons of mass destruction. This rather slim record may suggest that the SC cannot be counted on for collective enforcement of non-proliferation obligations, that the best it can do is manage the regime, through devices like resolution 1540 and weapons inspections. Yet the Iraq case demonstrates that the line between management and enforcement is blurry, that part of the management function is to send signals about enforcement, as the Council tried to do with the unanimous adoption of resolution 1441. The SC's resolutions on interdiction of cargo to and from North Korea illustrate the same point.

SC action on North Korea dates back to 1993, but for present purposes, we need only go back as far as 2006. In October of that year, after a nuclear test by the DPRK, the SC adopted resolution 1718 under Chapter VII, imposing targeted sanctions. The resolution also "calls upon" all states "to take, in accordance with their national authorities and legislation, and consistent with international law, cooperative action including through inspection of cargo to and from the DPRK, as necessary" (para. 8(f)). An outline agreement on North Korea's nuclear program was then reached in the Six-Party talks, but further negotiations on details broke down in December 2008. In April 2009, the DPRK tried to put a satellite in space. The SC declared this to be a violation of resolution 1718 and "called upon all Member States to comply fully with their obligations under resolution 1718 (2006)," which could be read as including paragraph 8(f) on inspections.[54] North Korea asked for an apology from the SC for this statement and said that if it did not get one, it would engage in nuclear and ICBM tests. On May 25, 2009, North Korea made good on its promise by conducting a second nuclear test. The SC responded by unanimously adopting resolution 1874 on June 12, 2009, under Chapter VII, expanding the sanctions and setting out a number of provisions on inspections of ships.

To understand the context of resolution 1874, some background on the Proliferation Security Initiative (PSI) is necessary. When resolution 1540 was adopted in 2004, the United States sought to include a provision on the interdiction of ships, aircraft, or trucks suspected of carrying WMD or related material. The threat of a Chinese veto led to the deletion of that paragraph. Instead, the Bush Administration launched the PSI, the most important feature of which is a set of interdiction principles. There is no organization to monitor compliance nor even legally-binding obligations. The core principle is that PSI participants undertake to interdict any suspicious ship, plane, or truck within their territory. (The most common scenario is to board and inspect a ship in territorial waters.) Close to 100 countries are now participants in the PSI (including Russia but not China and India). In addition, eight flag of convenience states (including Liberia, Panama, and

---

[54] UN PRST/2009/7, April 13, 2009.

Marshall Islands) have signed ship-boarding agreements with the United States, authorizing the latter to board any suspicious vessels flying their flags *on the high seas.*

The PSI rests on uncertain legal grounds. Even within the territorial sea of a participating state, the right to board and seize items from traversing ships may conflict with the "right of innocent passage" guaranteed by the Law of the Sea Convention.[55] What counts as noninnocent passage is set out in Articles 17 and 21 of the Convention: "any threat or use of force," "any act aimed at collection information," "any act of serious or willful pollution"—none of which explicitly prohibit the transport of WMD, and indeed Article 23 explicitly permits the transport of "nuclear or other inherently noxious or dangerous substance." On the other hand, the chapeau to Article 19 of the Convention states that "passage is innocent so long as it is not prejudicial to the peace, good order or security of the coastal state." An argument could be made that the transport of WMD-related material is prejudicial to the peace and security of the coastal state.

Interdiction *on the high seas* is almost certainly illegal unless the interdicting country has the permission of the flag state. A 2005 Protocol to the Convention on the Suppression of Unlawful Acts against the Safety of Maritime Navigation would allow for interdiction on the high seas, but the Protocol is not yet in force and, in any case, will be binding only on the states that sign and ratify it. In addition to the legal uncertainties, the PSI lacks clear standards as to when an interdiction would be warranted—which states and non-state actors are "of proliferation concern" (terminology used in the statement of PSI principles), when to interdict the ships of other states, how much proof is necessary to justify an interdiction, who gets to see the evidence, and what redress there is when an interdiction is not justified?[56] Moreover, even if legal, the PSI in itself is not a full solution because it only applies in the territorial waters of participating states or on the high seas with respect to flag states that have agreed to allow this. It does not apply on the high seas generally.

The legal uncertainty and concerns about biased implementation could be mitigated by having the PSI enshrined in a SC resolution obliging all states to board suspicious vessels in their territorial waters and authorizing states to board any vessel on the high seas. There was no will for such a generic resolution in 2004, nor is there in 2010. There is will, however, to increase pressure on North Korea in this way, which brings us back to resolution 1874. The key provisions of the resolution read as follows:

> 11. *Calls upon* all States to inspect, in accordance with their national authorities and legislation, and consistent with international law, all cargo to and from the DPRK, in their territory, including seaports and airports, if the State concerned

---

[55] Law of the Sea Convention, Articles 17 and 21.
[56] Jack Garvey, "The International Institutional Imperative for Countering the Spread of WMD: Assessing the PSI," 10 *Journal of Conflict and Security Law* 125 (2005).

has information that provides reasonable grounds to believe the cargo contains items the supply, sale, transfer, or export of which is prohibited...;

12. *Calls upon* all Member States to inspect vessels, with the consent of the flag State, on the high seas, if they have information that provides reasonable grounds to believe that the cargo of such vessels contains items the supply, sale, transfer, or export of which is prohibited...;

13. *Calls upon* all States to cooperate with inspections pursuant to paragraphs 11 and 12, and, if the flag State does not consent to inspection on the high seas, *decides* that the flag State shall direct the vessel to proceed to an appropriate and convenient port for the required inspection by the local authorities pursuant to paragraph 11.

Does it authorize military action? While the language could be interpreted that way, the better argument is that it does not. Paragraphs 11 and 12 use the term "calls upon", which in the context does not impose binding legal obligations, let alone enforceable ones.[57] Paragraph 13, on the other hand, is different. It stipulates that if a flag state does not consent to an inspection, the SC *"decides* the flag state shall" direct the vessel to a nearby port. That is a binding obligation. What if the flag state (e.g., North Korea) refuses? Can military action be employed to force the ship into the territorial waters of a sympathetic country (or to board and inspect the ship)? The United States or others may someday seek to interpret resolution 1874 that way, but China voted for the resolution based on the opposite understanding (stated in its explanation of vote).[58] No other SC member—not Russia, not Vietnam, not Libya—made a similar statement. In their explanation of votes, neither the United States nor any other country explicitly stated they had the legal authority to use force to interdict ships, but nor did they preclude it.

It is conceivable that there will be a row over how to interpret this resolution in the future (like 1441 on Iraq and the resolutions on Kosovo pre-1999), but practice so far has been consistent with a narrow reading. The United States, China, and Russia reportedly agreed in mid-June 2009 that they would implement the resolution by ordering ships to stop but *not* board them by force.[59] This does not preclude a more robust interpretation of the resolution later but does suggest that the matter will not come to a head soon.

On the other hand, North Korea is on notice that the SC could take the next step and authorize coercive interdiction. This strong political signal is a good illustration of how the SC can move in the direction of authorizing coercive action, incrementally and not

---

[57] The term "calls upon" has been used by the SC in the past to impose binding obligations, as affirmed by the International Court of Justice. *Legal Consequences for States of the Continued Presence of South Africa in Namibia (Southwest Africa) Notwithstanding Security Council Resolution 276 (1970)*, ICJ Advisory Opinion of June 21, 1971. However, in the context of resolution 1874, in which the words "demands," "decides," and "requires" are used in other paragraphs, the term "calls upon" cannot reasonably be read as a binding obligation.

[58] United Nations (2009) S/PV.6141, Meeting Record: New York Security Council, June 12, 2009.

[59] David Sanger, "U.S. to confront, not board, North Korean ships," *New York Times*, June 17, 2009.

necessarily according to any design on the part of a particular SC member. It occurs piecemeal, in reaction to crises as they erupt and as a function of the political dynamics within the SC at a given moment. Arguably, China is now closer to accepting coercive interdiction of suspicious North Korean vessels than it was five years ago. High level diplomacy combined with arms and economic sanctions were the best option for dealing with the problem when resolution 1874 was adopted, but diplomacy backed by the implicit threat of limited force—from the SC—may well pay dividends in the ongoing effort to contain North Korea. Reports that a North Korean freighter destined for Myanmar and tracked by the United States navy turned back suggest that this has already started to happen.[60]

V. CONCLUSION

The text of the NPT is the source of many legal disputes, most of which play out below the radar of those watching the larger political dynamics. As I have sought to show in this chapter, those dynamics are affected by legal considerations. They can shift the burden of persuasion, simplifying or complicating efforts to win support for a policy. By endorsing the U.S.-India nuclear deal, it will be harder for states in the IAEA or Nuclear Suppliers Group to stop China from making a similar deal with Pakistan on the grounds that it violates Article I. The ability to impose incremental pressure on the DPRK, through sanctions and interdiction, is affected by the debates over its NPT status.

Not all legal argumentation is below the radar screen of course. It was highly public in the period leading to the 2003 intervention in Iraq. The United States and the United Kingdom had something to gain—and to lose–by seeking a second resolution in the SC. The failure meant costs were incurred, and there were many in the Bush Administration who wished the effort had not been made for that reason. It is hard to be sure what portion of the costs can be attributed to the decision to act outside the legal and SC framework,[61] but a hard-headed empiricist would surely have more trouble making the case that there were no costs associated with the lack of clear legal authority.

In addition to its enforcement role, the SC plays a management role in the field of non-proliferation. The academic literature on compliance with international norms

---

[60] Choe Sang-Hun, "South Korea Says Freighter from North Turns Back," *New York Times*, July 7, 2009.
[61] Lael Brainard and Michael O'Hanlon estimated in 2003 that the security and reconstruction of Iraq would cost the United States $100 billion more than what it would pay for a multilateral reconstruction effort in Iraq along the lines of Bosnia or Kosovo.; Lael Brainard, and Michael O'Hanlon, "The heavy price of America's going it alone," *Financial Times*, August 6, 2003, p. 17.

distinguishes the "enforcement" model from the "management" model.[62] The former holds that states comply with deep commitments only if they fear the prospect of sanctions. The management model sees much non-compliance as the result of uncertainty about what compliance requires or limitations on the capacity of parties to carry out their undertakings, rather than deliberate defiance. Resolution 1540, discussed in Chapter 5, is an example of SC management. Managing the non-proliferation regime also entails using the SC as a pulpit, from which both reassuring and threatening signals can be sent. In 1992, at its first-ever summit meeting, the SC declared the proliferation of WMD to be a threat to international peace and security,[63] repeated in the preamble to resolution 1887 (2009). A more robust message was sent by resolution 1874, which carries an implicit threat—collectively issued by the SC—that forcible interdiction of North Korean cargo is on the table. On the other side of the ledger, resolutions that reaffirm the NPT goal of nuclear disarmament, like 1540 and 1887, send reassuring signals as do those on a nuclear weapons free zone in the Middle East. Because the P5 have enforcement powers and capacity, a warning from them is likely to be taken seriously by the target; because the legitimacy of strategic leadership by the NWS is questioned, reassuring signals on their end of the grand bargain can shore up the non-proliferation regime.

---

[62] Abram Chayes and Antonia Handler Chayes, *The New Sovereignty: Compliance with International Regulatory Agreements* (1995); George Downs, David Rocke and Peter Barsoom, "Is the Good News About Compliance Good News About Cooperation?" 50 *International Organization* 379 (1996).

[63] Statement of the President of the Security Council S/23500, January 31, 2002.

7

PEACE OPERATIONS

I. INTRODUCTION

THE ENTERPRISE OF peacekeeping, improvised from the start, is in a constant state of evolution. Certain principles have been identified and doctrine for peace operations is being developed, but for the most part, practice has been ahead of theory. The two most distinctive features of recent operations are increasingly ambitious peacebuilding tasks and increasingly robust protection of civilians mandates. These practices are tied to normative expectations that stem from democratic norms and human rights. In turn, the practice of peacekeeping affects those expectations: when the promotion of democracy and human rights are demonstrably successful in helping to secure peace, those norms are reinforced. The process is dynamic, involving influential states, key figures within international institutions, and nongovernmental entities. These external actors interact with internal actors in complex ways, shaping our understanding of what peace operations are and what they can and should be doing to help societies emerge from violent conflict.

In the next section of this chapter, I set out the legal framework for peace operations and introduce some concepts to help explain how peacekeeping practice has evolved. In the following section, on the peacebuilding agenda, I argue that the goal of participatory governance is best understood in terms of deliberative rather than representative or electoral democracy, at least in the early stages of peace consolidation. I turn to the protection of civilians in the final section: first by looking at its connection to the "responsibility to protect" norm, then by considering how the interpretation and implementation of the mandate has impacted that norm. My central argument is that the practice of peacekeeping both shapes and is shaped by the normative climate in which it occurs.

II. LEGAL AND CONCEPTUAL FRAMEWORK

A. A Short History of Peacekeeping

The term peacekeeping is not found anywhere in the UN Charter. Described by former Secretary-General Dag Hammarskjold as falling in Chapter VI1/2, it combines the peaceful dispute settlement mechanisms of Chapter VI with the enforcement provisions of Chapter VII. The first peacekeeping operations were small unarmed observer missions deployed in the Middle East, the Balkans, and on the border between India and Pakistan. The first armed peacekeeping mission was the United Nations Emergency Force (UNEF I), deployed in the aftermath of the Suez Canal crisis in 1956 to monitor the withdrawal of French, British, and Israeli forces from Egypt and the creation of a buffer zone. A number of guiding principles were established, and UNEF I became the prototype for so-called traditional peacekeeping that characterized the Cold War era.

With the end of the Cold War, the range of conflicts on which the superpowers could agree expanded, and the SC was able to work more cohesively. The total number of personnel deployed in UN operations went from 11,000 in 1988 to 78,000 in 1994, and the annual budget rose from $230.4 to $3.6 billion. Because the nature of the conflicts changed, the nature of the missions changed as well. Most post–Cold War conflicts were not between states but within states, fought between armies and irregular forces, or among irregular forces. They were often accompanied by humanitarian catastrophes, systematic human rights abuses, and the breakdown of law and order. Instead of interposition between two regular armies, peacekeepers were deployed either to monitor implementation of comprehensive peace agreements or in environments where there was no peace to keep. Robust operations (sometimes called "peace enforcement") were often subcontracted by the UN Security Council to regional organizations or coalitions of the willing. There was a lull in the late 1990s, but at the turn of the millennium, the UN once again began taking on ambitious peace operations, from the transitional administrations in Kosovo and East Timor, to the robust missions in the Sierra Leone, the DRC, and Sudan. Meanwhile, NATO remained in Kosovo and Afghanistan, the EU throughout the Balkans and in parts of Africa, and the AU in Somalia in so-called sub-contracted operations, authorized by the SC but not commanded by the UN.

Some leveling off in the number and size of peace operations began in 2010 as UN missions in Liberia, Chad, and the DRC started to scale down, and talk of NATO's withdrawal from Afghanistan began in earnest. Yet more than 120,000 military, police, and civilians were deployed in UN operations at the end of October 2010.[1] Combined with the 150,000 in non-UN operations (mainly Afghanistan), peace operations were still big business and seemed destined to remain an important instrument in the toolkit of many international organizations.

B. UN Charter Framework

Peacekeeping was invented because the collective security scheme embodied in the UN Charter could not be realized. That scheme relies heavily on unanimity among the great powers who, along with other members of the UN, were meant to join forces to prevent any country from using or threatening force in its international relations, other than in self-defense. Article 43 of the Charter stipulates that military action should be undertaken by member states who provide forces pursuant to "special agreements" negotiated with the SC. The idea in 1945 was that once the agreements were signed, those states would be bound to provide troops if called upon by the SC. A Military Staff Committee (composed of the chiefs of staff of the five permanent members plus others on an ad hoc basis) would plan and provide strategic direction to military operations. Because of the Cold War, the scheme never worked as intended, and no Article 43 agreements were ever signed. Instead, peacemaking and peacekeeping became the standard tools the SC employed to maintain international peace and security.

Three chapters of the UN Charter are relevant to peacekeeping: Chapter VI, Chapter VII, and Chapter VIII. The key difference between action under Chapter VI and action under Chapter VII is that the former is largely based on consent, while the latter can be coercive—or at least does not require the consent of the target of the action. Chapter VIII provides that regional organizations may also act to maintain international peace and security. If the action is firmly consent-based (that is, Chapter VI-style peacekeeping), then no SC authorization is required. According to Article 53, however, enforcement measures require such authorization. Therefore, whether a particular peace operation (UN or non-UN) requires SC approval depends on where it falls on the spectrum between Chapter VI and VII. Much has been written on the gray area between peacekeeping and enforcement action—the contested ground of "peace enforcement"—and there has been some doctrinal effort to clarify the distinction.[2] Yet a multitude of political and operational questions remain, few of which can be resolved by doctrinal precision.

---

[1] *United Nations Peacekeeping Operations, Background Note,* October 31, 2010. Available at http://www.un.org/en/peacekeeping/bnote.htm.
[2] The latest effort is *United Nations Peacekeeping Operations, Principles and Guidelines* (2008) [hereinafter the *Capstone Doctrine*]. See, in particular, p. 19 where the difference between peacekeeping and peace enforcement is explained on the basis of tactical v. strategic level consent.

Article 2(7) is also part of the legal framework for peacekeeping. It prohibits the UN from intervening in matters that are essentially within the domestic jurisdiction of a state but specifies that the prohibition does not apply to enforcement measures under Chapter VII upon a finding by the SC that a situation is a "threat to the peace." The SC has considerable, though not unfettered, discretion to decide whether that threshold has been met. Since the end of the Cold War, it has been employing an expanding definition of what constitutes a threat to international peace and security, to include support for terrorism (discussed in chapter 5), internal conflicts, and humanitarian catastrophes or human rights atrocities (discussed in Chapter 4 and below).

As important as the SC's expansion of Chapter VII is the expanding scope of activities undertaken in the context of Chapter VI operations. Multidimensional missions today not only help to provide basic security, but also engage in security sector reform, facilitate the return of refugees and internally displaced persons, monitor human rights, supervise elections, and support governments in the building of institutions, and extending state authority. While these functions clearly infringe on state sovereignty, much of this has occurred under the radar screen of the'sovereigntists' because it has been on the basis of consent, typically embodied in a peace agreement between the parties to a conflict.

Are those elements of Chapter VI peacekeeping and peacebuilding interference in internal affairs and therefore a violation of Article 2(7)? The formal legal answer is that if the activities are undertaken with the consent of the government concerned, then they are not "intervention". But as I discuss below, consent is often brought about under intense pressure. Some states, including some on the SC, view democratization and human rights promotion under that kind of pressure as being interference in internal affairs. Rosalyn Higgins (former International Court of Justice judge) has another way of looking at the problem. Though not writing about peace operations, in 1994, she observed that some historically domestic matters are now treated as matters of international concern.[3] Thus for example human rights are now truly matters of international concern and so peacekeeping and peacebuilding activities designed to promote them cannot be challenged on the grounds that they conflict with Article 2(7).

A final legal point: many UN peace operations have both Chapter VI and VII mandates. It is now standard practice to include Chapter VII provisions authorizing "all necessary means" to protect civilians in the context of what are essentially consent-based operations, like the UN Mission in the DRC (MONUC) and the UN Mission in Sudan (UNMIS). The mandate of the UN mission in Haiti (MINUSTAH) includes Chapter VII powers to support the transitional government in providing a secure and stable environment.[4] The entire mandate of the United Nations Mission in Liberia (UNMIL) is under Chapter VII, even though it was conceived as a consent-based multidimensional

---

[3] Rosalyn Higgins, *Problem and Process: International Law and How We Use It* 254 (1994).
[4] UN SC Res 1542 (2004).

operation.[5] The same was true for Burundi.[6] Conversely, the expanded UN mission in Lebanon (UNIFIL) includes the authority to "take all necessary action to ensure that its area of operations is not utilized for hostile activities of any kind. . . and to protect civilians," yet was placed entirely under Chapter VI for political reasons.[7] The final mandate for the UN mission in the Central African Republic and Chad (MINURCAT) shifted from Chapter VII to VI in deference to the wishes of the government and yet still includes the authority to protect civilians.[8]

It is tempting to conclude from this that the Chapter VI/Chapter VII distinction is not important. While that may be true in abstract legal terms, it does have political and operational significance. Some members of the SC are less inclined to authorize Chapter VII than Chapter VI missions, and many troop contributors prefer not to engage in peace enforcement. Plus, host states typically do not want the peacekeepers to have Chapter VII powers. (This was the Government of Sudan's position on any operation in Darfur although it ultimately gave in.) If the mandate is under Chapter VII, there is no need for the consent of the host state as a matter of law. As a matter of policy, it is necessary to deploy with that consent in order to avoid crossing the line from peacekeeping to war.

C. The Meaning of Consent

The art of contemporary peacekeeping is to strike the right balance between consent and coercion. While formal consent is always granted in some manner, it is often qualified in one of three ways: it is unreliable, brought about by external pressure, or open-ended. Unreliable consent is typical in conflicts involving more than two actors or factions not under the complete control of the main protagonists. In the DRC, MONUC was first deployed in 2000 to monitor the Lusaka Agreement, but the cooperation of the eight signatories (six governments and two rebel groups) was always tenuous, and many armed groups posed—and still do—a perpetual challenge to the peacekeepers.

Bosnia after Dayton, Kosovo, and East Timor are cases of consent under pressure. In the first two, consent followed NATO bombing campaigns; in East Timor, Indonesia consented to the International Force in East Timor (INTERFET) only after ten days of intense diplomatic pressure, threats of economic sanctions and warnings by the Secretary-General of international criminal prosecution. In all three places, the consent granted was hardly an act of volition and indeed verged on duress.

Open-ended consent is illustrated by the peace operations in Cambodia, El Salvador, and Mozambique, where the parties invited the UN to monitor and support implementation of comprehensive peace agreements. No peace agreement, no matter how

---

[5] UN SC Res 1509 (2003).
[6] UN SC Res 1545 (2004).
[7] UN SC Res 1701 (2006).
[8] UN SC Res 1923 (2010).

comprehensive, can provide for every contingency. Gaps in the accords materialize, problems of interpretation arise, and circumstances change throughout the life of a peace process. Signing these peace agreements, with obligations that are not well specified and that will take time to implement, is, in effect, a gesture of faith that later problems can be worked out on a consensual basis.

The UN has sought to account for the qualified nature of consent in its peacekeeping doctrine. The *Capstone Doctrine,* building on the *Brahimi Report*[9], is notable for two innovations. First, it stresses that the consent required is not only to the presence of a peacekeeping operation but also to a political process.[10] More helpful than the truism that peacekeeping is not the right instrument when there is no peace to keep is the notion that peacekeeping can only succeed if accompanied by a viable political process. Second, it distinguishes between "tactical" and "strategic" consent.[11] The idea is that a UN mission must gain and keep the consent of the main parties to the conflict but can act robustly against spoilers at the local level without losing its character as peacekeeping. While a step forward in doctrinal thinking, it is not clear how workable the distinction is in the field. Determining whether a particular "spoiler" is a minor actor operating locally or a proxy for one of the main parties is no easy task. In the DRC and Sudan (both Darfur and the South), there are many groups that could fall in one category or the other; whether to take them on militarily or negotiate for their cooperation is a difficult judgment call.

It should not be surprising, therefore, that managing consent—even in the context of an operation that rests on a comprehensive peace agreement—is difficult. It is further complicated by the fact that there is growing uncertainty about how transformative peacekeeping and peacebuilding should be. What exactly are the parties consenting to, the presence of an impartial referee to monitor their behavior, or deep external involvement in transformation of their society? Doctrinal thinking in the UN describes "sustainable peace" as the goal of any peace process, requiring progress in five areas: safety and security, political dialogue and support to political processes, rule of law and human rights, governance and the extension of state authority, and socioeconomic development. Precisely how these are defined, and what are the particular attributes of each varies among the missions, but the extent to which they permeate policy documents and mandates is striking.[12]

---

[9] United Nations, *Report of the Panel on United Nations Peace Operations,* 21 August 2000, A/55/305-S/2000/809 [hereinafter the *Brahimi Report*]

[10] *Capstone Doctrine,* p.31.

[11] *Id.* This terminology is used on p. 19, and the idea is developed at pp. 31–32. It echoes the British notion of "wider peacekeeping" introduced in 1993, which drew on recent experience in Bosnia, Cambodia, and from observing the United States in Somalia.

[12] In the UN context, see for example, *Report of the Secretary-*General, *No exit without strategy: Security Council decision-making and the closure or transition of UN peacekeeping operations* S/2001/384 (April 20, 2001)

This ambitious agenda raises conceptual questions (are peace operations neocolonial exercises in social engineering based on liberal democratic models?) and pragmatic ones (even if building democratic states in the aftermath of conflict is a worthy goal, to what extent can outside intervention contribute to the achievement of that goal?)[13] It also raises questions about the scope and limits of *peacekeeping* itself. What is it that peacekeepers as opposed to other external actors (like development agencies and bilateral partners) can be expected to do during the limited period when they are deployed? The *Capstone Doctrine* focuses on security, rule of law, political processes, and coordination as the "core business" of a peacekeeping operation.[14] *New Horizon* specifies that among the priorities established in the Secretary-General's 2009 report on peacebuilding, "support to national political processes and the provision of safety and security" are areas of UN peacekeeping's comparative advantages. This may include "the reestablishment of frameworks for governance," but leaves out things like the provision of basic services and the socioeconomic dimensions of peacebuilding—where peacekeepers are primarily in the role of supporting other external actors.[15] In practice, the distinctions drawn in the policy documents remain contested and implementation has been inconsistent.[16]

[hereinafter *No exit without strategy*]; Center on International Cooperation, *Building on Brahimi: Peacekeeping in an Era of Strategic Uncertainty* (2009); Department of Peacekeeping Operations and Department of Field Support, *A New Partnership Agenda: Chartering a New Horizon for UN Peacekeeping* (July 2009) [hereinafter *New Horizon*]; Department of Peacekeeping Operations and Department of Field Support, *The New Horizon Initiative : Progress Report No. 1* (October 2010) [hereinafter *New Horizon Progress Report*];Report of the Secretary-General, *Peacebuilding in the immediate aftermath of conflict*, A/63/881-S/2009/304 (June 11, 2009); Report of the Secretary-General, *Security, Peace and Development: The Role of the United Nations in Supporting Security Sector Reform* (A/26/659-S/2008/39). For thinking outside the UN context, see United States Institute for Peace and U.S. Army Peacekeeping and Stability Operations Institute, *Guiding Principles for Stabilization and Reconstruction* (2009), a comprehensive report that synthesizes a large number of strategic policy documents from government ministries (United States and other), intergovernmental organizations (including the African Union, European Union, NATO, OECD, OSCE, Word Bank, as well as the UN) and nongovernmental organizations.

[13] Some of these questions were debated, if obliquely, at the Security Council Open Debate on Transition and Exit Strategies in February 2010. United Nations (2010) S.PV/6270 and S.PV.6270 (Resumption 1), Meeting Records: New York, Security Council, February 12, 2010. In the academic literature, see Roland Paris and Timothy Sisk eds., *The Dilemmas of Statebuilding: Confronting the Contradictions of Postwar Peace Operations* (2009); Oliver Richmond, *The Transformation of Peace: Rethinking Peace and Conflict Studies* (2007); Michael Pugh, Neil Cooper and Mandy Turner eds., *Whose Peace? Critical Perspectives on the Political Economy of Peacebuilding* (2009).

[14] *Capstone Doctrine*, *supra* note 2 at 23.

[15] *New Horizon*, *supra* note 12 at 23. See also *New Horizon Progress Report*, *supra* note 12, at 14.

[16] I elaborate on this point in Ian Johnstone "Peacekeeping's Transitional Moment" in *Annual Review of Global Peace Operations 2011* (Center on International Cooperation, 2011).

D. The Peacekeeping Bargain

A second conceptual issue concerns the peacekeeping "bargain." Whether under Chapter VI, Chapter VII, or some combination, a peacekeeping mandate functions as a "bargain" between internal and external actors. In simple (and highly stylized) terms, the bargain looks like this: local elites want security and development assistance in exchange for which they are willing to tolerate governance reforms, human rights monitoring, and other elements of the liberal peace.[17] This is a caricature, but it does illuminate a recurring problem. Since security and development assistance are likely to reinforce the power of elites, and governance and human rights monitoring are likely to undermine it, there is built-in tension and therefore the need for ongoing negotiation in implementation of the mandate. In this sense, a peace agreement is more of a multilateral "relational contract" (discussed below) among the parties to the conflict and the external actors than a one-off bilateral transaction.

The problem for external actors is that the bargain obsolesces. As Michael Doyle and Nicholas Sambanis explain, the authority of the UN and leverage of the peacekeepers is greatest in the early stages of a peace process because that is when the parties are most dependent on the UN, and the UN has less of its prestige and resources on the line.[18] David Edelstein adds that the host population's welcome of intervening forces tends to diminish over time.[19] This "obsolescing welcome" is matched by diminishing will in troop, police and finance contributing countries, especially as the perceived costs of continued deployment start to outweigh benefits.

Adding a further layer of complexity, the dynamics of the bargain depend on the strength of the host government. Typically, the UN starts out dealing with weak transitional governments, as in Haiti, Burundi, and the Democratic Republic of the Congo. The governments need the UN and other external actors for security assistance and therefore are willing to tolerate significant external interference in exchange. But as the government becomes stronger, it becomes less tolerant of international tutelage—content to accept a small peacebuilding presence if that means greater financial resources but less interested in a military presence and governance advice. This dynamic played out in Burundi after the 2005 elections and in the DRC after the 2006 elections. In Sudan, the UN has been dealing with a relatively strong government from the start, and it got even stronger after the 2010 elections. President Bashir consolidated his power and gained new confidence in dealing with UNAMID, illustrated by an announcement that the peacekeepers would have their bags searched at airports and would have to inform the

---

[17] Michael Barnett and Christoph Zurcher, "The peacebuilders contract: how external statebuilding reinforces weak statehood," in Paris and Sisk eds., *supra* note 13 at 23–52.

[18] Michael Doyle and Nicholas Sambanis, *Making War and Building Peace* 309 (2006).

[19] David Edelstein, "Foreign Militaries, Sustainable Institutions and postwar statebuilding," in Paris and Sisk eds., *supra* note 13 at 81 and 83.

Sudanese government before moving on roads, even within cities.[20] This contravention of peacekeeping principles is part of a pattern that has emerged in Sudan and elsewhere: the presence of peacekeeping missions is not challenged directly, but they face so many small obstructions that their ability to fulfill the mandate is seriously jeopardized—amounting in some cases to the *de facto* withdrawal of consent.[21]

III. PEACE OPERATIONS AND DEMOCRATIC NORMS

The notion of a peacekeeping bargain begs the question: whose consent matters? There is a premium on local ownership in a peace process, both as a normative stance (people ought to have control over the decisions that affect their lives) and as a requirement for effectiveness (no peace process will succeed if there is not broad buy-in). But which local actors should 'own' the process, those who hold power only–typically the parties to the conflict – or a broader range of stakeholders? Factional leaders do not necessarily represent broad constituencies, and the governing arrangements they put in place may not be seen as legtimate by all who have a stake in the peace process. Thus, sustainable peace is thought to require inclusive politics, which for the peacekeeping operation means engaging with opposition parties, parliamentarians, mid-level government officials, local governors and administrators, civil society and the private sector. Yet pressure for inclusive politics bumps up against sovereign authority if the peacekeeping mission is seen as by-passing governmental channels to engage directly with the population on politically sensitive matters. So is the bargain with the host government and local elites only, or is it a social compact with the population as a whole? That question invites an inquiry into the relationship between peacekeeping and democratic norms.

A. A Right to Democracy?

Peacekeeping and peacebuilding do not occur in a normative vacuum. What is seen as a matter of international concern has evolved, to include human rights for example (discussed further below).[22] More controversial is the form of governance. Is a lack of participatory or democratic governance a matter of international concern? According to Boutros-Ghali's *Agenda for Democratization*, there is an emerging consensus on the legitimacy of democracy promotion by international organizations; others have declared

---

[20] "Sudan to monitor movements of UN peacekeepers," BBC July 31, 2010, available at http://www.bbc.co.uk/news/world-africa-10829620.

[21] *Capstone Doctrine, supra* note 2 at 32. In addition to Sudan, this occurred in Eritrea and Chad.

[22] For a good analysis of the relationship between human rights and peacekeeping, see Christine Bell, *Peace Agreements and Human Rights* (2006). See also, Michael Doyle, Ian Johnstone and Robert Orr, *Keeping the Peace: Multidimensional UN Operations in Cambodia and El Salvador* (1995).

a right to democracy.[23] Like peacekeeping, the word democracy does not appear in the UN Charter, but it was written in the name of "we the peoples" and affirms the principles of self-determination, human rights, and fundamental freedoms. The Universal Declaration of Human Rights and many human rights treaties grant a right to political participation.[24] In April 1999, the Commission on Human Rights adopted a nonbinding resolution entitled "Promotion of the Right to Democracy."[25] In March 2005, the Secretary-General declared that democracy is a universal right,[26] and in a striking statement at the World Summit later that year, the General Assembly "reaffirmed that democracy is a universal value" and established a democracy fund to promote it.[27] The constitutive instruments of the EU, NATO, OSCE, OAS, AU, ASEAN, Commonwealth, Mercosur, Andean Community, and ECOWAS all list democracy promotion as a goal. The OAS's 2001 Inter-American Democratic Charter states that "unconstitutional interruption of the democratic order shall lead to suspension" from the organization, invoked in respect of the attempted coup against President Chavez of Venezuela in 2002 and most recently in 2009 to suspend Honduras.[28] The OAU adopted a similar instrument in 1999, reaffirmed in Article 30 of the Constitutive Act of the African Union. Comoros, Côte d'Ivoire, and Madagascar have all been suspended on the basis of that Article.

These norms have had an impact on peacekeeping. "Participatory governance" is a stated goal, and peace operations have sought to promote it in various ways.[29] But the connection between peacebuilding and democratic norms has not played out quite as the "liberal peace" agenda would predict. Creating electoral democracies and market-oriented economies has proven to be difficult, and the neocolonial flavor of liberal peacebuilding

---

[23] Boutros Boutros-Ghali, *An Agenda for Democratization* (United Nations 1996), para. 28. On the right to democracy, see generally the compilation of essays in Gregory Fox and Brad Roth eds., *Democratic Governance and International Law* (2000). See also Thomas Zweifel, *International Organizations and Democracy* (2006); M. Archibugi, D. Held and M. Kohler eds., *Reimagining Political Community: Studies in Cosmopolitan Democracy* (1998); Richard Burchill ed., *Democracy and International Law* (2006); Thomas Carothers, *Critical Mission: Essays on Democracy Promotion* (2004).

[24] Article 25 of the International Covenant on Civil and Political Rights guarantees a "right to political participation," including the right to take part in public affairs, to vote and to be elected in "genuine periodic elections" by secret ballot. Various regional human rights documents set out the right in similar terms: the First Protocol to the European Convention on Human Rights, the American Convention on Human Rights, the African Charter of Human Rights and the OSCE Charter of Paris.

[25] United Nations, Commission on Human Rights resolution1999/57.

[26] United Nations, *Report of the Secretary-General, In Larger Freedom: Towards Development, Security and Human Rights for All* (March 21, 2005), A/59/2005, para.149.

[27] United Nations General Assembly, *World Summit Outcome*, A/RES/60/1 (October 24, 2005), para. 135.

[28] On July 21, 2010, the Central American Integration System, a regional political block, readmitted Honduras. The OAS had not done so by then, but there was movement in that direction. "Patching things up: Honduras's post-coup President," *The Economist*, July 24, 2010, p. 40.

[29] *No Exit Without Strategy*, supra note 12 at para. 10. Peace operations hold the promise of "participatory peace." Doyle and Sambanis, *supra* note 18 at 18–19.

has been criticized.[30] An alternative approach is starting to gain ground, one that draws more on deliberative than liberal democracy. Rather than assuming there is some predetermined end-state toward which all post-conflict societies must be pushed, deliberative principles are aimed at informing the process that determines what the end-state should be and how to get there.[31] This less-ambitious approach is reflected in recent peacekeeping practice.

B. *The Impact of Deliberative Norms on Peacekeeping*

The consolidation of peace is an inherently political exercise, whose central goal is to channel conflict from violent into peaceful forms of settlement.[32] Peace operations play a variety of roles in achieving that goal, ranging from active patron informed by international standards of legitimacy, to passive observer, deferring at every step to local ownership and local conceptions of legitimacy.[33] The range of roles highlights a basic dilemma that all peace operations face: on one hand, the more proactive the external role, the harder it is for local governing institutions to gain credibility; on the other hand, rigid adherence to "local ownership" can mean deferring to powerful actors who may lack the legitimacy and capacity to deliver sustainable peace. Where the balance should lie is rarely self-evident from the start of an operation, and never static. Because neither internal nor external actors have privileged insight into how to strike the balance, the process of peace consolidation tends to be interactive, among local actors, and between local and external actors. A review of recent practice in three areas illustrates the point: governance, security, and justice.[34]

The nature of *governance* arrangements between the end of the worst fighting and the establishment of permanent institutions can have a profound effect on the prospects for sustainable peace. Transitional arrangements shape the political landscape for competing

---

[30] Richmond, *The Transformation of Peace, supra* note 13; Pugh, Cooper and Turner eds., *supra* note 13. One of the first to worry about the impact of rushed elections and liberalization in post-conflict societies is Roland Paris, *At War's End: Building Peace After Civil Conflict* (2004). But he did not oppose liberal peacebuilding per se and recently wrote an article defending the agenda from critics. Roland Paris, "Saving Liberal Peacebuilding," 36 *Review of International Studies* 337 (2010). For good reviews of the debates, see Alex Bellamy, Paul Williams and Stuart Griffin, *Understanding Peacekeeping* (2004); and Paris and Sisk, *supra* note 13.

[31] Michael Barnett, "Building a Republican Peace: Stabilizing States After War," 30 *International Security* 27 (2006).

[32] See the Secretary-General's Address to Opening Session of Peacebuilding Commission, UN General Assembly PBC/1 (June 23, 2006); Elizabeth Cousens and Chetan Kumar, *Peacebuilding as Politics: Cultivating Peace in Fragile Societies* (2000).

[33] Richard Caplan, *International Governance of War-Torn Territories* (2005).

[34] I draw in this section on Ian Johnstone, "Consolidating Peace: Priorities and Deliberative Processes", in *Annual Review of Global Peace Operations 2007*, 13-88 (Center on International Cooperation, 2007). See also, Katia Papagianni, "Political Transitions after Peace Agreements: The Importance of Consultative and Inclusive Political Processes", 3 *Journal of Intervention and Statebuilding* 47 (2009).

groups in a post-conflict society: they prepare for elections, write constitutions, manage the budget, and appoint people to the ministries that administer the transition, such as defense, the interior, and justice. The process by which all this occurs is as important as the outcome. An inclusive, deliberative approach to constitution making, for example, is important because the future governance of the country cannot be left entirely in the hands of those who fought the war.[35] Afghanistan is illustrative. The "interim authority" selected to govern Afghanistan at the 2001 Bonn meeting handed over to a more inclusive transitional government that came out of the Emergency Loya Jirga of 1051 elected and 500 appointed delegates held in 2002. That set the stage for the drafting of a constitution by a 35-member commission, following extensive public consultations with an estimated 178,000 people. The constitution was formally adopted in a Constitutional Loya Jirga of 502 representatives in 2004, paving the way to elections in 2004–2005. While this transitional exercise involved back-room deals and pressure tactics, as well as traditional forms of consultative governance, it did produce a government that enjoyed substantial respect among the Afghan population—at least until the lack of progress in improving security became apparent.[36] By way of comparison, the rushed and improvised constitutional process in Iraq was far less successful in animating an inclusive debate about the future of that country.[37]

In the early days of a peace process, *security* is not up for discussion: either outsiders impose it, or a peace agreement obliges it. The primary function of most peace operations is to help provide security, and increasingly they are being given robust mandates–if not always the capacity–to do so. But eventually they must hand over to local forces. As Barnett Rubin argues, the negotiation of the security transition and political transition are mutually reinforcing; control over security institutions is central to building a legitimate state, while building effective security institutions requires credible political leadership.[38] And because security sector reform (SSR) is not only about equipping and training, but also about governance—about who oversees the security sector and whose interests it protects—the parties to the conflict and security establishments should not make decisions behind closed doors. Representative assemblies, local governments, and

---

[35] Vivien Hart, "Constitution-Making and the Transformation of Conflict," 26 *Peace and Change* 153 (2001).
[36] Richard Ponzio, "Transforming Political Authority: UN democratic peacebuilding in Afghanistan," 13 *Global Governance* 255 (2007); see also Hamish Nixon and Richard Ponzio, "Building Democracy in Afghanistan: The Statebuilding Agenda and International Engagement" 14 *International Peacekeeping* 26 (2007).
[37] For critiques of the constitutional process in Iraq, see Hamid Barrada and Philippe Gaillard, "Le Grand Interview: Lakhdar Brahimi," *Jeune Afrique* No. 2375, July 16–22, 2006; International Crisis Group Middle East Briefing No. 19, "Unmaking Iraq: A Constitutional Process Gone Awry," September 26, 2005; United States Institute for Peace Special Report No. 155 "Iraq's Constitutional Process: An Opportunity Lost," December 2005.
[38] Barnett Rubin, "The Politics of Security in Post-Conflict Internationalized State Building," in *Building States to Build Peace* 31 (C. Call and V. Wyeth eds, 2008); Barnett Rubin, "Peace Building and State-Building in Afghanistan: constructing sovereignty for whose security?" 27 *Third World Quarterly* 175, 180 (2006).

the broader population must be engaged. This lesson was well learned in Sierra Leone where the Office of National Security took the lead in facilitating inclusive decision-making processes, including consulting local communities.[39] Talks on SSR in Afghanistan, on the other hand, lacked transparency.[40] In contrast to the constitution-making process described above, the security arrangements in Afghanistan were driven more by a desire to enlist allies in the war against Al-Qaeda and the Taliban than a genuine effort to build national security institutions dedicated to supporting the central government.

Policing is a further illustration of the deeply political nature of security sector reform. Many peace processes entail a transition from security provided by external military forces, to external police forces (typically formed police units), to local police forces. The success of the transition depends on the extent to which a social contract between the local police and population is forged. It does not emerge spontaneously but rather in an interactive, evolutionary manner, in which an ethos of community policing is cultivated, and effective oversight institutions are built. Good security sector governance means ensuring all security forces are under civilian control, meeting basic standards of accountability and transparency, and insisting on respect for basic human rights.[41] These standards cannot be imposed by outsiders, nor can they be adopted wholesale by national security forces in the early stages of a peace process. But they can be the starting point for an inclusive dialogue about the security requirements of a given society. Ideally, the dialogue engages all national and international "stakeholders," as occurred in Timor Leste after the crisis of 2006 – a crisis that was caused by inattentiveness to security sector reform.[42]

There is a tendency in peace operations to defer action on *justice*, given the more pressing security and governance demands in the immediate post-conflict period. This assumes a tradeoff between peace and justice that is based on too narrow of a reading of both concepts. Broadly speaking, there are three goals of transitional justice: accountability, truth and reconciliation, and restoration. A close look at each of the three goals illustrates the complexity of the relationship between local and external actors. Whether based on a theory of retribution or deterrence, accountability reaffirms the shared norms of a society by expressing condemnation of those who committed the crimes and of the crimes themselves. But rushing to punishment can undermine a peace process. Fear of arrest by peacekeepers and being handed over to the International Criminal Court is one

---

[39] See Conflict Prevention and Peace Forum, "Workshop on Peace Consolidation in Sierra Leone," Freetown Sierra Leone, June 30–July 1, 2006.

[40] Rubin, "Politics of Security," *supra* note 38 at 24.

[41] See OECD DAC Guidelines and Reference Series: Security System Reform and Governance, 2005; EU Concept for ESDP Support to Security Reform, 2005; United Nations DPKO Policy Directive on Law Enforcement Agencies; UNDP 2002, *Strategic Approaches to Justice and Security Sector Reform*.

[42] *Report of the Secretary-General on Timor-Leste pursuant to Security Council resolution 1690 (2006)*, August 8, 2006, para. 114; UN SC Res 1704 (2006).

of the reasons why the Sudanese government opposed the transition from the AMIS to UNAMID in Darfur.

Truth telling is important when the facts about past human rights abuses are in doubt or in order to "lift the veil of denial" about widely known or unspoken truths.[43] Unlike trials that depend on making a choice between individual guilt and innocence, truth commissions can hear different points of view about the pattern of abuses and the political, social, and economic conditions that may have led to them. If truth commissions promote reconciliation, as advocates claim, it is not because they lead to forgiveness about the past but because they are exercises in deliberative politics—a way to stimulate public debate about how to address the past and carry on.[44] The truth commissions in Sierra Leone and Liberia served this purpose to an extent, though not without controversy.

Societal restoration, a third goal of transitional justice, is about reconstructing the social, political, and legal systems destroyed by violence.[45] It may involve building institutions virtually from scratch, as in Timor; it may involve resurrecting traditional "community-based" approaches to justice, as in Liberia and southern Sudan.[46] Either way, as Secretary-General Kofi Annan put it, "planning rule of law reforms and agreeing on transitional justice processes are... necessary subjects of serious public consultation and debate."[47] Experience shows that deciding on mechanisms for achieving each of the goals of transitional justice, and when, should be a collaborative process, with domestic and foreign actors working together to map the range of options and to catalyze policy and public deliberations on which to pursue.

C. The Impact of Peacekeeping on Deliberative Norms

Picking up on the notion of peacekeeping as a 'bargain', it is useful to think of a peace agreement as a long-term relational contract. In contract theory, a contract is relational "to the extent that the parties are incapable of reducing important terms of the arrangement to well-defined obligations, [either] because of the inability to identify uncertain future conditions or because of inability to characterize complex adaptations adequately even when the contingencies themselves can be identified..."[48] A transactional contract, by

---

[43] Priscilla Hayner, *Unspeakable Truths: Facing the Challenge of Truth Commissions* 25 (2002).
[44] Amy Gutmann and Dennis Thompson, *Why Deliberative Democracy?* 185 (2004).
[45] Martha Minnow, "The Hope for Healing: What can Truth Commissions Do?" in *Truth v. Justice* 253 (R. Rotberg ed., 2000).
[46] On Liberia, see International Crisis Group, "Liberia: Resurrecting the Justice System," April 6, 2006, p. 1. My conclusion on southern Sudan is based on interviews in Juba, September 2006.
[47] United Nations, *Report of the Secretary-General on the Rule of Law and Transitional Justice in Post Conflict Societies*, S/2004/16 (August 3, 2004), para. 19.
[48] Charles Goetz and Robert Scott, "Principles of Relational Contracts," 6 *Virginia Law Review* 1089, 1091 (1981). See also Melvin Eisenberg, "Relational Contracts," in, *Good Faith and Fault in Contract Law* (J. Beatson, and D. Friedmann eds.1995).

way of contrast, involves a discrete, one-time exchange of goods. To illustrate, in the context of economic relations, a collective bargaining agreement between a union and management is relational; buying a tank of gasoline from a gas station on a highway far from home is a one-off transaction. In the context of personal relations, a marriage is a relational contract; a one-night stand is a transaction.[49] The two are on a spectrum: almost all contracts are "relational" to an extent, and even the most relational contracts have "transactional" qualities."[50] At the risk of over-stating the analogy, peace agreements are like relational contracts in various ways. First, even if they emerge from a hostile relationship, the parties understand that they have committed to a shared project and expect the arrangement to endure. Second, the terms of the agreement are necessarily open-ended. The contract is not simply an exchange of obligations, but a framework for managing an on-going relationship of unspecified duration and in that sense a "living document" that must be interpreted and implemented in light of changing circumstances.[51] Third, this interpretation and implementation occurs through interaction between the parties over the course of the relationship. Deviations are inevitable and expected (tacitly if not explicitly) in a peace process of any duration, but the agreement remains the foundation for managing a relationship that is full of uncertainties. Fourth, peace agreements, like relational contracts, implicate stakeholders other than the immediate parties. Opposition groups, vulnerable segments of the population and neighboring countries are stakeholders as well. So may be the broader population, suggesting that the contract is not simply a bargain between the parties. Fifth, a peacekeeping mission with a mandate to support implementation of the peace agreement is not a party, but tends to find itself in a bargaining relationship with the parties, as noted above. Moreover, that bargaining relationship is situated in a pre-existing normative framework, embodied in the UN Charter and other legal instruments as well organization practices. The content of that normative framework is fluid and contested, but it is not inconsequential. It can be a source of leverage for the parties to the agreement, for other stakeholders and for the leadership of a UN operation.

Combining these insights with deliberative principles suggests two broad strategies for managing peace operations. First, the notion of relational contracts suggests an expansive vision of whose consent to a peace process matters. It counsels an inclusive form of political engagement. When and how to cultivate inclusive politics will vary from place to place (and, indeed, there is a risk of "delegitimizing" a government if a

---

[49] Robert Leckey, "Relational Contracts and Other Models of Marriage," 40 *Osgoode Hall Law Journal* 1 (2002).
[50] The leading relational contract theorist is I.R. MacNeil, *The New Social Contract: An Inquiry Into Modern Contractual Relations* (1980); I.R. MacNeil, "Relational Contract Theory: Challenges and Queries" 94 *Northwestern University Law Review*, 877 (2000).
[51] The notion of peace agreements as 'living documents' highlights their quasi-constitutional nature. See Christine Bell, *On the Law of Peace: Peace Agreements and the Lex Pacificatora* 149–52 (2008).

peace operation seems to be going around it by engaging directly with the population), but to assume that the only voices that matter are the signatories to the peace agreement overlooks the "social compact" character of peace agreements. Moreover, keeping some political distance from the host government is justifiable because consent as a peacekeeping principle is tied to the notion of impartiality, understood as fair application of a mandate.[52] Deferring to the preferences of the host government at any price is not managing consent but abdicating responsibility for ensuring the mandate is fulfilled in a principled manner. If a peace agreement indeed is a social compact, then the UN is justified in insisting on compliance even if the parties themselves are disposed to accept less than full implementation.

Second, deliberative principles can provide a useful framework for guiding the engagement of all actors in a peace process. The ideal of deliberation set out in Chapter 2—that participants have equal standing and voice and that the debates occur unaffected by relationships of power and coercion—is not met in any society, let alone one coming out of conflict. But two of its underlying principles, participation and public scrutiny, can usefully inform the relationships among the relevant actors. The process of formulating and implementing a peace consolidation strategy should be as participatory as circumstances permit. Typically, this will be limited to the parties to the conflict and the most powerful outside actors in the early stages but can become more inclusive as the post-conflict situation stabilizes. While it is never possible to consult all who are affected in every decision, opening the process to public scrutiny is an indirect way of engaging a broader range of stakeholders. This is a device for converting parliamentarians, opposition groups, and civil society, into an audience at whom the justifications must be directed. Direct participation is not necessary for deliberative principles to have an impact: the audience effect impels the speaker to account for the concerns of all who have a stake in the outcome of the deliberations.[53]

IV. PROTECTION OF CIVILIANS

Consent-based multidimensional peacekeeping is one kind of post–Cold War operation. Ideally, it takes place in a relatively permissive environment when there is considerable willingness among the parties to carry through on their commitments and ultimately make peace. Unfortunately, many post–Cold War conflicts have been messier, and peace operations have been deployed when the "peace to keep" is unreliable. Examples include

---

[52] *Capstone Doctrine, supra* note 2. See also the *Brahimi Report*, para. 50.
[53] As discussed in Chapter 2, even if the public reason-giving is insincere, paying lip service to shared interests can moderate behavior, because the speaker feels impelled to make some effort to match words with deeds. Jon Elster calls this the "civilizing force of hypocrisy." Jon Elster "Introduction" in *Deliberative Democracy* 12 (J. Elster ed, 1998).

Sierra Leone in 2000 and the DRC and Darfur today. The distinguishing feature of these operations is that they do not depend on the full and reliable consent or cooperation of all of the local actors, and the use of force is contemplated for purposes beyond self-defense. The UN *Capstone Doctrine* separates robust peacekeeping from peace enforcement, based on the line between tactical and strategic consent. For robust peacekeeping, force may be used against a minor spoiler, at the tactical level; for peace enforcement, it may be necessary at the strategic level, against one of the main parties to the conflict. Both are distinct form war, where the use of force is to defeat a designated enemy. In peacekeeping and peace enforcement, force is used for more limited objectives, the most common of which is the "protection of civilians."

A. Normative Roots

That human rights are a matter of international concern is beyond question. The UN Charter designates the promotion of human rights as one of the purposes of the organization. The adoption of the Genocide Convention and Universal Declaration of Human Rights in 1948 was the harbinger of a dense web of legal instruments, including the Geneva Conventions and the two human rights covenants. These were accompanied by important regional developments, like human rights treaties in Europe, the Americas, and Africa, all of which now have courts to induce compliance with the obligations they impose. The post of High Commissioner for Human Rights has been created in the UN system, and the OSCE has its influential High Commissioner for National Minorities. The SC established ad hoc criminal tribunals for former Yugoslavia and Rwanda, paving the way for the International Criminal Court. Humanitarian and development agencies involved in peacebuilding, like UNHCR, UNICEF, and UNDP have adopted a "rights-based" approach to their work. EU and OSCE missions are meant to act in conformity with the principles of their respective organizations, which include human rights. The Constitutive Act of the African Union proclaims human rights a value and gives the organization the right to intervene to stop mass atrocities.

Thus, it is no longer seen as exceptionable, or even exceptional, when human rights concerns are pressed in the context of peace processes. Add to this the sense of collective guilt associated with the failure to stop the genocide in Rwanda in 1994 and the fall of Srebrenica in 1995, and it is not surprising that every peacekeeping operation authorized by the SC since 1999 has a "protection of civilians" (POC) mandate, either explicit or implicit. The concept was first introduced in UN circles in 1998 in the Secretary-General's report on "The Causes of Conflict and the Promotion of Durable Peace and Sustainable Development in Africa," where protecting civilians was described as a "humanitarian imperative."[54] This coincided with a number of workshops convened by the International Committee of the Red Cross in the late 1990s, out of which came the

---

[54] UN Doc. S/1998/318-A/52/871 (April 13, 1998).

following definition of protection adopted by the Inter-Agency Standing Committee (a network of intergovernmental and nongovernmental humanitarian actors chaired by the UN): "...all activities aimed at obtaining full respect for the rights of the individual in accordance with international humanitarian, human rights and refugee law."[55] This definition, used by most humanitarian and human rights actors, encompasses a wide range of activities undertaken in peace operations, from preventive diplomacy to human rights monitoring, to the building of justice institutions. Others employ a narrower definition, restricting POC to action that ensures civilians are safe from physical harm.[56]

The origin of POC is also tied to the responsibility to protect (R2P). The first time the Security Council authorized the protection of civilians was in late 1999, in Sierra Leone, just prior to the release of *The Responsibility to Protect* report. The Canadian government was instrumental in both. When violence broke out in Sierra Leone, Canada took the lead in pushing for a robust mandate, having learned from its experience in Rwanda, where the force commander, Canadian General Romeo Dallaire, was restrained by his mandate from taking forceful action to prevent the genocide. The Canadian Minister of Foreign Affairs pushed hard to place UNAMSIL under Chapter VII with a mandate it to protect civilians, saying that he would not allow another Rwanda "on his watch."[57] The Netherlands, Malaysia, Argentina, Botswana, Brazil, and the Government of Sierra Leone, all pushed for a strong protection of civilians mandate in light of the crimes that were being committed, particularly against children. The resolution adopted was a compromise between those who wanted a Chapter VII mandate for the entire mission and those who were concerned about raising expectations that could not be fulfilled. A single chapter VII paragraph, limited by objective (protection from imminent threats), geography (within the mission's area of deployment), and function (within capabilities) was a way of managing those expectations.

Although POC and R2P are connected normatively, for political reasons they have been dissociated. As objections to the latter arose among NAM countries, proponents of the protection of civilians feared that the peacekeeping mandate would be sacrificed on the altar of sovereignty. So the Secretariat and supportive member states have gone to considerable lengths to insist that protection of civilians is not the thin edge of the wedge of R2P or humanitarian intervention. The concepts are quite different, even in their most

---

[55] Quoted in "Draft DPKO/DFS Operational Concept on the Protection of Civilians in United Nations Peacekeeping Operations," p. 3 (Submission to the Special Committee on Peacekeeping, January 29, 2010).

[56] To these two "paradigms" of protection, Holt and Taylor add a third: POC is the inherent end result of peacekeeping, and is therefore redundant as a distinct mandated task. Victoria Holt and Glyn Taylor with Max Kelly, *Protecting Civilians in the Context of UN Peacekeeping Operations: Successes, Setbacks and Remaining Challenges*, Independent Study Commissioned by the Department of Peacekeeping Operations and Office for the Coordination of Humanitarian Affairs (2009), 170–71 [hereinafter *Protecting Civilians*].

[57] This comes from a study commissioned by OCHA and DPKO on the protection of civilians, quoting an internal government memo of one of the Permanent Five Members of the Security Council (P5). *Protecting Civilians, id.* at 37, footnote 10.

coercive form: R2P connotes military intervention to end genocide, crimes against humanity, war crimes and ethnic cleansing, without the consent of the host government; the POC mandate authorizes peacekeepers to use limited force to protect civilians against any threats to their physical well-being in the context of peace operations that are primarily consent-based. Objections to R2P on sovereignty grounds, therefore, need not translate into objections to the protection of civilians by peacekeepers. But the two concepts are rooted in the same humanitarian impulse and similar bodies of law.

Another factor that has shaped the context for protection of civilians is its institutionalization in UN mechanisms and doctrine. The earliest thematic statements on protection of civilians came not out of the peacekeeping department but out of the humanitarian agencies. The Secretary-General's report on the causes of conflict in Africa was followed by five Security Council resolutions and seven Presidential Statements on POC.[58] Other resolutions are on themes that are closely related to the protection of civilians: women, peace, and security; children; and sexual and gender-based violence. The Council has held several open debates on POC, following one of which an aide-memoire was adopted as "a practical tool that provides a basis for improved analysis and diagnosis of key protection issues during deliberations on peacekeeping mandates."[59] This was updated in December 2003 and then again in January 2009.[60] An Informal Security Council Working Group on the Protection of Civilians was established in 1999 and an expert group in 2009. The UN Office for the Coordination of Humanitarian Affairs has responsibility for developing policy on protection of civilians and, in 2005, protection became one of the "clusters" of functions performed by the humanitarian part of the UN system.

As for peacekeeping, protection of civilians practice has been ahead of coherent policy. Following UNAMSIL, nine more UN missions have been given protection of civilian mandates, in substantially the same terms: "to take the necessary action. . . within its capabilities and areas of deployment, to afford protection to civilians under imminent threat of physical violence, taking into account the responsibilities of the Government. . ."[61] Several non-UN missions also have the mandate, though without using the precise language.[62] This necessarily leaves room for interpretation and

---

[58] UN SC Res 1265 (1999); UN SC Res 1296 (2000); UN SC Res 1674 (2006);UN SC Res 1738 (2006); UN SC Res 1894 (2009);UN S/PRST/1999/6 (2009); UN S/PRST/2002/6 (2002);UN S/PRST/2002/41 (2002); UN S/PRST/2003/27; UN S/PRST/2004/46 (2004);UN S/PRST/2005/25 (2005); UN S/PRST/2009/1 (2009).

[59] The Aide-Memoire was adopted in March 2002 as UN S/PRST/2002/6 (2002).

[60] UN S/PRST/2003/27 (2003); UN S/PRST/2009/1 (2009).

[61] UN SC Res 1270 (1999), para. 14.

[62] In addition to UNAMSIL and ONUB, both of which are terminated, the following current UN missions have the mandate: MONUC, UNMIL, UNOCI, MINUSTAH, UNMIS, UNAMID, MINURCAT, and UNIFIL. Non-UN missions with protection functions authorized by the Security Council include KFOR in

considerable discretion on implementation to the peacekeepers. Not surprisingly, these clauses have been interpreted differently in different missions. "Imminent threat," for example, has been interpreted narrowly in some missions, restricting it to moments when an aggressor confronts civilians with the immediate intent of doing them harm.[63] MONUC, on the other hand, has been engaging in robust operations in eastern DRC based on a more expansive reading of the protection mandate, including pre-emptive action on the grounds that hostile pronouncements and a pattern of behavior makes some armed groups a constant threat to civilians.[64] In Darfur, POC became a priority when it was apparent that the Darfur Peace Agreement signed by only one rebel group was not a viable basis for the peace process. Yet, even with more than 20,000 uniformed personnel on the ground, its ability to do so through coercive action has been severely constrained: lack of mobility and obstruction by the Government of Sudan left the mission "wholly ill-situated and ill-equipped to provide protection in cooperation with the host government, and that on the basis of a flawed peace agreement." [65]

UNMIS's protection of civilians' mandate was not conceived as a priority for what is largely a consent-based multidimensional mission deployed in the south of Sudan. When the Lord's Resistance Army committed attacks in 2006, UNMIS took the position that it was configured as a Chapter VI mission and therefore did not have the capacity to protect civilians.[66] However, after a serious clash in the volatile Abyei region in 2008, protection of civilians became a more conspicuous function of UNMIS, and the SC called for the development of a "comprehensive protection strategy" involving multiple components of the mission and partners.[67]

UNMIL, deployed to Liberia in 2003, faced a tense period n the lead-up to and during the 2005 elections. That security did not become an issue was due in part to the Chapter VII mandate of UNMIL, its substantial presence of 15,000 troops in relation to the size of the country, and signals by the SRSG that it would react robustly to any effort to destabilize the polls, a threat made good on when UN police fired tear gas to disperse a stone-throwing crowd of supporters of the losers in the elections.[68]

Kosovo, INTERFET in East Timor, Operation Artemis and EUFOR Congo in the DRC, Operation Licorne and ECOMICI in Côte d'Ivoire, AMIS in Darfur, and EUFOR in Chad.

[63] DPKO/DFS Lessons Learned Note on the Protection of Civilians in UN Peacekeeping Operations: Dilemmas, Emerging Practices and Lessons, (Submitted to the Special Committee on Peacekeeping Operations, January 27, 2010), p. 2.

[64] Center on International Cooperation, *Annual Review of Global Peace Operations 2006* 73-80 (2006).

[65] In 2009, deteriorating security conditions meant the peacekeepers had to make self-protection a priority, leaving fewer of them available to patrol and offer "presence" to populations. *Protecting Civilians, supra* note 56 at 159.

[66] *Report of the Secretary-General Pursuant to Resolutions. 1653 (2006) and 1663 (2006)*, S/2006/478 (June 29, 2006).

[67] UN S/PRST/2008/24, June 24, 2008; UN SC Res 1870 (2009), para. 15.

[68] Annual Review 2006, *supra* note 64 at 57 and 59.

B. Normative Impact of Protection of Civilians

Challenges in implementation stimulated a push for protection of civilians doctrine. This proved to be a political battle because the notion of 'doctrine' is anathema to many UN member states who see it as the first step towards turning UN peacekeeping in to an exercise in war-fighting. To try to move the debate forward, in 2008 the Department of Peacekeeping Operations and Office for the Coordination of Humanitarian Affairs commissioned a major study on protection of civilians by the Stimson Center, released in November 2009.[69] Meanwhile, the *Capstone Doctrine* sounded a cautionary note by stressing the importance of matching resources to mandate, knowing the danger of generating expectations that can not be fulfilled. The SC reinforced the point in resolution 1894 (2009):

> 19. *Reaffirms* its practice of ensuring that mandates of UN peacekeeping and other relevant missions include, where appropriate and on a case-by-case basis, provisions regarding the protection of civilians, *stresses* that mandated protection activities must be given priority in decisions about the use of available capacity and resources, including information and intelligence resources, in the implementation of mandates. . .
>
> 20. *Reaffirms also* the importance of entrusting peacekeeping and other relevant missions that are tasked with the protection of civilians with clear, credible and achievable mandates. . . *further reaffirms* the importance of a greater awareness in the Security Council of the resource and field support implications of its decisions..;

The SC is only 15 members so the next step was to take it to the Special Committee on Peacekeeping (C-34), comprised of more than 100 contributors to peace operations. The Department of Peacekeeping Operations submitted two 'non-papers' to the C-34 in February 2010. Debate in the committee was much less contentious than in previous years, out of which came the following carefully crafted statement on protection of civilians:

> 147. The Special Committee appreciates the efforts of the Secretariat to provide Member States with the input to enhance common understanding regarding the implementation of protection of civilian mandates by relevant United Nations peacekeeping missions, including through the non-papers "Lessons Learned Note on the Protection of Civilians" and "Draft Operational Concept on Protection of Civilians", bearing in mind that these do not create legal obligations for Member

---

[69] *Protecting Civilians, supra* note 56.

States or their contingents. The Special Committee encourages the Secretariat to engage with Member States, host countries, regional organizations and troop- and police-contributing countries to further advance in this endeavour.

148. The Special Committee reiterates its request to the Secretary-General to provide detailed information for its consideration, based on lessons learned, on concepts of operations and the provision of resources, in existing peacekeeping missions regarding the mandate of protection of civilians, and requests an assessment of their adequacy in effectively achieving this mandated task. . .

149. The Special Committee requests the Secretariat to develop a strategic framework containing elements and parameters for mission-specific strategies to guide senior mission leadership in elaborating a comprehensive protection strategy aligned with the mission's concept of operations.[70]

Thus by the middle of 2010, UN member states had finally reached a rough consensus on the promise and peril of protection of civilians mandates. R2P is part of the normative context in which that consensus emerged, despite the sensitivities alluded to above. In Chapter 8, I consider how the operational activities of international organizations can lead to the hardening of soft law, perhaps even create new law. In principle, this could happen with R2P. As peacekeepers successfully engage in protection, and as doctrine is further developed, the inchoate norm is given content. Conversely, the failure to protect civilians could undermine the R2P norm: if peacekeepers are not authorized or are unable to protect civilians being slaughtered before their eyes, what hope is there for the deeper concept of an R2P to ever take hold?

A separate but related legal question is whether peacekeepers have an *obligation* to protect civilians. As discussed in Chapter 4, R2P does not impose a legal obligation on outsiders to intervene through coercive military action, even to stop genocide. But what about the narrower circumstances when peacekeepers are already deployed? Do they have positive duty to act? Siobhan Wills answers that question in the affirmative, but only when the UN is in charge of a transitional administration or in localized areas subject to their authority such as prisons and military camps.[71] This is based on international humanitarian law (in particular, Article 1 of the Geneva Conventions) and human rights law. Outside of that context, the C-34 was explicit that the non-papers produced by the Secretariat do not create legal obligations for states (see paragraph 147 above). This disclaimer is unnecessary (Secretariat non-papers can not create legal obligations) and was probably inserted to drive home the point that peacekeepers do not have a general responsibility to protect civilians. The position is not surprising, since it would imply legal accountability for the failure to do so, a prospect that would discourage countries from

---

[70] *Report of the Special Committee on Peacekeeping Operations (C-34)*, 10 May 2010, UN GA Doc A/64/19.
[71] Siobhan Wills, *Protection of Civilians: The Obligations of Peacekeepers* 266–67 and 283 (2009).

sending their troops to these operations. As for any special obligation the P5 and other SC members may have, the notion of a blanket obligation would require them to make sure an operation with a protection of civilians mandate was large and robust enough to actually succeed. The SC has never ordered a state to participate in military action or provide equipment, and it is doubtful that it has the competence to do so without first entering into an Article 43 agreement.

Though not a legal obligation, there is a strong normative expectation of protection that derives from peacekeeping practice. It would be hard politically for the SC not to grant a POC a mandate in circumstances where there is a danger of mass violence against civilians. Even without the mandate, after Rwanda and Srebrenica, it would be hard for peacekeepers to stand by as civilians are killed before their eyes. In the year 2000, the Brahimi Report stated: "UN peacekeepers who witness violence against civilians should be *presumed* to be authorized to stop it, within their means, in support of basic UN principles."[72] Despite 10 difficult years of trying to live up to that aspiration from Haiti to Timor to the DRC, failing as often as not, the expectation of protection remains—giving content to the notion of peacekeeping as a "social compact."

V. CONCLUSION

This chapter considered the normative climate associated with peacekeeping and how that climate has affected and been affected by peacekeeping practice. In a sense, every operation established by an international organization is an implicit interpretation of the constitutive act of the organization and related law. Either through a rational application of lessons learned or the inertial force of precedent, what seems to work in one operation will often be tried in the next. Demonstrably successful cases of international intervention reinforce inchoate norms. Unsuccessful cases—or cases where the norms are ignored—undermine them.

Sovereignty norms are still important to peacekeeping, and host government consent is still a defining principle. But our understanding of what that means in practice has evolved, pushing the boundaries of intervention in internal matters through the instrument of peacekeeping. The debate between those who would place democratization and human rights at the center of peacebuilding, and those who see it as a pipedream has not been resolved.[73] While we are starting to see a backlash against the liberal peace agenda, a return to the days when the only goal of peacekeeping was the absence of war (negative peace) is not on the horizon. Nor is abandonment of protection of civilians mandates, despite the well-known obstacles to fulfilling the mandate effectively.

---

[72] *Brahimi Report, supra* note 9 at para. 62.
[73] For a summary of the debate, see Ponzio, "Transforming Political Authority," *supra* note 36.

The backlash against ambitious peace operations is a partly a matter of money and loss of political will. It is also the product of serious reflection on how to balance "local ownership" with the normative expectations that outsiders bring to the practice of peacekeeping. Deliberative politics is a way of managing the tension that dilemma creates. It is consistent with democratic norms and principles of peaceful conflict resolution. It is a way of reconciling external engagement and international standards of legitimacy, with local ownership and local conceptions of legitimacy. There are obvious limits on how "deliberative" a peace process can be. Most decisions in post-conflict societies are the result of hard bargaining, arm twisting, and less subtle forms of coercion, though hopefully not violence. But deliberative habits and institutions can be cultivated over time. For external actors, deliberative interaction with local authorities and stakeholders is a way to practice what they preach, enhancing the legitimacy of their intervention while fostering the sort of democratic practices that successful peace consolidation requires.

8

OPERATIONAL ACTIVITIES

I. INTRODUCTION

THIS CHAPTER PICKS up on a point introduced in Chapter 7, that the operational activities of IOs can contribute to the hardening of soft law, analogous to the manner in which customary law hardens through state practice.[1] The term "operational activities" describes the programmatic work of international organizations carried out as part of their overall mission or in fulfillment of a specific mandate. These are to be distinguished from the more explicitly normative functions of IOs, such as treaty making or the adoption of resolutions, declarations, and regulations by inter-governmental bodies. The impact on development of the law occurs as follows: operational activities are undertaken against the backdrop of widely acknowledged but not well-specified norms. In carrying out those activities, IOs are not seeking to enforce the norms per se but typically act in a manner that conforms to them; these activities generate friction, triggering bouts of legal argumentation; the reaction of affected governments—and the discourse that accompanies the action and reaction—can cause so-called soft law to harden. Having hardened, the discourse about compliance becomes more demanding, making it more difficult for states

---

[1] This chapter is a revised and updated version of Ian Johnstone, "Law-making through the operational activities of international organizations," 40 *George Washington International Law Review* 87 (2008). I am grateful for comments I received on an earlier draft from David Kennedy, Beth Simmons, Joel Trachtman and other participants in the Harvard International Law/International Relations Workshop in November 2008.

to evade their obligations by claiming that the status of the relevant norm is uncertain. This pattern is connected to the traditional sources of law identified in Article 38 of the Statute of the International Court of Justice—treaties, custom and general principles—but to the extent that international organizations act autonomously in engaging in these practices, the process is one step removed from state consent. As such, it signifies a new form of lawmaking.

This chapter begins by examining the crystallization of soft law: first, by defining the concept soft law and then sketching how it can harden through IO operational activities.[2] I then review three areas of IO practice that illustrate the trend: the impact of election monitoring and electoral assistance on the right to political participation; how the conflict prevention activities of the Organization for Security and Cooperation's (OSCE) High Commissioner for National Minorities have helped to crystallize minority rights; and the effect of humanitarian action and human rights advocacy on the Guiding Principles on Internal Displacement. In the third part, I analyze the law-hardening process that occurred in each of the three areas of practice. I do not claim that the law in fact has hardened in all three areas (although a strong argument can be made for the right to political participation); my purpose is to make a plausible case that the law *can* harden in this way. Part IV highlights two theoretical implications of the process: first, that it indicates a more fluid and less state-centric form of lawmaking, in which international organizations play an autonomous role; and second, that argumentation between IO officials, governments, and nonstate actors is central to that process.

II. SOFT LAW AND LEGAL ARGUMENTATION

The term soft law describes norms that are formally nonbinding but habitually obeyed.[3] They fall between recommendations and purely political statements on one hand, and

---

[2] The analysis of the legal import of operational activities is related to the growing interest in global administrative law. See, for example, the Special Issue of the journal *Law and Contemporary Problems*, Benedict Kingsbury, Nico Krisch, Richard Stewart and Jonathan Wiener, "The Emergence of Global Administrative Law," 68 *Law and Contemporary Problems* (2005); and José Alvarez, *International Organizations as Law-Makers* 217–56, 596–600 (2005). The difference is that global administrative law is mainly about standard-setting by international organizations in textual form other than treaties, such as regulations, guidelines and policy directives. This article is about incremental standard-setting through the *practices* of international organizations and thus is closer to customary law formation than treaty making or regulation.

[3] Paul Szasz, "General law-making processes," in *The United Nations and International Law* 32 (Christopher Joyner ed., 1997); Edith Brown Weiss "Introduction" in Edith Brown Weiss ed., *International Compliance with Nonbinding Accords*, ASIL Studies in Transnational Legal Policy No. 29 (1997), p. 3. On soft law generally, see Dinah Shelton ed., *Commitment and Compliance: The Role of Non-Binding Norms in the International Legal System* (2000); Dinah Shelton, "Normative Hierarchy in International Law," 100 *American Journal of International Law* 291 (2006); Alvarez, *supra* note 2; Alan Boyle, "Soft Law in International Law-Making," 141

the binding law typically found in treaties and well-established customary law on the other. Soft law comes in various forms: norms expressed in hortatory language in an otherwise binding instrument; norms expressed in obligatory language, but contained in a nonbinding instrument; general principles set out in a framework convention without detailed obligations or specifics on how to implement the principles; norms enshrined in a binding treaty but in vague or imprecise terms; or guidelines that supplement a treaty.[4] It is a contested concept in legal circles because it implies what a strict legal positivist would deny—that there is a continuum between political and legal commitments, and that the difference between the two is a matter of degree.[5] According to the authors of an influential volume on "the legalization" of world politics, they fall on a spectrum, with the hardest law being clearly obligatory, precise, and subject to judicial or some other form of dispute settlement delegated to third parties, while the softest law is nonbinding, vague, and subject to diplomatic dispute settlement.[6] This spectrum has been criticized for relying on too narrow of a conception of international law, missing out on its broader nature as a "social phenomenon deeply embedded in the practices, beliefs and traditions of societies and shaped by interaction among societies."[7] But if modified to include

---

International Law (Malcolm Evans ed., 2006); Jan Klabbers, "The Redundancy of Soft Law," 65 *Nordic Journal of International Law* 167 (1996).

[4] See Christine Chinkin, "Normative Development in the International legal system," in *Commitment and compliance, supra* note 3, at 21, 30; Alvarez, *supra* note 2, at 248–49; Szasz, *supra* note 3, at 32–33; Frederic L. Kirgis, "Specialized Law-Making Processes" in *The United Nations and International Law* 65, 82–85 (Christopher C. Joyner ed., 1997); Sean Murphy, *Principles of International Law* 96–107 (2006).

[5] One of the earliest and most forceful objections to the notion of "soft law" is in Prosper Weil, "Towards Relative Normativity in International Law," 77 *American Journal of International Law* 413 (1983). More recently, Jan Klabbers has argued that the concept of soft law is redundant, precisely because law and nonlaw are on a continuum and there is no need for a middle category. Klabbers, *supra* n. 3. On the debates over the nature and reality of soft law, see Shelton ed., *supra* n. 3; Steven Ratner, "Does International Law Matter in Preventing Ethnic Conflict?," 32 *NYU Journal of International Law and Politics* 591, 612 (2000); Michael Riesman, "The Concept and Functions of Soft Law in International Politics," in *Essays in Honour of Judge Taslim Olawale Elias* 135–36 (E. Bello and Bola Ajibola eds., 1992); John Kirton and Michael Trebilcock eds., *Hard Choices, Soft Law: Voluntary Standards in Global Trade, Environment and Social Governance* (2004).

[6] Judith Goldstein, Miles Kahler, Robert Keohane and Anne-Marie Slaughter eds., "Legalization and World Politics," 54 *International Organization* 1 (2000), republished as a book in 2001. The concept of legalization is set out briefly in the introduction to the volume, and then elaborated more fully in Kenneth Abbott, Robert Keohane, Andrew Moravcsik, Anne-Marie Slaughter and Duncan Snidal, "The Concept of Legalization," 54 *International Organization* 401 (2000); and Kenneth Abbott and Duncan Snidal, "Hard and Soft Law in International Governance," 54 *International Organization* at 421 (2000). Georges Abi Saab identified similar criteria: the circumstances of the adoption of the instrument, including the amount of support for it; the concreteness of the language; and the existence of follow-up procedures. Georges Abi-Saab, "Cours General de Droit International Public" 207 *Recueil des Cours* 160–61 (1987).

[7] Martha Finnemore and Stephen Toope, "Alternatives to Legalization: Richer Views of Law and Politics," 55 *International Organization* 743–58 (2001). For the authors' response to the critique, see Judith Goldstein, Miles Kahler, Robert Keohane and Anne-Marie Slaughter, "Response to Finnemore and Toope," 55 *International Organization* at 759–60 (2000).

perceived legitimacy as an element of the felt sense of obligation and the implicit authority to interpret and implement the law as an element of delegation, then the three criteria are useful for assessing the movement from soft to hard law.

As I argued in Chapter 3, legal discourse within interpretive communities helps to explain both compliance with and incremental evolution of the law. The starting point is the idea that law is an interpretive concept.[8] Legal interpretation, other than in the form of authoritative decisions rendered by tribunals, is largely a matter of argumentation between interested actors. Good arguments—as opposed to merely plausible ones—are those that cohere best with the broader normative context in which the discourse occurs.[9] The staunchest proponents of soft law claim that compliance does not depend on where a norm falls on the spectrum[10] Yet what this misses is that hard law invokes a more demanding form of discourse, compelling states to justify their behavior on the basis of the text, context, underlying purpose, negotiating history, precedent, and subsequent practice: standard techniques of legal interpretation and argumentation. This, in turn, raises reputational costs when states are unable to justify their actions in legal terms.[11]

What triggers this argumentation? Typically, it is state conduct, but increasingly, it is the practices of IOs. The operational activities of international organizations can generate friction if those affected by the activity object. When humanitarian agencies, for example, insist on a right of access to displaced persons, the government may object on grounds of sovereignty or simply because they do not want their weaknesses exposed – consider Myanmar's reaction to offers of assistance after Cyclone Nagris in 2008. Such friction triggers legal argumentation: those engaged in the activity often make their case in terms of relevant norms; those on the receiving end react. If the ensuing back and forth results in an agreed solution, it serves as an implicit interpretation of the law. As Oscar Schachter put it: "UN interpretation does not usually have an adjudicative character. The task faced by most UN bodies is practical and instrumental—that is to prepare a plan

---

[8] Ronald Dworkin, *Law's Empire* 410 (1986). The literature on law as interpretation is voluminous. For a review of the debates, see Andrei Marmor *Interpretation and Legal Theory* (revised 2d ed., 2005).

[9] Crawford talks about coherence as an element of the persuasiveness of any argument. Neta Crawford, *Argument and Change in World Politics, Ethics, Decolonization and Humanitarian Intervention* 79 (2002). Thomas Franck says coherence is one of four features that gives legal norms their "compliance pull." See Thomas Franck, *The Power of Legitimacy Among Nations* (1990). Other theories of legal interpretation built on the notion of coherence are Ronald Dworkin, *Law's Empire supra* note 8; Stanley Fish, *Doing What Comes Naturally: change, rhetoric and the practice of theory in literary and legal studies* (1988); and Stanley Fish, *Is there a text in this class? the authority of interpretive communities* (1990).

[10] *See* Kirgis, *supra* note 4, at 91–92. For a multi-author study of the impact of "hardness" on compliance, see generally *Commitment and Compliance, supra* note 3.

[11] On the significance of reputation to law compliance, see Chapter 3 above. See also, Andrew Guzman, *How International Law Works* (2005); Oona Hathaway, "Between Power and Principle: An Integrated Theory of International Law," 71 *University of Chicago Law Review* 469 (2005); Robert Keohane, "International Relations and International Law: Two Optics," 38 *Harvard Journal of International Law* 487, 496–98 (1997).

of action or to... achieve a goal... Problems are analyzed, proposed solutions negotiated, decisions reached. Interpretation is implicit in the measures adopted."[12]

Moreover, this interpretative process is creative: not a straightforward application of rules whose meaning is self-evident but rather giving content to inchoate norms. Activities by IOS, like those of states, can create international law if carried out "in a regular manner and in the conviction that even if not responding to positive requirements of international law they are at least authorized by and in conformity with such law."[13] The activity, subject to international scrutiny and discursive interaction, can cause the norm to harden.

III. OPERATIONAL ACTIVITIES

Operational activities are carried out as part of the overall mission of an international organization. They may be authorized by intergovernmental bodies, but the functions performed often go beyond what is explicitly mandated. I will examine three areas of recent IO practice in which this has occurred and, as result, the hardening of law seems to be underway.

A. The Right to Political Participation

Gregory Fox makes a strong case that the right to political participation as enshrined in the International Covenant on Civil and Political Rights (ICCPR) has been refined, elaborated, and given content through election monitoring and other forms of electoral assistance by IOs.[14] His thesis has been reinforced by recent developments in multidimensional peace operations that, as discussed in Chapter 7, almost invariably include an electoral process, and the good governance agenda of development organizations like the World Bank and UNDP. Article 25 of the covenant reads in relevant part:

Every citizen shall have the right and the opportunity...
   a) To take part in the conduct of public affairs, directly or through freely chosen representatives;

---

[12] Oscar Schachter, "The UN Legal Order: An Overview," in *The United Nations and International Law* (Christopher Joyner ed., 1997).

[13] Szasz, *supra* note 3 at 43.

[14] Gregory Fox, "The Right to Political Participation in International Law," in *Democratic Governance and International Law* 48–90 (G. Fox and B. Roth eds., 2000). Fox's analysis is part of a growing body of literature that considers whether there is a right to democratic governance in international law. See for example, Thomas Franck, "Legitimacy and the Democratic Entitlement", in *Democratic Governance and International Law* 25-47 (G. Fox and B. Roth eds, 2000); Tom Farer, "The Promotion of Democracy: International Law and Norms", in *The UN Role in Promoting Democracy: Between Ideals and Reality* (E. Newman and R. Rich eds., 2004).

b) To vote and to be elected at genuine periodic elections which shall be by universal and equal suffrage and shall be held by secret ballot, guaranteeing the free expression of the will of the electors. . .

This language leaves open some important interpretative questions, the most important of which is whether "genuine" periodic elections require party pluralism. This was a point of contention between West and East during the Cold War; neither the text of the ICCPR nor *travaux preparatoires* provide a definitive answer. Similar ambiguity appears in Article 3 of the First Protocol to the European Convention on Human Rights and Article 23 of the Inter-American Convention on Human Rights.

These provisions have been interpreted in various judicial and quasi-judicial bodies, all pointing toward party pluralism, though only the European Court of Human Rights has issued an authoritative ruling to that effect.[15] The Human Rights Committee (HRC), a quasi-judicial body composed of 18 independent experts with the authority to issue nonbinding "General Comments" on the ICCPR, expressed skepticism that one-party elections would be "genuine," stating in 1996 that the right to form and join political parties "is an essential adjunct to the rights protected by Article 25."[16] Article 23 of the Inter-American Convention on Human Rights is phrased almost exactly like Article 25, and the Inter-American Commission—another expert body that lacks binding powers—has determined that one-party elections are not "authentic" within the meaning of the article. The Helsinki Final Act and other CSCE/OSCE documents, none of which are legally binding, include language that could be read as endorsing multiparty democracy. Thus, these bodies have been consistent in holding that participatory rights require party pluralism, but they have done so in equivocal and generally nonbinding terms.

The "soft law" on party pluralism has been reinforced by years of electoral assistance by IOs. Fox examines two forms of UN practice in this area: (a) General Assembly resolutions on the standards to be followed in the decolonization process (culminating in the election that led to Namibia's independence in 1989); and (b) the monitoring and verification missions in the post-colonial period, which consistently insisted on certain common features before declaring an election free and fair. For some monitoring missions, the General Assembly outlined specific standards. In other cases, the standards were the basis of agreement among several states, for example, with respect to Namibia (the five Western members of the Contact Group and the government of South Africa) and Nicaragua (the Esquipula II agreement among the five Central American presidents). In Haiti, neither the General Assembly nor a peace agreement provided clear terms of

---

[15] Article 3 of the First Protocol to the European Convention on Human Rights uses language that is even narrower than Article 25 but has been interpreted broadly by the European Court of Human Rights to prohibit the banning of political parties. Fox, *id.*

[16] The Committee relies on persuasion and dialogue rather than coercion to induce compliance, sometimes through tough questioning on the periodic reports ICCPR parties are obliged to submit.

reference, but virtually the same participatory rights—including party pluralism—were insisted on by the monitoring mission. By the mid-1990s, Fox argues, "burgeoning international standards had been repeated so frequently that the particulars of any given electoral monitoring mission had become essentially uncontroversial."[17] The criteria for free and fair elections had been reduced to boilerplate, and no state complained that by insisting on these standards, the UN was interfering in internal affairs.

In addition to these stand-alone monitoring missions, elections and democratic institution building are now staples of multidimensional peace operations. A stated goal of peacebuilding is participatory governance, on the theory that conflict needs to be channeled from violent to nonviolent forms of contestation and resolution.[18] Accordingly, the post-conflict peacebuilding work of the UN and regional organizations includes a range of measures to cultivate democratic governance, including the conversion of rebel groups into political parties, as well as multiparty elections. The organizations have conducted, certified, or helped with numerous elections in peace processes. The forms of assistance they offer range from organizing the entire election (as the UN did in Cambodia, Eastern Slavonia, and East Timor; and the OSCE has done in Bosnia and Kosovo), to supervision and verification (as the UN did in Namibia and El Salvador, and Liberia; and the OAS has done in Haiti), to coordination and support of international and national observers, to the provision of technical assistance by reviewing electoral laws and training electoral officials. Party pluralism has been a feature of every case; indeed it is hard to imagine any IO being associated with an electoral process that did not include party pluralism, let alone certifying it as free and fair.

Democratization is also part of the broader good governance agenda of the UNDP, World Bank, EU, and other development agencies and donor governments. The UNDP's 2002 Human Development Report calls for "deepening democracy" by building governance institutions, including political parties, an independent electoral system, and vibrant civil society. Many of these are activities undertaken in the context of post-conflict peacebuilding, but democratic governance has become a guiding principle for a broad range of UNDP programs. Interestingly, UNDP has gone beyond the World Bank's concept of good governance, whose roots were in economic liberalization and public sector management, to emphasize the political and civic dimensions of governance.[19]

---

[17] Fox, *supra* note 14 at 81.

[18] Report of the Secretary-General, *No Exit Without Strategy: Security Council Decision-Making and the Closure or Transition of United Nations Peacekeeping Operations*, April 20, 2001, S/2001/391. The transition period in a peace process is an opportunity to design institutions that foster nonviolent, political, and legal contestation, holding the promise of what Michael Doyle and Nicholas Sambanis call "participatory peace." Michael Doyle and Nicholas Sambanis, *Making War and Building Peace* 18–19 (2006). See also Terrence Lyons, "Transforming the Institutions of War: Post-Conflict Elections and the Reconstruction of Failed States," in *When States Fail: Causes and Consequences* (Robert Rotberg ed., 2003).

[19] On the good governance agenda of the World Bank, see, in particular, the World Development Report of 1997, "The State in a Changing World." For a good comparison of the UNDP and World Bank approaches to good

These two parallel processes—the interpretation of relevant treaty provisions by judicial and quasi-judicial bodies on one hand; and operational activities in the form of election monitoring, peacebuilding and development assistance, on the other—have converged on a position that strongly supports the notion that participatory rights require multiparty elections. While not directly linked (the operational activities are not engaged in to enforce treaty rights, nor are the treaty bodies purporting to set standards for the monitoring, peacebuilding, or development projects), there was substantial cross-pollination. The net result is the emergence of an "international law of participatory rights," founded in human rights treaties, but with more precision and determinacy than the treaties themselves.[20]

To recap, a vague principle was set out in treaties, giving it the character of soft law. The principle was interpreted in quasi-judicial bodies, which operate on the basis of dialogue and persuasion. Meanwhile, election monitoring and related operational activities by IOs converged on a set of standards for what constitutes a "free and fair election" and, implicitly, what the right to political participation requires. An increasing number of states request this assistance, anxious for the legitimacy it can bestow. No governments have complained that the criteria constitute interference in internal affairs. Many states have tacitly endorsed them by authorizing the operational activities or not objecting when the activities are undertaken. States are involved in the process, but IOs play an autonomous role as operational actors who initiate the activities and insist on the electoral standards in carrying them out.

B. Minority Rights

The impact of the conflict prevention role of the OSCE High Commissioner for National Minorities (HCNM) on ethnic minority rights is another example of this law-hardening process, though focused on one region and less advanced than the right to political participation. The post of HCNM was created in 1992 with a mandate to investigate problems relating to national minorities before they reach crisis proportions, precipitated by the outbreak of hostilities in Yugoslavia. The title High Commissioner *on* rather than *for* minorities indicates that the job is not to serve as an advocate but rather as a mediator in ethnic disputes.[21] First occupied by Max van de Stoel, then Rolf Ekeus and now Knut

---

governance, see Thomas Weiss, "Governance, good governance and global governance: conceptual and actual challenges," 21 *Third World Quarterly* 795 (2000).

[20] Fox, *supra* note 14. The standard, it should be stressed, applies only to parties to the ICCPR and regional treaties with similar language. (Few would argue that multiparty democracy is required by international customary law, even if a more general right to political participation may be.)

[21] Erika Schlager, "A Hard Look at Compliance with 'Soft Law'; the Case of the OSCE," in *Commitment and Compliance: The Role of Non Binding Norms in the International Legal System* 363 (Dinah Shelton ed., 2000).

Vollebaek, the individual promotes conflict prevention, using norms as an integral part of his strategy to resolve incipient conflicts.[22]

The Conference on Security and Cooperation in Europe (CSCE) began with the Helsinki Final Act of 1975, which created three "baskets" of activity. Basket three dealt with "the human dimension," which included human rights, the rule of law and democracy, as well as cooperation in the humanitarian field. The human rights provisions in the Helsinki Final Act became a yardstick for nongovernmental organizations to measure government performance, while CSCE meetings became venues for public diplomacy and "shaming."[23] The impact was hard to discern in the 1970s and 1980s, but some have credited the Helsinki process with helping to bring an end to the Cold War by contributing to the emergence of a civil society in Eastern Europe, while playing a catalytic role in delegitimizing Soviet hegemony.

As the Cold War ended and the Soviet Union split apart, the CSCE adopted a number of documents that pertain to minorities; the Vienna Concluding Document of 1989, the Cophenhagen Document of 1990, the Charter of Paris later that year, and the Moscow Document of 1991. The Copenhagen Document listed detailed protections for minorities, reinforced by formal mechanisms for implementation set out in the other three. The norms embodied in the OSCE instruments are at the soft end of the "legalization" spectrum.[24] The documents are "politically" rather than legally binding, an uncertain distinction but which at a minimum means there are no automatic legal consequences for violation of their provisions.[25] Some of the language is precise, but much is open textured. The instruments do not include binding dispute settlement provisions and, while they do include some formal government-to-government review mechanisms, these have not been used often.[26]

Other international law pertaining to minorities is also quite soft. The International Covenant on Civil and Political Rights and the International Covenant on Economic Social and Cultural Rights both contain protections for minorities, but the focus is on

---

[22] Steven Ratner, "Does International Law Matter in Preventing Ethnic Conflict?," 32 *NYU Journal of International Law and Politics* 591, 621 (2000); John Packer states "The HCNM's reference to standards is not expressly foreseen in the mandate, and the extent to which he uses the standards is for the sole purpose of conflict prevention." John Packer, "Making International Law Matter in Preventing Ethnic Conflict: A Practitioner's Perspective," 32 *NYU Journal of International Law and Politics* 715, 716 (2000).

[23] Schlager, *supra* note 21, at 355.

[24] This is the terminology of Goldstein et al., *supra* note 6.

[25] Peter Van Dijk, "The Implementation of the Final Act of Helsinki: The Creation of New Structures or the Involvement of Existing Ones?" 10 *Michigan Journal of International Law* 110, 114 (1989). The distinction is artificial because no obvious legal consequences flow from noncompliance with any human rights instrument. Most human rights treaties are not enforced coercively; the sole sanction is publicity (naming and shaming), the impact of which is political.

[26] With the end of the Cold War, states became less willing to use the CSCE/OSCE as a forum for "naming and shaming" in respect of human rights commitments. Ratner, *supra* note 22, at 605–06.

nondiscrimination against individuals rather than the preservation of minority groups or identity.[27] The UN General Assembly adopted a Declaration on the Rights of Persons Belonging to National or Ethnic, Religious and Linguistic Minorities in 1992, but it is formally nonbinding, and the language itself is less demanding than the OSCE documents. The Council of Europe's 1995 Framework Convention for the Protection of National Minorities is a binding treaty, but the provisions on implementation are weak, for example, requiring states to "endeavor to ensure" certain rights "as far as possible."[28] Both the ICCPR and European Convention on Human Rights have received some elaboration in the Human Rights Committee and European Court of Human Rights respectively, but many aspects of minority rights remain unaddressed by either.[29]

This is the context in which the HCNM operates. His conflict prevention mandate includes the power to collect information, visit countries (with their consent), promote dialogue between government and minority groups, warn of impending conflict and find solutions through "early action."[30] In carrying out his functions, he meets with government leaders, representatives of minorities, others involved in the particular issue (e.g., education leaders), representatives of the kin state of the relevant minority, and other OSCE states whose influence may be needed to help resolve the problem.[31] He works within a well-developed institutional framework and is ultimately accountable to OSCE member states but remains in many ways a free agent.[32]

The HCNM uses norms consciously and actively in his conflict prevention strategy. As Steven Ratner explains:

> The norms of the OCSE, the Council of Europe and the United Nations have provided both a starting point for many of his interventions and a continued reference point during the discussions. He has invoked and interpreted them constantly, especially if one party is seeking to ignore or mischaracterize them. He has proposed solutions in which states explicitly acknowledge duties to undertake behavior required or at least encouraged by the norms. And he has used a variety of strategies to support outcomes consistent with norms and to oppose policies inconsistent with them. In short, he uses norms to achieve solutions, and seeks solutions consistent with the norms. . . [T]he High Commissioner has made norm compliance a necessary (though not sufficient) element of his problem-solving approach.[33]

---

[27] *Id* at 600.
[28] *Id* at 611, citing Articles 10 and 14 of the Framework Convention.
[29] *Id* at 623.
[30] High Commissioner on National Minorities, "Overview" at <http://www.osce.org/hcnm/13019.html>.
[31] Ratner, *supra* note 22, at 619.
[32] *Id* at 620.
[33] *Id* at 622.

One technique the High Commissioner uses is to explain to the disputing parties what the norms require and to offer concrete proposals to accommodate the concerns of both sides in a manner consistent with the standards.[34] These functions—clarification and policy recommendation—"translate" vague norms into practical guidance, making them "meaningful and relevant to domestic actors."[35] Ratner does not consider whether soft law can harden through this process, but the two functions illustrate how this may occur. To begin with, there is necessarily an element of interpretation in the first. Thus, for example, in a dispute in Macedonia about the education opportunities for ethnic Albanians, the HCNM explained both privately and publicly that international norms ensured the right of minorities to establish education institutions in their own language but did not require public funding of those institutions.[36] In other words, he elaborated on the meaning of a vague principle in the particular circumstances of the case at hand. The second function—offering concrete proposals consistent with the standards—contributes to a hardening of the law to the extent that acceptance of the policy proposals by all concerned signifies acquiescence to the norms.

Another causal pathway identified by Ratner is the development of new international norms based on general principles: legal concepts common to different legal systems. For example, in Latvia, the High Commissioner put pressure on the government to employ language and residency requirements for citizenship, based on standard practices of other CSCE states. He took a "soft" general principle and sought to have it applied throughout the region, which, if accepted, would have the effect of hardening the norm.

Thus, in various ways, the HCNM's actions produce authoritative interpretations of existing OSCE law and demonstrate how new law can be created through operational activities. As John Packer puts it:

> ... the HCNM has become a source of 'soft jurisprudence,' drawing upon textual instruments, doctrine and state practice in the composition of his own argumentation to arrive at a specific recommendation. While his status is important in bringing the HCNM into a situation, it is ultimately his power of argumentation that moves a state to alter policy or law bearing on the situation of minorities.[37]

The High Commissioner's mediation is largely an exercise in argumentation and persuasion. Through that argumentation, not only are solutions to particular problems found, but the norms that were invoked in finding those solutions actually sharpen.

---

[34] *Id* at 627–29.
[35] *Id* at 694.
[36] *Id* at 627.
[37] Packer, *supra* note 22, at 718.

C. The Rights of Internally Displaced Persons

The "hardening" of the Guiding Principles on Internal Displacement is an especially interesting case because those most directly involved have been acutely conscious of the unusual normative process in which they are engaged. The Guiding Principles (GPs) were drafted by a group of independent experts, under the direction of the Representative of the Secretary-General on Human Rights for Internally Displaced Persons (RSG), a post created by the UN Commission on Human Rights (CHR). They are explicitly nonbinding but reflect and are consistent with international human rights and humanitarian law. According to the first RSG, Francis Deng, they restate relevant legal principles applicable to the internally displaced, clarify gray areas, and address gaps that may exist.[38] Determined to counter accusations of making new law "through the back door," the second RSG insisted that the GPs simply "identify those guarantees and concepts implicit in the rich body of existing international law that respond to the special needs of IDPs, and make this protection explicit."[39] The reality, however, is that the 1996 "Compilation and Analysis of Legal Norms" presented to the Human Rights Commission in spring 1996 identified 17 areas in which the law was imprecise and 8 areas with clear gaps.[40]

The GPs originated in an NGO campaign to pressure the CHR to appoint a special representative whose mandate would be to promote an institutional and normative framework for the protection of IDPs.[41] The first RSG, Francis Deng, was appointed in 1993. Between then and 1995, he worked with a team of legal experts to survey the state of existing international law applicable to IDPs. This group included academics and nongovernmental activists, mainly from the United States and Europe, as well as representatives of UN human rights and humanitarian organizations. A study produced by the Ludwig Boltzmann Institute in Vienna and another produced under the joint auspices

---

[38] Report of the Representative of the Secretary-General submitted pursuant to Human Rights Commission resolution 1997/39, Addendum, Guiding Principles on Internal Displacement, E/CN.4/1998/53/Add.2, February 11, 1998, Introductory Note to the Guiding Principles, paras. 9 and 10. See also Walter Kälin, "The Guiding Principles on Internal Displacement as International Minimum Standard and Protection Tool," 24 *Refugee Survey Quarterly* 27–36 (2005); Roberta Cohen, "The Guiding Principles on Internal Displacement: An Innovation in International Standard Setting," 10 *Global Governance* 459–80 (2004). See generally,Thomas Weiss and David Korn, *Internal Displacement: Conceptualization and its Consequences* (2006).

[39] Kälin, *id* at 28.

[40] *Report of the Representative of the Secretary-General, Mr. Francis Deng, submitted pursuant to Commission on Human Rights resolution 1995/57. Compilation and analysis of legal norms* E/CN.4/1996/52/Add.2 (December 5, 1995) [hereinafter *Compilation and Analysis*].

[41] The main NGOs were the Friends World Committee for Consultation, the World Council of Churches and the Refugee Policy Group. Recent accounts of the implementation of the Guiding Principles can be found in Forced Migration Review Special Issue *Ten Years of The Guiding Principles on Internal Displacement* (December 2008). See, for example, articles by Elizabeth Ferris, Francis Deng, Roberta Cohen and Walter Kälin. See also, Phil Orchard, "Protection of Internally Displaced Persons: Soft Law as a Norm-Generating Mechanism", 36 *Review of International Studies* 281 (2010).

of the American Society of International Law and International Human Rights Group were merged by Walter Kalin (who later became the RSG). Kalin took the U.S. text as the starting point, which included a good amount of "soft law" based on UN resolutions and related texts, and filled it in with "hard law" from the more positivist Austrian text.[42] The resultant compilation found that existing law provided many protections to IDPs, but there was a need to "restate the general principles of protection in more specific detail" and to address gaps "in a future international instrument."[43]

The next step was to seek support from the CHR in developing a legal framework for enhancing the protection of IDPs. Francis Deng and Walter Kalin preferred a declaration of principles rather than a binding treaty because negotiating a treaty could take years and would open up opportunities for recalcitrant states to weaken existing rights.[44] Austria and various Nordic countries took the opposite view, but their attempt to win support among states for a treaty-drafting exercise got nowhere and indeed was opposed by UNHCR and the International Commission of Jurists. So these countries backed off and threw their support behind Deng's call for a set of guiding principles.

In early 1996, the CHR endorsed Deng's approach and called on him to "continue on the basis of his compilation and analysis of legal norms, to develop an appropriate framework in this regard for the protection of internally displaced persons." The drafting process involved a progressively expanding group of nongovernmental experts, humanitarian agencies, and representatives of international and regional organizations.[45] The draft principles were then presented to the Inter-Agency Standing Committee in 1998, a body comprised of most of the major humanitarian agencies within and outside the UN system. The IASC adopted a decision welcoming the GPs and encouraging its members to apply them. The principles were then submitted to the CHR in 1998, with no guarantee that they would be approved. Because they had been drafted by nongovernmental actors and endorsed by representatives of international organizations, there was real concern that states would object to this way of producing a quasi-legal text. Russia, India, China, Cuba, and Sudan were all potential spoilers, with Mexico taking the lead in expressing reservations about "standard setting by the back door."[46]

Ultimately, Russia and Mexico insisted on removing the words "with appreciation," but they did not stand in the way of a consensus resolution "taking note" of the GPs and of Deng's intention to use them in his dialogue with government, IGOs, and NGOs.[47]

---

[42] Korn and Weiss, *supra* note 38, at 61.

[43] *Compilation and Analysis, supra* note 40. For a comprehensive review of the process by which the Guiding Principles were formulated, see Simon Bagshaw, *Developing a Normative Framework for the Protection of Internally Displaced Persons* (2005).

[44] Korn and Weiss, *supra* note 38, at 61.

[45] Bagshaw, *supra* note 43, at 96. Weiss and Korn, *supra* note 38, at 62–65.

[46] Bagshaw, *supra* note 43, at 102.

[47] Weiss and Korn, *supra* note 38, at 67.

Roberta Cohen, a key member of Deng's team, reflected on the decision to go the "guiding principles" route rather than seek a treaty:

> First, there was no governmental support for the development of a legally binding treaty on a subject as sensitive as internal displacement. Second, treaty making could take decades, whereas there was urgent need for a document *now* to address the emergency needs of IDPs. Third, sufficient international law existed to make it possible to bring together in one document, adapted to the needs of the internally displaced, the myriad of provisions dispersed in a large number of instruments.[48]

In short, there was insufficient support for the drafting of an IDP convention, but the political climate was conducive to endorsement of existing international law and to a process of dialogue about operational programs that states knew could lead to incremental expansion and deepening of the law.

While some of the principles are embodied in hard law instruments, those that clarify gray areas or fill gaps are soft law at best.[49] It is possible to cite legal provisions that underpin most of them, but some are novel.[50] Principle 15, for example, prohibits the forced return or resettlement of IDPs to places where their lives may be in danger. Walter Kalin claims that this is firmly rooted in human rights law, but others see it as a creative reinterpretaiton of the law.[51] Principle 25 stipulates that states shall not arbitrarily withhold consent to offers of assistance from international humanitarian organizations or obstruct access to IDPs by those organizations.[52] The 1995 compilation states that international law did not explicitly recognize those duties, but they can be read as flowing from various instruments. Article 1(3) of the UN Charter requires states to cooperate in "solving international problems of an economic social, cultural or humanitarian character and in promoting respect for human rights and fundamental freedoms for all."[53]

---

[48] Roberta Cohen, "Developing an International System for Internally Displaced Persons," 7 *International Studies Perspective* 87–101 (2006).

[49] Bagshaw, *supra* note 43, at 72–74. Walter Kälin says they are not even typical soft law because they were not drafted by states and therefore did not rest on state consensus when they were formulated. Kälin, *supra* note 38, at 29.

[50] *Id.* at 29. Similarly, the ICRC concluded that *most* of them restate customary law. Jean-Marie Henckaerts and Louise Doswald-Beck, "Customary International Humanitarian Law" 1 *Rules ICRC* (2005).

[51] Catherine Phuong, *International Protection of Internally Displaced Persons* 61 (2004); Orchard, *supra* note 41, at 298.

[52] I am grateful to Simon Bagshaw, Senior Humanitarian Affairs Officer in the Office for the Coordination of Humanitarian Afffairs, Geneva, for providing this example of a guiding principle that may be hardening. Interview, Simon Bagshaw, November 2006.

[53] Bagshaw, *supra* note 43 at 78. See also Cohen, *supra* note 38, at 467. General Assembly resolutions invite states to work with humanitarian organizations, but the right to provide assistance was based on the consent of the state concerned. This issue was actively debated when GA Res 46/182 (1992) was adopted, which created the post of Emergency Relief Coordinator.

The "right to life" guaranteed by global and regional human rights treaties is also a source, as is Article 2(1) of the ICESCR, which obliges states to "take steps, individually and through international assistance and cooperation. . . to the maximum of available resources, with a view to achieving the full realization of the rights recognized" in the covenant. The ICRC commentary on relevant provisions of the Geneva Conventions and Protocols states that it is not entirely up to the discretion of each state whether to consent to international relief actions.[54] Finally, the compilation considered that SC resolutions on Northern Iraq, Bosnia, and elsewhere had obliged the authorities to permit UN agencies and NGOs access to civilians in need.[55] Thus, Principle 25 did not have an explicit basis in international law when the GPs were formulated, nor was it pulled out of thin air.[56]

The stated objective of the principles is to provide guidance to the RSG in implementing his mandate; to states when confronted with situations of displacement; to all other authorities and groups in their relations with internally displaced persons; and to inter-governmental and nongovernmental organizations in carrying out their work.[57] Those purposes are being achieved: increasingly, the principles are being cited and used by UN agencies, regional organizations, NGOs, and governments.[58] They have been disseminated to the field staff of UN agencies and, through those agencies, to nongovernmental and governmental partners. The IASC has prepared a training package for all its members, based on the principles. The UN High Commissioner for Refugees applies them in a manual for use by field staff. The Office for the Coordination of Humanitarian Affairs has also produced field manuals and has urged UN Resident Coordinators (who coordinate all UN agencies in a particular country) to disseminate the principles among governmental and nongovernmental partners. The UN High Commissioner for Human Rights, human rights rapporteurs, and nongovernmental organizations like Amnesty International and Human Rights Watch use them in their advocacy work. The Inter-American Commission on Human Rights applies them as a benchmark for evaluating conditions in member states. UN agencies have drawn on the principles in designing programs for IDPs in Sri Lanka, Angola, and Burundi. The Brookings Institute convened workshops on them in Ethiopia, Colombia, Thailand, Georgia, Indonesia, Armenia,

---

[54] Walter Kälin, *Guiding Principles on Internal Displacement,* 116, 119 (Revised ed., 2008).

[55] Bagshaw, *supra* note 43 at 80; Kälin *id.* at 117.

[56] A similar principle is 15(2), which concerns protection against forcible return of IDPs to places of danger, which can be inferred from the more general norm prohibiting cruel and inhuman treatment. Principles that have an even less firm basis, i.e., those designed to fill clear gaps in the law, include enforced disappearances (principle 10), property restitution (principle 29), and detention in closed camps (principle 12).

[57] Guiding Principles on Internal Displacement, "Introduction: Scope and Purpose," available at <http://www.reliefweb.int/ocha_ol/pub/idp_gp/idp.html>.

[58] Cohen, *supra* note 38, at 467. The following account comes mainly from Bagshaw, *supra* note 43, at 117–29 and Cohen, *supra* note 38, at 469–71. See also, Orchard, *supra* note 41.

Azerbaijan, Russia, West Africa, Sudan, Mexico, and Botswana. In addition to those it co-sponsored with Brookings, the Norwegian Refugee Council has convened workshops in the Philippines, Angola, and Sierra Leone. National NGOs in those and other countries have begun using them as advocacy tools, both with respect to their own governments and UN agencies.[59]

These operational activities took place against the backdrop of debates in inter-governmental bodies, typically culminating in expressions of support for the GPs, with varying degrees of enthusiasm. After "taking note" in 1998, the CHR recognized the value of the IDPs in 1999 and welcomed their wide use by the operational agencies. In 2003, it declared that the principles had become a "standard" in international efforts to protect IDPs.[60] Similarly, beginning in 1999, the UN General Assembly adopted progressively more effusive resolutions, culminating with the claim at the 2005 World Summit that the principles provided "an important international framework for the protection of internally displaced persons."[61] The Secretary-General drew attention to them in a report to the Security Council in 1998. The Council itself began referring to them in its debates on the protection of civilians and formally acknowledged their utility in a Presidential Statement in the year 2000.[62] Institutional developments that emerged from these debates were the creation of an internal displacement division in the UN Office for the Coordination of Humanitarian Affairs and the appointment of UNHCR as the cluster lead for IDP protection.

The principles have also been welcomed in various regional and subregional bodies: the Organization of African Unity (OAU) Commission on Refugees, the OAU Council of Ministers, the OAS, the Council of Europe, the European Union, and ECOWAS. The Inter-American Commission on Human Rights described them as "authoritative guidance to the Commission on how the law should be applied during all phases of displacement."[63] The OSCE's Maastricht Declaration of December 2003 referred to them as "a useful framework for the work of the OSCE and the endeavors of participating states in dealing with displacement."[64] The states of Africa's Great Lakes Region adopted a 2005 Declaration on Peace, Democracy and Development, with a number of Protocols including one on internal displacement that incorporated the Guiding Principles en bloc.

Most significantly, the AU has adopted a Convention for the Protection and Assistance of Internally Displaced Persons in Africa (the Kampala Convention). The Convention was adopted unanimously by 46 states in October 2009. As of June 2010, it

---

[59] Cohen, *supra* note 38, at 471. See also Bagshaw, *supra* note 43, at 127.
[60] Cohen, *supra* note 38, at 469.
[61] UN GA Res 60/1, October 24, 2005.
[62] UN SC Presidential Statement, S/PRST/2000/1.
[63] Weiss and Korn, *supra* note 38, at 108.
[64] *Id.* at 114.

had been signed by 27 and ratified by 1 (Uganda). Fifteen ratifications are required for it to enter into force. The process leading to the Convention was strongly influenced by the Guiding Principles, as the AU Commissioner for Human and People's Rights stated in a speech made in October 2008: "The African Union, recognizing the growing displacement problem on the continent, has embarked on a bold initiative of codifying a legal instrument on the prevention and suppression of internal displacement in Africa. *The instrument traces its roots to the principles enunciated by the Guiding Principles.*"[65][Emphasis added]

Debates about the principles were sharpest in the year 2000, with Algeria, Egypt, Sudan, and India questioning the process by which they were made and casting doubt on their normative status. (Mexico, under newly elected President Vicente Fox, had become a supporter.[66]) India and Egypt in particular were reluctant to see internally displaced persons as a special category that needed protection beyond what was provided in existing human rights law. Both underscored that the GPs were not legally binding.[67] In the 2000 session of ECOSOC, they sought to delete any reference to them in the "agreed conclusions." Their opposition was even more public in the GA, calling for a vote on the operative paragraph of a resolution on the Office of the UN High Commissioner for Refugees that referred to the "continuing relevance of the Guiding Principles." The result in the Third Committee of the GA was 118 for, 0 against, and 31 abstentions; in the GA plenary, it was 139 for, 0 against, and 31 abstentions.

In the course of those debates, it became apparent that concern about the GPs had more to do with the broader debate about humanitarian intervention (triggered by Kosovo) than strong opposition to the principles themselves.[68] While Egypt and India were fighting this relatively lonely battle in the UN, the OAU (with Egyptian support!), the East African Inter-governmental Authority on Development (following a conference on IDPs hosted by Sudan), ECOWAS, the OAS, OSCE, and the Council of Europe all formally acknowledged the principles and expressed support for their usefulness as a tool for humanitarian action and advocacy.[69] Meanwhile, a substantial number of states with IDP problems have adopted legislation or policies based on them, including Angola,

---

[65] Statement by Bahame Tom Nyanduga, Commissioner, African Commission on Human and Peoples' Rights, "10th Anniversary of the Guiding Principles on Internal Displacement: An African Perspective" Oslo Conference, Oct. 16–18 2008. Available at http://www.internal-displacement.org/8025747B0037BAC5/ (httpPages)/27358963822E83E4C12574E200482E9C?OpenDocument&parentunid=2A570681A064057280 25747B003B5D4A. See also Allehone Mulugeta Abebe, "Legal and Institutional Dimensions of Protecting and Assisting Internally Displaced Persons in Africa," 22 *Journal of Refugee Studies* 155 (2009).

[66] Cohen, *supra* note 38, at 473.

[67] Bagshaw, *supra* note 43, at 113–14.

[68] Bagshaw, *supra* note 43, at 115–16; see also Cohen, *supra* note 38, at 472; Weiss and Korn, *supra* note 38, at 113.

[69] Cohen, *supra* note 38, at 469–71; Bagshaw, *supra* note 43, at 122–24; Kälin, *supra* note 38, at 27. SAARC and ASEAN bucked the trend.

Azerbaijan, Bosnia, Burundi, Colombia, Georgia, Guatemala, Iraq, Peru, the Philippines, Sri Lanka, Turkey, and Uganda.[70] Of particular interest, the Constitutional Court of Colombia delivered a number of judgments that cite the GPs in claims by IDPs, ruling that the principles should be used "as parameters for the creation of rules and for the interpretation of national law on forced displacement."[71] The Sudan People's Liberation Movement used the GPs to draft a policy on IDPs in Southern Sudan. Representatives of civil society and opposition groups in Sierra Leone, Sri Lanka, Colombia, India, Russia, and Liberia have used them to seek better protection from governments.[72] The Government of Uganda was criticized by international and national NGOs for not effectively implementing its IDP policy.[73]

It would therefore seem that the debates triggered by the dissidents who questioned the legal status of the GPs helped to solidify them. India and Egypt retreated from their hard-line positions; Mexico did an about face; and during Francis Deng's visit to Russia in 2003, the government acknowledged the principles were applicable to the displaced in Chechnya.[74] The resolutions coming out of those many meetings do not themselves convert the GPs into hard law[75] but, along with the surrounding argumentation, provide grounds for claiming that a sense of legal obligation is emerging alongside the consistent practice of IOs. An important step has been taken in Africa with the adoption of the Kampala Convention. If and when it comes into force, it will be binding only on the states that ratify it, but the GPs were an important element of the discourse leading to its unanimous adoption in 2009, suggesting that those principles could harden in the mode of customary law alongside ratifications of the Convention. More generally, widely used and commented upon throughout the world, the GPs are becoming the normative framework for protection and assistance activities on behalf of the internally displaced.[76]

---

[70] A total of 20 states had policies and 13 had legislation by the year 2008. Orchard, *supra* note 41, at 295-96. See also, Cohen, *supra* note 38, at 470; Kälin, *supra* note 38, at 33.

[71] Bagshaw, *supra* note 43, at 125.

[72] Weiss and Korn, *supra* note 38, at 139.

[73] Orchard, *supra* note 41, at 296-97.

[74] Weiss and Korn, *supra* note 38, at 113-14.

[75] On the legal status of UN General Assembly resolutions and similar instruments, see Alvarez, *supra* note 2; Rosalyn Higgins, *Development of International Law Theory Political Organs of the UN* (1963).

[76] Bagshaw, *supra* note 43, at 12 and 137. See also Patrick Schmidt, "The Process and Prospects for the Guiding Principles on Internal Displacement to Become Customary Law" 35 *Georgetown Journal of International Law* 483 (2004).

IV. THE HARDENING OF SOFT LAW: THEORETICAL IMPLICATIONS

The operational activities described above are loosely regulated by soft law. Like much of IO practice, they occur against the backdrop of widely acknowledged but not well-specified norms. The IOs are not trying to enforce the norms but carry out their mandated activities in a manner that coincides with them. The purpose is to achieve programmatic goals; the effect may be to harden international law. The extent to which that has happened in the areas surveyed in this chapter varies, but they all offer at least suggestive evidence that the law *can* harden in this way.

In terms of the legalization criteria introduced by Abbott and his co-authors (obligation, precision and delegation), the right to political participation has become more *precise* as a result of election monitoring and related activities. Multiparty elections are increasingly seen as *obligatory* in the sense that governments are anxious to claim the external and internal legitimacy that certification of "free and fair" elections bestows— so much so that the demand for election monitoring vastly outstrips what IOs are willing and able to provide—and that certification will only be forthcoming if political parties are allowed to form. This occurred as a result of two parallel phenomena: interpretation of the ICCPR and regional human rights treaties by nonjudicial bodies that operate on the basis of dialogue and persuasion; and election monitoring on the basis of criteria for what constitutes a free and fair election, to which no government objected, and many tacitly endorsed by authorizing the operational activities. States are involved in the process, but international organizations play an autonomous role as operational actors who initiate the activities and insist on the electoral standards in carrying them out.

Ethnic minority rights embodied in nonbinding instruments are being given more *precise* meaning ("translated," in Ratner's terms) by the activities of the HCNM. The High Commissioner has become an implementing agent of those norms, serving as an intermediary who not only explains the meaning of minority rights to the parties to a conflict but also puts pressure on them to resolve their differences in a manner that is consistent with the norms. Implicitly, the HCNM has been *delegated* the authority to interpret and implement the norms. While the sense of *obligation* to comply with the relevant instruments has not been internalized in all OSCE states, the actions of the High Commissioner are a form of external scrutiny that arguably is pushing the norms up the spectrum from soft to hard law.

At least some of the GPs on Internal Displacement—already a relatively *precise* set of standards–are coming close to being seen as *obligatory*, like Principle 25 on humanitarian access. For example, a press statement delivered by the president of the SC, following an open debate on the protection of civilians, included the following paragraph: "Members of the Security Council recalled the obligations of international humanitarian law regarding the protection of civilians. They urged all concerned parties to allow full, safe and unimpeded access by humanitarian personnel to civilians in need of assistance in situations of armed conflict."[77] To the extent that international humanitarian organizations invoke the principles in their day-to-day work, some responsibility for implementing them has implicitly been *delegated* to those organizations. The process has not been smooth or linear, in part because the GPs bump up against a powerful countervailing norm; sovereignty. In Africa, where the sovereignty principle had already been substantially compromised by the Constitutive Act of the African Union, it was possible to take the first step toward a binding convention on IDPs. Seeking to have the GPs enshrined in a *global* treaty would likely be counter-productive because it would give resistant states the opportunity to object. As with other international norms (like humanitarian intervention), states seem to be willing to acquiesce in incremental expansions of the law on a case-by-case basis (or find it harder to resist such expansion) even if they would resist codification of that expansion in a formal text. The framework of rights that protect IDPs is being stretched and deepened incrementally, through a diffuse lawmaking/law implementation process that combines IO practice with argumentation about that practice.

Two important theoretical implications follow from the above analysis. First, it suggests a more flexible and pluralistic, though less predictable, form of lawmaking than state-to-state interactions. In 1963, Rosalyn Higgins pointed out that resolutions of the political organs of the UN do not fit neatly into any of the primary sources of law enumerated in Article 38 (1) of the Statute of the International Court of Justice.[78] This is even truer of the operational activities of international organizations.[79] Analogies can be drawn to customary law formation (for example, IDP Guiding Principle 25), treaty interpretation (the right to political participation), and the identification of general principles of law (OSCE-member state citizenship requirements), but the practices of IOs are not simply a variation on these traditional sources. Though the resolutions of inter-governmental organs and rulings of quasi-judicial bodies are relevant, international officials are the driving force. That this has occurred across a range of areas signifies a trend away from traditional lawmaking, to less state-centric, more innovative approaches.[80] International officials—like the HCNM, Representative of the Secretary-General for IDPs, and the heads of electoral assistance missions—act autonomously, one step removed from state consent.[81] Moreover, nongovernmental actors are more

---

[77] "Security Council Press Statement on Protection of Civilians in Armed Conflict," SC/9058, June 22, 2007. Although the Council only "urged" unimpeded humanitarian access, the placement of that sentence in the statement suggests the principle is close to being a legal obligation if not quite there yet.

[78] Higgins, *supra* note 75.

[79] Benedict Kingsbury, "Operational Policies of International Institutions as Part of the Law-Making Process: The World Bank and Indigenous Peoples," in *The Reality of International Law: Essays in Honour of Ian Brownlie* (G. Goodwin Gill and S. Talmon eds., 1999).

[80] Bagshaw, *supra* note 43, at 1.

[81] On the autonomy of international organizations, see. M. Barnett and M. Finnemore, *Rules for the World: International Organizations in Global Politics* (2004).

directly involved than in normal international legal processes. Many of the operational activities are targeted primarily at nonstate actors, not states.[82] NGOs play a greater role in making the law, as the formation and implementation of the Guiding Principles for Internal Displacement illustrates. The impetus behind the international recognition of internal displacement came from NGOs, not states or inter-governmental actors, and NGO representatives have been involved at every step of the way, working alongside the RSG.[83]

The second theoretical implication concerns the impact of argumentation (legal and otherwise) on the conduct of international affairs. There are two dimensions to this: the hardening occurs as a result of argumentation about the status of the norm; and the harder the norm, the more demanding is the discourse about compliance. Combined, these two dimensions show the dynamic nature of lawmaking and law compliance: legal discourse promotes compliance with soft norms and, in the process, the norm hardens making it more difficult to counter demands for compliance next time the law is invoked. Whether the law actually hardens depends on the extent of compliance and the tenor of argumentation: the operational activities of IOs could lead to a softening of hard law if they provoke widespread resistance. Thus, as discussed in Chapter 7, it is possible that the difficulty in implementing the protection of civilians mandate in peace operations, and the resistance to connecting it to the responsibility to protect, may result in the 'softening' of that norm.

IO practice alone is not enough for the law to harden; there must also be something analogous to *opinio juris*—a sense that the practice is accepted as law. The only way of ascertaining that sense of legal obligation is through the argumentation that surrounds the practice. The argumentation occurs directly, between the IO, the target state, and affected people, and more diffusely in deliberative forums where the norms are being debated. Thus, for example, while UN electoral assistance missions were insisting on the right to form political parties as a condition of free and fair elections, the Human Rights Committee was expounding the view that party pluralism is an element of the right to political participation. While OCHA and other humanitarian actors were insisting on access to IDPs, debates were underway in inter-governmental bodies about whether states could arbitrarily withhold consent to offers of humanitarian assistance. Interpretation of the norm is implicit in the action taken; it becomes more explicit in the discourse and deliberation surrounding the practice.

The discourse involves a wide range of states and other actors, with IOs serving as both agents that engage in argumentation and as venues for argumentation between states. The discourse, moreover, occurs within the shared background assumptions and understandings that underpin the organization, setting the boundaries of reasoned exchange

---

[82] Alvarez, *supra* note 2, at 245; Chinkin, *supra* note 4 at 35–37.
[83] Bagshaw, *supra* note 43, at 63.

about the meaning and status of norms.[84] The extent to which these shared understanding exists varies from organization to organization. But the specialized discourse of international law provides an additional layer of cohesiveness, regardless of the setting, through the operation of the interpretive community—the governmental, inter-governmental, and nongovernmental actors who speak the language of law in seeking to advance the programmatic goals of the organization.

Once the law hardens, compliance is far from automatic, but the burden of persuasion shifts to those who would seek to defy it. Reverting again to the three "legalization" criteria, it becomes harder to argue that compliance with the norm is optional, not *obligatory*. States that commit to a norm become trapped by their own rhetoric: purely self-serving arguments based on power and self-interest are no longer adequate; to be persuasive, legal counter-arguments—applicable to all like cases—must be advanced. Moreover, to the extent that the law-hardening process is seen as legitimate, the felt sense of obligation does not depend entirely on the content of the law: the compliance pull exists simply because it is law.[85] Second, if the law if more *precise*, it is more difficult to avoid compliance based on conflicting interpretations. Third, if the hardening process results in IO officials tacitly being *delegated* the task of following up on the norm, then the opinion of those officials as to what the law means and its implementation entails carries special weight; their views tend to be more influential than for softer norms, where expertise and bureaucratic authority count for less.

V. CONCLUSION

The operational activities of IOs occur in the context of a diffuse normative process, in which claims and arguments are made, challenged, defended, and elaborated in the course of interactions among IOs, governments, and affected peoples.[86] The process does not

---

[84] As discussed in Chapters 2 and 3 of this book, IOs provide the "common lifeworld" that makes rational discourse possible. See generally Habermas and IR theorists who have applied his theory of communicative action to international politics: Thomas Risse, "Let's Argue: Communicative Action in World Politics" 54 *International Organization* 10–11 (2000); Friedrich Kratochwil, *Rules, Norms and Decisions* (1989); Harald Mueller, "Arguing, Bargaining and All That: Communicative Action, Rationalist Theory and the Logic of Appropriateness in International Relations," 10 *European Journal of International Relations* 395 (2004); Corneliu Bjola, "Legitimating the Use of Force in International Politics: A Communicative Action Perspective," 11 *European Journal of International Relations* 266, 279 (2005).

[85] As Allen Buchanan and Robert Keohane explain, by way of analogy to a club: "I have a content-independent reason to comply with the rules of the club to which I belong if I have agreed to follow them and this reason is independent of whether I judge any particular rule to be a good or useful one." Allen Buchanan and Robert Keohane, "The Legitimacy of Global Governance Institutions," 20 *Ethics and International Affairs* 405, 409–11 (2006). See also, Jutta Brunnée and Stephen Toope, *Legitimacy and Legality in International Law: An Interactional Account* 53 (2010), who refer to fidelity to the rule of law itself rather than specific rules.

[86] Kingsbury, "Operational Policies," *supra* note 79 at 340.

entirely bypass state consent, because the member states of the organization give a broad mandate to engage in the activity; those same members can put a stop to it if they so choose; and if governments respond positively or do not object, then that signifies acquiescence. But nor is the process entirely or even primarily driven by states in the manner of traditional lawmaking. It is more pluralistic and fluid, involving international and NGO officials, as well as representatives of governments. From the perspective of IO officials, the harder the norms they can point to the better: it gives them a more solid foundation on which to push for changes in state behavior. And when the norms are "soft," a far from incidental by-product of this interactive, dialogic process is that the law can harden. Thus, the discursive power of IO officials serves not only to persuade states to behave in accordance with accepted norms but also to sharpen those norms and thereby shape the climate within which future behavior will occur.

9

TRADE

I. INTRODUCTION

INTERNATIONAL ORGANIZATIONS ARE often criticized for being dominated by technocratic elites. Expertise counts for a great deal in the making of public policy, but it must be balanced against democratic representativeness and accountability. The IMF and World Bank have come in for particular criticism as staff-driven organizations.[1] The charge is less often leveled against the WTO, a member driven organization where the Secretariat plays a lesser role. The main legitimacy critique there focuses on the hegemonic influence of the great trading powers whose "green room" consultations tend to exclude the majority of member states. Yet trade law does have an impact on the environment, health, and human rights, for example, limiting the regulatory autonomy of states in these areas.[2] The further trade decisions are removed from direct citizen input the

---

[1] Andrew Baker, "Deliberative Equality and the Transgovernmental Politics of the Global Financial Architecture," 15 *Global Governance* 195 (April–June 2009); Ngaire Woods and Amrita Narlikar, "Governance and the Limits of Accountability: the WTO, the IMF and the World Bank," 53 *International Social Science Journal* 569-583 (2001).

[2] Patricia Nanz, "Democratic Legitimacy and Constitutionalisation of Transnational Trade Governance: A View from Political Theory," in *Constitutionalism, Multilevel Trade Governance and Social Regulation* 59, 67 (C. Joerges and E. Petersmann eds., 2006),; M. Krajewski, "Democratic Legitimacy and Constitutional Perspectives of WTO Law" 35 *Journal of World Trade* 170 (2001).

longer the lines of delegation between the citizen and those who make decisions the sharper the questions about democratic legitimacy. One aspect of the critique is that decision making is dominated by a trade elite "not particularly interested in the larger political and social conflicts of the age."[3] For that reason, according to the critics, it has been difficult for environmental, labor, and other "nontrade" considerations to penetrate the narrow agenda of the trade organizations. The response of the "trade elites" is that there is little conflict between trade and other values, and that the best way to realize the other values is through instruments outside the trade area.

In this chapter, I look at whether the WTO really is a "technocracy" through the lens of "trade-environment" issues, focusing on the *Shrimp-Turtle* case. The notion of a technocratic elite stands as a direct challenge to the thesis that the power of interpretive communities enhances democratic deliberation. If those in the interpretive community are closely associated with the organization and are prone to block out perspectives from outside the mainstream of thinking about trade issues, then its contribution to deliberation may be valuable, but it can hardly be called democratic. This is not to suggest that the contribution of experts is necessarily undemocratic, but that the legitimacy of decisions about most matters of public policy requires a mix of expert and more democratically representative decision making. Because trade affects so many areas of social policy, a highly technocratic, closed decision-making process would not be legitimate.

The interpretive community functions differently in the trade field than in most other areas of international law because there is a strong dispute settlement system designed to render authoritative interpretations of the law. The WTO Appellate Body (AB) is empowered to issue binding rulings that result in enforcement by the WTO Dispute Settlement Body, including authorization for retaliatory measures. There would seem to be less room or need for an interpretive community as the functional equivalent of a court, given that the system itself includes a well-functioning judicial process. Yet even a definitive judgment of the AB does not end all debate. As I aim to demonstrate in this chapter, reconciling the tension between free trade and other values is a discursive process in which the AB is a weighty voice but not the only one. This makes the WTO an interesting venue for testing the theory of interpretive communities, because if the communities are influential there, presumably they would be even more influential in areas where tribunals figure less prominently.

I begin this chapter with an overview of the democratic deficit critique as it applies to the WTO. I then turn to describing the deliberative features of two of the three principal functions of the WTO—dispute settlement, and what has been called the "missing

---

[3] Robert Howse, "From Politics to Technocracy—and Back Again: The Fate of the Multilateral Trade Regime," 96 *American Journal of International Law* 94 (2002). See also Deborah Cass, *The Constitutionalization of the World Trade Organization: Legitimacy, Democracy and Community in the International Trading System* 10, 15 (2005).

middle" between the negotiation of treaties (not covered in this chapter) and dispute settlement. The fourth section is devoted to an analysis of the *Shrimp-Turtle* case. I conclude with an assessment of how "technocratic" the WTO really is. I argue that it is not dominated by a trade elite to the extent that critics have charged, but the impact of environmental activists does not necessarily make it a more deliberatively democratic institution.

II. DEMOCRATIC DEFICIT CRITIQUE OF THE WTO

Complaints about the legitimacy of the WTO tend to be along two lines. The first and more common critique is that the organization—and the international trade regime in general—is dominated by states with the largest market shares, leaving little room for weaker states to set the terms of debate, let alone determine outcomes. The rise of China, India, Brazil, and other emerging economies changes the equation but does not undercut the fundamental critique that some countries are "decision-makers" and other are "decision-takers."[4] This structural inequality, moreover, is exacerbated by perceived procedural flaws: a negotiating process characterized by closed "green room" consultations restricted to a few states with the greatest power and, they would argue, stake in the issues under discussion; a still-secretive dispute settlement process that favors the powerful who can better bear the burden of litigation and the costs of retaliation; and technical assistance and capacity building programs that tend to serve the status quo rather than facilitate challenges to the hegemonic power of the few.[5]

A second related critique concerns the individuals involved in making, interpreting and implementing WTO law. The argument is that a small group of trade experts has dominated the system. Robert Howse, for example, wrote in 2002 of an "insider network": a specialized policy elite comprising WTO Secretariat officials, former or current government trade officials, GATT-friendly academics who often sit on dispute settlement panels and attend GATT/WTO meetings; World Bank, IMF and OECD officials; and a few private attorneys, consultants, and former politicians.[6] They created the GATT

---

[4] Woods and Narlikar, *supra* note 1, at 573.

[5] On the last point, see Greg Shaffer, "Can the WTO Technical Assistance and Capacity Building Serve Developing Countries," in Erns-Ulrich Petersmann ed., *Reforming the World Trading System: Legitimacy, Efficiency and Democratic Governance* 245–74 (2005).

[6] Howse, *supra* note 3. See also J.H.H. Weiler, "The Rule of Lawyers and the Ethos of Diplomats: Reflections on WTO Dispute Settlement" in *Efficiency, Equity, Legitimacy: The Multilateral Trading System at the Millennium* (R. Porter, P. Sauve, A. Subramanian and A. Beviglia Zampetti eds., 2002); Cass, *supra* note 3, at 10–23. But cf. Debra Stager, "Afterword: The 'Trade and. . .' Conundrum—A Commentary" 96 *American Journal of Internationl Law* 135, 139 (2002), See also Elizabeth Fischer "Beyond the Science/Democracy Dichotomy: The World Trade Organisation Sanitary and Phytosanitary Agreement and Administrative Constitutionalism" in *Constitutionalism, Multilevel Trade Governance and Social Regulation supra* note 2.,

system, staff the WTO Secretariat, sit on the arbitration panels, and generally controlled the dispute settlement process, at least until recently. This technocratic "interpretive community" share understandings and expectations of what the system is all about and is highly influential in determining outcomes when trade values conflict with nontrade values.

At one level, this is simply a description, not a criticism of how the interpretation of trade law works, especially during the GATT days. The cohesiveness of the trade policy elite is what enabled consensus on the meaning of typically vague dispute settlement rulings on necessarily imprecise texts.[7] In one of his earlier articles, Howse praises the legitimating role of experts who enhance the quality of "rational democratic deliberation" by providing accurate information about risks and control strategies.[8] But for the most part, critics do not see the power of so-called experts as benign. They describe a GATT "elite cohesion strategy," characterized by secrecy, centralized management of interpretation by bureaucrats, the exclusion of controversial material, and the rejection of participation by interested stakeholders like environmental NGOs.[9] The counterargument, elaborated below, is that the exclusion of NGOs is based on objections from the least developed countries, not the "trade elite." The critics acknowledge that this cohesion is less true of the WTO than the GATT but still complain that the elite has a one-dimensional understanding of the purpose of the WTO as a trade liberalizing organization, as opposed to one that should also be attentive to development, the environment, and other social and economic values.[10] Under the guise of "expertise," dissenting voices have been silenced and broader interests suppressed.

This critique is tied to a deeper claim about the growing power of technocrats in global public policy. Andrew Baker complains that the agenda and priorities of the entire global financial architecture (the G-20, the IMF, the Basel Committee on Banking Supervision, the Financial Stability Forum, etc.) is established among a limited number

---

Gregory C. Shaffer, "The World Trade Organization Under Challenge: Democracy and the Law and Politics of the WTO's Treatment of Trade and Environment Matters," 25 *Harvard International Law Review* 1 (2001).

[7] Robert Hudec, *Enforcing International Trade Law: The Evolution of the Modern GATT System* 12 (1993).

[8] Robert Howse, "Democracy, Science and Free Trade: Risk Regulation on Trial at the World Trade Organization," 98 *Michigan Law Review* 2329, 2330 (2000).

[9] Robert Howse, "Adjudicative Legitimacy and Treaty Interpretation in International Trade Law: The Early Years of WTO Jurisprudence," in *The EU, The WTO and the NAFTA: Towards a Common Law of International Trade* 35, 39 (J.H.H. Weiler ed, 2000); Monica Garcia-Salmones, "Taking Uncertainty Seriously: Adaptive Governance and International Trade: A Reply to Rosie Cooney and Andrew Lang," in 20 *European Journal of International Law* 167, 182–85 (2009). Outside the trade area, the main critic of expert rule at the international level is David Kennedy. See David Kennedy, "Challenging Expert Rule: The Politics of Global Governance" 27 *Sydney Law Review* 5 (2005).

[10] See, for example, Ulrike Ehling, "Environment Policies and the WTO Committee on Trade and Environment: A Record of Failure?" in *Constitutionalism, Multilevel Trade Governance and Social Regulation supra* note 2, at 452–53.

of regulators and central state agencies.[11] David Kennedy, Marti Koskenniemi, and other critical legal theorists claim that international law and politics are influenced to a much greater extent than we appreciate by a "technocratic background" field of experts, as opposed to the "political foreground" of presidents, diplomats, and Secretaries-General.[12] Of course, expertise itself is not a bad thing. The effectiveness of functional regimes like health and the environment depends on using expertise for public policy purposes. Expertise can even enhance the democratic character of deliberations, by providing impartial, evidence-based reasons for decisions. But taken too far, reliance on expertise can become hegemonic in the Gramscian sense, dressing up political and value choices in seemingly neutral language and obstructing if not making impossible consideration of alternatives.

These two lines of criticism (great power hegemony and technocratic elitism) bump up against each other. The first boils down to a North *versus* South debate; the second boils down to a trade elite *versus* multiple stakeholder debate. Developing countries are generally not enthusiastic about the trade-environment linkage or about opening up the WTO to greater NGO and civil society participation, which they see as the agenda of northern NGOs primarily.[13] Their main concern is with market access and they are, on balance, suspicious of attempts to limit that access through environmental regulation.[14] One must take care not to overgeneralize on either count—developing country governments are not of one mind on trade issues, and environmental NGOs are not all from the North—but in reflecting on the legitimacy of the WTO, it is important to remember that the critiques and solutions may point in opposite directions.

---

[11] Andrew Baker, "Deliberative Equality and the Transgovernmental Politics of the Global Financial Architecture," 15 *Global Governance* 195 (April–June 2009).

[12] Kennedy, "Challenging Expert Rule," *supra* note 9. See also David Kennedy, "The Mystery of Global Governance" in *Ruling the World?: Constitutionalism, International Law and Global Governance* 37, 53–54 (J. Dunoff and J. Trachtman eds., 2009); David Kennedy, *Of War and Law* 25–26 (2006). Martti Koskenniemi, "The Fate of International Law: Between Techniques and Politics," 70 *The Modern Law Review* 1, 8 (2007); Martti Koskenniemi, "The Politics of International Law–Twenty Years Later," 20 *European Journal of International Law* 7 (2009).

[13] Shaffer, *supra* note 6, at 61–68.

[14] Jagdish Bhagwati, "Afterword: The Question of Linkage," 96 *American Journal of International Law* 127 (2002). Bhagwati stressed this point in commenting on a symposium in the *American Journal of International Law*, in which he complains that no developing country scholar is represented and none of authors who contributed or commented on the North-South dimension of the trade-environment linkage. He is especially critical of Robert Howse, who is one of the strongest critics of "insider network" (i.e., neoliberal trade elite) that dominates the trading regime. Bhagwati has high praise for Greg Shaffer, who has written extensively on the North-South dimension. See, for example, Shaffer, *id.* Other participants in the symposium who highlight the North-South split are Debra Steger, *supra* note 2 and José Alvarez, "The WTO as Linkage Machine" 96 *American Journal of International Law* 146, 157–58 (2002).

III. FUNCTIONS OF THE WTO: DISPUTE SETTLEMENT AND THE "MISSING MIDDLE"

The principal functions of the WTO are the negotiation of trade agreements and the settlement of disputes between its members. Pascal Lamy, in his foreword to the World Trade Report 2007, asked whether and to what extent a third function exists—"a missing middle"—where the WTO is engaged in fostering dialogue on matters of common interest to the membership.[15] The negotiation of trade agreements is beyond the scope of this chapter. The second and third functions, dispute settlement and nonbinding deliberation, will be discussed with a view to assessing the nature, scope, and power of the interpretive community that shapes trade law.

A. Dispute Resolution

Dispute resolution is at the center of trade governance.[16] Arguably, the most important systemic outcome of the Uruguay Round of trade negotiations was the tightening of the WTO's dispute settlement mechanism. Trade law is not only enforced (if that term is understood to mean binding judicial decisions plus the prospect of retaliatory sanctions), it is also elaborated and expanded—even made—through the interpretation of treaties.[17] This is especially true in the so-called "trade and..." cases when the dispute resolution bodies are required to consider whether environment, labour rights and other values limit the scope of trade law under Article XX of GATT. That Article allows states to derogate from their GATT obligations in order to protect social, political, or economic values, specified in seven sub-paragraphs. Two of those relate to the environment: Article XX(b), on measures "necessary to protect human, animal or plant life or health" and Article XX(g), on measures "relating to the conservation of exhaustible natural resources...").[18] If a national regulation falls within one of those subparagraphs, then the tribunal must consider whether the standard set in the Article XX chapeau is satisfied:

> Subject to the requirement that such measures are not applied in a manner which would constitute a means of arbitrary or unjustifiable discrimination between

---

[15] World Trade Organization, *World Trade Report 2007* vi (2007).

[16] Joel Trachtman, "The Domain of WTO Dispute Resolution," 40 *Harvard International Law Journal* 333, 339 (1999).

[17] Richard Steinberg, "Judicial Lawmaking at the WTO: Discursive, Constitutional and Political Constraints," 98 *American Journal of International Law* 247, 250–57 (2004). For an analogous study of the relationship between parties to treaties and dispute settlement tribunals in the investment area, see Anthea Roberts, "Power and Persuasion in Investment Treaty Interpretation: The Dual Role of States," 104 *American Journal of International Law* 179 (2010). Roberts argues that how states interpret treaties affects how tribunals decide cases, and how tribunals decide cases affects the interpretation and thus creation of the law.

[18] WTO. GATT 1947, Article XX, pp. 37–38. Annexed to the *Marrakesh Agreement Establishing the World Trade Organization*. See http://www.wto.org/english/docs_e/legal_e/gatt47_02_e.htm, accessed 8/18/09.

countries where the same conditions prevail, or a disguised restriction to international trade, nothing in this Agreement shall be construed to prevent the adoption or enforcement by any contracting party of [those] measures. . . .[19]

The move to binding, compulsory dispute settlement in the WTO would seem to mark a shift away from the diplomatic style of dispute settlement under the GATT, characterized by Joseph Weiler as dominated by a small community of actors that:

> . . .successfully managed relative insularity from the 'outside' world of international relations, and it established among its practitioners a closely knit environment revolving around shared normative values (of free trade) and shared institutional ambitions. GATT operatives became a classical 'network' of first-name contacts and friendly relationships.[20]

In other words, the GATT was driven by a narrow and fairly cohesive interpretive community. Disputes would be settled diplomatically or by panelists who were often diplomats or ex-diplomats belonging to the same trade network, little attention was paid to nontrade consequences of decisions, panel reports were often drafted by the Secretariat and hard to come by. Yet despite the transformed and "juridified" WTO, Weiler asserted in 2005 that diplomatic practices and habits continued to pervade the dispute settlement framework.[21] If the old process was "diplomacy through other means," the new process was meant to import elements of legal culture, characterized by adherence to principles of natural justice (such as no person can be a judge in his or her own case) as well as softer norms that are seen as indispensable to a legitimate legal process such as "sound legal reasoning, coherence, consistency and communicativeness."[22] In practice, the profile of the panelists had not changed much; an aura of secrecy still permeated the proceedings, the Secretariat still wielded a lot of power in giving supposedly "objective legal advice," and—at least before the *Shrimp-Turtle* case–NGOs had little input.

In a telling observation, Weiler states about the process: "for lawyers, and particularly judges, the notion of excluding voices affected by one's decision and not hearing arguments by them runs counter not only to the ethic of open and public process but to the principles of natural justice."[23] This highlights the connection between principles of democratic deliberation and of adjudication, alluded to in Chapter 2 and discussed in the context of the resolution 1267 targeted sanctions regime in Chapter 5. On their face, the two processes look different: deliberation is about the making of law (and policy); legal

---

[19] *Id.*
[20] Weiler, *supra* note 6, at 336.
[21] *Id.* at 336–37.
[22] *Id.* at 341.
[23] *Id.* at 344.

argumentation is about its interpretation and implementation. While it is true that the latter is a more bounded form of discourse, the difference should not be overstated. Deliberation in legislative bodies is constrained by the felt need to make principled, impartial arguments. Legal interpretation—especially when the lines between nonlaw, soft law, and hard law are blurry—is fundamentally a search for inter-subjective meaning. Weiler's point is that the legitimacy of both democratic deliberation and adjudication depends on adherence to certain procedural norms: namely, that those who are affected by a decision ought to be heard or at least their interests accounted for.

From this perspective, the WTO dispute settlement process, though as court-like as one can get in the international system, is embedded in a broader process of discursive interaction over the meaning and application of negotiated texts. As Richard Steinberg argues in response to complaints about judicial activism, the AB is constrained by international legal discourse as well as politics and constitutional structure.[24] The legal discourse is "intrinsically elastic," allowing for either restrained or expansive judicial lawmaking, and the constitutional constraints are less than they were under the old system because an AB report is adopted unless a consensus (including the winning party) favors blocking its adoption.[25] So the AB can opt for judicial activism, filling gaps in the law, clarifying ambiguities, and generally taking an evolutionary, dynamic approach to interpretation. This approach opens the door to the WTO accommodating a wide range of values, including environmental protection.[26]

The real constraints on the AB, Steinberg argues, are political. Powerful states have special privileges when it comes to the appointment of AB members; they can react to judicial lawmaking by threatening to rewrite the rules; they can send disapproving diplomatic signals or even defy decisions, both of which can "delegitimize" the AB.[27] Functioning in the shadow of this means that powerful states have ways to encourage or discourage judicial activism.[28] This, according to Steinberg, means there is no serious democratic deficit in the WTO with respect to powerful states.[29] That is not an argument that WTO dispute settlement is conducive to inclusive deliberation but rather that it is subject to control by a few states. Transposing Steinberg's analysis to the concept of an interpretive community, it suggests that a U.S.- and EU-dominated interpretive community existed in and around the WTO dispute settlement process. As the distribution of power in the global trading environment changes, the "interpretive community" that impacts WTO decisions would change as well.

---

[24] Steinberg, *supra* note 17 at 248.

[25] *Id.* at 249.

[26] *Id.* at 247.

[27] *Id.* at 264–67.

[28] *Id.* at 268 and 274.

[29] *Id.* at 275.

The implication is that an argument for the power of interpretive communities in the trade field must consider two conflicting lines of attack on the legitimacy of the WTO dispute settlement process. On one side are those who see it as dominated by a neoliberal, trade-oriented policy elite, unwilling to accommodate nontrade values. On the other are those who see the relevant "interpretive community" as dominated by voices from the most powerful states, who are more responsive to pressure from environmental activists than developing countries, and whose environmental policies are perceived by the latter as disguised protectionism. Before assessing which is closer to the truth, let me now turn to the so-called missing middle, which sheds further light on the relationship between lawmaking and dispute settlement in the WTO.

B. The "Missing Middle": the Committee on Trade and Environment

> We need to think more about the monitoring and surveillance functions of the institution—a good part of this task would be aimed at encouraging constructive discussion and engagement on common interests... As an institution we legislate and litigate, and I believe we do this reasonably well. But is there something of a 'missing middle' where we should be engaged more in fostering dialogue that can bolster cooperation?[30]

Pascal Lamy's question was not directed at the trade-environment issue per se, but it is relevant, not least because a Committee on Trade and Environment (CTE) was established to perform the sort of functions he describes. The thrust of this chapter (indeed of this book) is that deliberation is central to effective lawmaking, interpretation, and implementation, so I conceive of the "missing middle" as a complement to legislative and dispute resolution functions of the WTO, not separate from them.

The appeal for a more overtly deliberative function in the WTO implies that there is a problem. Simon Evenett illustrates its nature with three recent developments: the too-limited set of issues being addressed in the Doha Round, the impact of climate change negotiations, and the spread of regional trade agreements.[31] All three phenomena could have benefited and could still benefit from more deliberation. Evenett argues for more evidence-based discussion of matters that affect the world trading system in non-negotiation and non-litigious settings so that members of the organization could better set priorities, develop strategies, and engage with other IOs.

So-called trade and... issues lend themselves to deliberation because of the uncertainty about how to address these linkages—or even whether they should be addressed

---

[30] WTO, *supra* note 15.
[31] Simon Evenett, "Aid for Trade and the 'Missing Middle' of the World Trade Organization" 15 *Global Governance* 359, 361 (2009).

by the WTO.[32] The WTO is not a "free trade" organization; it has a broader purpose. A close reading of the opening clause of the 1994 Marrakesh Agreement establishing the WTO suggests that its overarching purpose was to promote development through freer trade but not at the expense of other values:

> Recognizing that their relations in the field of trade and economic endeavour should be conducted with a view to raising standards of living, ensuring full employment and a large and steadily growing volume of real income and effective demand, and expanding the production of and trade in goods and services, while allowing for the optimal use of the world's resources in accordance with the objective of sustainable development, seeking both to protect and preserve the environment and to enhance the means for doing so in a manner consistent with their respective needs and concerns at different levels of economic development. . .[33]

The trade-environment link was first identified by the GATT in 1971 when the Council of Representatives decided to establish a Group on Environmental Measures and International Trade (EMIT). The EMIT Group did not convene until the middle of the Uruguay Round in 1991, on the request of the European Free Trade Association states.[34] EMIT was given a narrow remit to focus on the trade impacts of environmental measures only, largely because developing countries insisted the WTO was a trade, not an environmental organization.[35] The CTE was an outcome of the EMIT Group discussions between 1991 and 1994, pushed mainly by the North, with the South going along on the understanding that its agenda would reflect development as well as trade and environment concerns.[36] The Committee's two-part mandate is "to identify the relationship between trade measures and environmental measures, in order to promote sustainable development," and "to make appropriate recommendations on whether any modifications of the provisions of the multilateral trading system are required." Its ten-item agenda was later clustered into one set of market access issues and a second set of environment-trade linkage issues.[37] At the same time that the CTE was created, a Trade and Environment Division was established in the WTO Secretariat to service it.

---

[32] An entire *American Journal of International Law* symposium was dedicated to this. José Alvarez ed., "Symposium: The Boundaries of the WTO" 96 *American Journal of International Law* 1–158 (2002).

[33] WTO, 1994. Marrakesh Agreement Establishing the World Trade Organization, 1994 (came into force 1995). See http://www.wto.org/english/docs_e/legal_e/04-wto_e.htm, accessed 8/18/09. Deborah Cass calls it a development organization. Cass, *supra* note 3, at 247–48.

[34] Ehling, *supra* note 10, at 442.

[35] Shaffer, *supra* note 6, at 23–24.

[36] *Id.* at 24.

[37] WTO Committee on Trade and Environment Adopts 1997 Report, Trade and Environment Bulletin No. 20, PRESS/TE020 (Dec. 3, 1997).

The CTE was established as a forum for political deliberation, not negotiation. Some saw it as having the potential to serve as the core venue for conducting the trade and environment debate at the global level.[38] It was not until the 2001 Doha Declaration that trade and environment linkages were put on the negotiating agenda of the WTO, to be undertaken in CTE Special Sessions. To this day, the regular sessions of the CTE (as opposed to the special sessions) are devoted to deliberations but not negotiations. It prepares reports, seeks agreement on broad policy, and has the authority to make recommendations on changes to trade rules. All WTO states are members; and the Secretariat, as well as observers from other organizations, participate in its sessions.

How successful has it been? Not very if the standard is how much it has contributed to changes in the trade rules. The report it presented to the first WTO Ministerial meeting in 1996 proposed no substantive changes to the law. Since then, the deliberations have been trapped in deadlock, largely because decisions are by consensus, and the conflicting interests of member states have prevented agreement on matters of substance.[39] The 1996 "failure," if it can be called that, was not because the issues were not fully explored, but because there were divisions within and between the United States and European Union, and because developing countries were suspicious not only of the environment agenda as a disguised form of protectionism but also of it being a precedent for labor standards.[40]

That being said, the 1996 report did have an impact. Its very failure to recommend modifications is evidence that deliberation matters. As a Nigerian delegate to the discussions stated, "words have consequences. . . . Delegates are wary of the WTO. GATT is a binding contract. People are not as open and freewheeling as in other international fora. In the WTO, everything you say matters and can be used against you."[41] It is worth asking, therefore, what the CTE tells us about the nature and power of the WTO-based "interpretive community." Is the CTE dominated by a cadre of international "trade technocrats"? Shaffer's answer was an unequivocal no, at least for the period of 1994–2000. It was an intergovernmental body, dominated by the United States, the European Union, and Canada, and even among them, trade delegates did not always dominate: agricultural ministries, for example, sometimes played a key role.[42] Transnational businesses played a role in shaping the debate, as did Northern environmental NGOs. While the WTO Secretariat may have been an "epistemic community" of trade economists and lawyers, only six were assigned to the CTE Secretariat in 1998, and their influence paled in

---

[38] J. Cameron and K. Campbell, "A Reluctant Global Policy Maker," in *The Greening of Trade Law: International Trade Organizations and Environmental Issues* 1, 25 (R. Steinberg ed. 2002).
[39] Ehling, *supra* note 10, at 451.
[40] Shaffer, *supra* note 6, at 36–41.
[41] Chiedu Osakwe, quoted by Shaffer, *id* at 38.
[42] *Id* at 48.

comparison to that of powerful states and powerful constituencies within states.[43] The position of developing countries, which generally did not like the CTE, certainly cannot be explained by the machinations of a neoliberal trade elite.

Ehling argues the opposite.[44] He stresses that trade ministries coordinate the interagency process that leads to national positions taken there; that participants in CTE meetings are mainly trade specialists, and that there is resistance to including other experts on national delegations; that while selected other intergovernmental organizations have observer status, there is strong resistance to granting NGOs that status. In sum, "the GATT and WTO can both be seen as prime examples of political institutions which function as a Club Model of experts that benefitted from the belief that international trade raises highly technical questions and should be left to technocratic decision-making by qualified experts."[45] The CTE was not designed as a problem-solving institution, let alone as a forum for genuine deliberation but rather for "symbolic politics"–to give the impression that the WTO and its members are concerned with the linkage issue.

Even if Ehling is right, that the CTE was created for appearances, the "civilizing force of hypocrisy" discussed in Chapter 3 suggests that sooner or later, deeds must be brought into line with words. Having given all states the opportunity to discuss the trade-environment link in a less-pressured context than trade negotiations or particular disputes, having opened up those deliberations to greater public scrutiny, having established a framework for coordination with Multilateral Environment Agreement Secretariats and those of other organizations, having begun interacting with NGOs, and having empowered the Secretariat to take some initiative through its studies and reports, the "symbolic politics" may yet result in real political agreement. If nothing else, the legitimacy of the WTO is enhanced. Moreover, as Joel Trachtman pointed out in 1999, while the CTE was a talking shop, it had an impact on WTO dispute resolution—both leading to and in the aftermath of the *Shrimp-Turtle* case.[46] I now turn to that dispute.

---

[43] *Id.* at 60–61. The WTO now has "in-house" environmental experts who can advise members on environmental impacts of trade liberalization. Daniel Esty, C. "Governing at the trade-environment interface," in *The WTO and Global Governance: Future Directions* 121(Sampson, Gary P. ed., 2008).

[44] Ehling, *supra* note 10.

[45] *Id.* at 455.

[46] Trachtman, *supra* note 16, at 365.

IV. THE *SHRIMP-TURTLE* CASE

A. Background

The creation of the CTE was prompted in part by one of the most high-profile disputes the GATT dispute settlement panel ever decided, the *Tuna-Dolphin* case. In two decisions, one in 1991 and another in 1994, panels found that U.S. embargoes on tunas violated Article XI of the GATT and were not exempted under Article XX.[47] The United States banned tuna imports from Mexico because Mexican boats used fishing methods that killed dolphins trapped in their nets. The 1991 panel found that the U.S. measure regulated a "process" rather than a product and so was subject to the prohibition of embargoes under Article XI. It also found that the Article XX(b) exemption did not apply because that provision did not permit protection of animals outside the territory of the state adopting the relevant measure. The 1994 panel was established to address the EC's challenge to the United States' secondary ban on tuna imports. That panel left open the possibility that Article XX could protect such animals but found that the U.S. measures were designed not to achieve environmental goals but to coerce other governments into adopting specific environmental policies.

Environmental groups were incensed – Greenpeace erected a banner at GATT headquarters depicting a dolphin being devoured by a shark named "GATT."[48] The decision came in the midst of the Uruguay Round and so, to preempt efforts by environmentalists to jeopardize the trade negotiations, the United States and EC supported activation of the EMIT group and creation of the CTE. The CTE, as has been noted, could have addressed the trade-environment interface by recommending "legislative" changes to the WTO rules, which one might have expected given the *Tuna-Dolphin* controversy. But it did not. It is in that context that the *Shrimp-Turtle* dispute arose.

B. The Shrimp-Turtle Case[49]

In October 1996, four countries—India, Malaysia, Pakistan, and Thailand—brought a complaint before the WTO dispute settlement body (DSB) regarding a U.S. law that banned the importation of shrimp from countries not certified by the United States as having adequate measures to avoid the incidental capture of sea turtles. In the United States, the shrimp industry was required by law to use "turtle excluder devices" (TEDs); the United States would not import shrimp from countries that did not have a comparable standard of protection. The four complainants plus a number of third-party observers

---

[47] The summary of the case is from Trachtman, *id*. at 357–58.

[48] Shaffer, *supra* note 6, at 20.

[49] My summary of the case draws on a paper prepared by Jason Yeager as my research assistant.

argued that the U.S. law was discriminatory, in violation of Article I (the Most Favored Nation principle), Article XI (on the general elimination of quantitative restrictions), and Article XIII (nondiscriminatory application of quantitative restrictions). The United States claimed that the law was legitimate under GATT Article XX(g), which allows countries to derogate from their obligations in order to protect "exhaustible natural resources."[50]

The Dispute Settlement Body (DSB) established a panel in February 1997 to settle the dispute. In May 1998, it concluded that the U.S. measure was inconsistent with GATT Article XI and was not justifiable as an exemption under Article XX.[51] The Panel ruled that the U.S. measure violated the chapeau of Article XX and was therefore not a legitimate exception to GATT obligations: the U.S. certification process was "discriminatory" because it effectively required countries to adopt sea turtle-protection policies identical to those of the United States, regardless of differing conditions. Applying the same coercive standard to different countries was tantamount to applying different standards to countries where the same conditions prevail, as prohibited by the chapeau to Article XX.[52]

The United States appealed the ruling. The AB report, issued on October 12, 1998, upheld the panel's ruling, but criticized its reasoning. It found that the U.S. measure was legitimate under subparagraph (g) of GATT Article XX (protection of "exhaustible natural resources"), but the way in which the measure was *implemented* did not meet the requirement of the chapeau of Article XX. In evaluating first—and solely—the chapeau of Article XX, the original panel effectively "erased" any possibility of an environmental trade measure being legitimate under the GATT. While the original panel's reasoning was rejected, the outcome was the same: the United States measure was GATT/WTO-inconsistent and had to be changed—not because its objective was illegal, but because it was "too broad and unnecessarily stringent" in its application, forcing other countries to adopt the same policy as the United States despite differing conditions in those countries. The AB affirmed that MEAs served as a potentially more effective environmental policy instrument and less-trade-restrictive measure.[53]

The *Shrimp-Turtle* dispute indicates a clear move by the AB toward a more flexible and environment-friendly approach to settling trade-environment conflicts.[54] It defined

---

[50] WTO Secretariat, Summary of *United States–Import Prohibition of Certain Shrimp and Shrimp Products*. From <www.wto.org/english/tratop_e/dispu_e/cases_e/ds58_e.htm> (Accessed 7/29/09).

[51] *Id.*

[52] Trachtman *supra* note 16, at 358. De la Fayette, Louise. "United States-Import Prohibition of Certain Shrimp and Shrimp Products-Recourse to Article 21.5 of the DSU by Malaysia," 96 *American Journal of International Law* 691 (2002).

[53] Trachtman, *supra* note 16, at 362–63.

[54] *Id.* at. 363–64.

"exhaustible natural resources" as being an "evolutionary" and not a "static" concept.[55] WTO treaty text ". . . must be read by a treaty interpreter in the light of contemporary concerns of the community of nations about the protection and conservation of the environment."[56] In doing so, the AB could consider broader, more progressive definitions of "exhaustible" and "natural resources" to include animal life. Indeed, it cites a number of environment treaties and the UN Convention on the Law of the Sea (UNCLOS) to support the notion that marine life qualifies as a "natural resource," and that under contemporary understandings of the term (including that implied by the preamble to the 1994 Marrakesh Agreement), it was not reasonable to argue otherwise.[57] The AB cited the "Convention on International Trade in Endangered Species of Wild Fauna and Flora (CITES), which listed sea turtles as endangered species in justifying that this particular natural resource (sea turtles) was "exhaustible."[58] The AB even cited MEAs to which not all the disputants were parties. This further supports the notion of international environmental protection rising in importance in relation to the objective of trade liberalization, legitimating efforts by countries to impose trade restrictions based on the environmentally harmful production methods of an exporting country. Finally, in a further sign of a more hospitable view toward consideration of environmental concerns, for the first time, the AB permitted the submission of unsolicited *amicus curiae* briefs–many of which came from environmental NGOs.

On the other hand, the AB's reasoning in *Shrimp-Turtle* is not a radical departure. It reflects a more balanced approach to trade-environment conflicts than had been the case in the past, but as Trachtman states, it is "measured," "conservative," and "politically sensitive."[59] The AB elevated the cause of environmental protection, while preserving the fundamental principles of the trade regime. In applying a "balancing test,"[60] the AB wrote that "the measures falling within the particular exceptions must be applied reasonably, with due regard both to the legal duties of the party claiming the exception and the legal rights of the other parties concerned."[61] The ruling does not prioritize a state's environmental policies over its multilateral trade obligations but rather broadens the scope for taking environmental and other nontrade concerns into consideration. It grants dispute

---

[55] WTO Appellate Body, "WTO doc. WT/DS58/AB/R," October 12, 1998, para. 127-28.7-2. Also cited in Shaffer, *supra* note 6. "United States-Import Prohibition of Certain Shrimp and Shrimp Products. WTO doc. WT/DS58/AB/R." 93 *The American Journal of International Law* 511 (1999).

[56] WTO Appellate Body.*supra* note 55, at para.129. Also cited in Trachtman *supra* note 16, at 361.

[57] *Id.* at paras. 128–31.

[58] *Id.* at para. 132. See also Trachtman, *supra* note 16, at 361.

[59] Trachtman *supra* note 16, at 363–64.

[60] Christiane Gerstetter, "The Appelate Body's 'Response' to the Tension and Interdependencies Between Transnational Trade and Social Regulation' in Joerges and Petersmann, *supra* note 2.

[61] Cited in Trachtman *supra* note 16, at 362. From WTO Appellate Body, *supra* note 55, at para.152.

settlement panels the right to accept amicus curiae briefs but not an obligation to do so.[62] Overall, the shift in approach from *Tuna–Dolphin* (a case that was criticized for its formalism[63]) was significant yet consistent with a broad reading of the language of WTO law and a system that is still first and foremost oriented toward promoting free trade.

C. Assessment From the Point of View of Deliberative Legitimacy

Four aspects of the case provide insight into the deliberative processes in the WTO. First, to the extent that an "insider network" ever dominated the WTO and GATT dispute panels' use of interpretive techniques to arrive at only trade friendly decision, the AB has rejected their approach.[64] The AB endorsed an "organic" or "evolutionary" approach to interpretation by reading the words "exhaustible natural resources" in light of "the contemporary concerns of the community of nations about the protection and conservation of the environment."[65] It referred to environmental treaties to support its interpretation of Article XX and adopted a balancing test, giving the dispute settlement bodies considerable discretion in how to search for the least trade restrictive measures compatible with environmental law. It referred to the language on sustainable development in the preamble of the WTO agreement to interpret the chapeau of Article XX. Along with the *Beef Hormones* case decided earlier in the year, the AB expanded the scope of admissible reasons member states could plead in support of regulatory policies to protect life, health, the environment, and other social values.[66] If the resolution of trade disputes was ever insulated from broader political considerations, 1998 marked a turning point.

Second, by allowing unsolicited amicus curiae briefs for the first time, the WTO opened the door to participation by NGOs in the management of international trade. Article 13 of the Dispute Settlement Understanding allows a panel to "seek information and technical advice" from outside sources. The panel in the *Shrimp-Turtle* case interpreted this to mean it was prohibited from receiving information that it had not requested. The AB reversed this decision, ruling that *unsolicited* briefs could also be taken into account at the panel's/AB's discretion.[67] This willingness to accept a wider range of

---

[62] Arthur Appleton, "Shrimp/Turtle: Untangling the Nets," 2 *Journal of International Economic Law* 477, 484 (1999).

[63] David Leebron, "Linkages" in *American Journal of International Law* Symposium: Boundaries of the WTO, 96 *American Journal of International Law* 5 (2002). But cf. Baghwati in *supra* note 14.

[64] Robert Howse's "insider network" thesis has been called "preposterous" by Debra Steger, at least to the extent that it implies a deliberate attempt on the part of GATT operatives to keep the system closed to real world interests and politics. Steger, *supra* note 6 at 139. In any case, it is Howse who argues that the Shrimp/Turtle dispute is the harbinger of the end of "insider network" domination, *supra* note 3, at 108-17.

[65] Trachtman, *supra* note 16, at 361.

[66] Nanz, *supra* note 2, at 77–78.

[67] Gregory Shaffer, "United States Import Prohibition of Certain Shrimp and Shrimp Products", 93 *American Journal of International Law* 505, 508 (1999); LaFayette, *supra* note 52, at 691.

opinions and views from outside the WTO is consistent with principles of natural justice, and with "the ethic of an open and public process"[68]—a response to the charge that the WTO is dominated by corporate interests and trade technocrats and lacks democratic legitimacy. By receiving relevant information and points of view that the parties to the dispute, or third parties, would not necessarily provide, the deliberative quality of the proceedings are enhanced. But before celebrating this "democratization" of the WTO, it is important to remember that the ruling comes on the heels of a bitter North-South debate over whether to permit amicus briefs, which most developing countries had opposed and indeed dozens protested at the following WTO Council meeting.[69] On balance, Southern governments do not view greater nongovernmental input as a democratizing force; to the contrary, they worry that it will further skew the process in favor of northern elites, both business and environmental.[70] Those considerations may be why the AB ruled that dispute settlement panels have the right but not the obligation to accept such briefs.

Third, what the AB did in *Shrimp-Turtle* was a form of lawmaking in the sense that it clarified ambiguities and filled gaps in the law. For example, once it decided that the U.S. measures in question fell within Article XX(g), it established five factors relevant to deciding whether the measure violated the chapeau of Article XX, none of which are tied directly to the text.[71] This sort of dynamic interpretation is not unusual in the common law tradition, but how creative a court should be is a source of bitter dispute (and a standard line of questioning) when appointees to the U.S. Supreme Court go through confirmation hearings. In the context of trade and environment issues, such "judicial lawmaking" by the AB is justified, at least in part, because trade law is not clear, and the CTE had the chance but failed to clarify it.[72] The "legislature," so to speak, did not do its job, so the "judiciary" had to step in.

This highlights the larger point that the line between "legislative" reasoning and judicial reasoning is not all that sharp. As noted above, deliberative democrats question the distinction made between courts as forums for principled deliberation and legislatures as brokers of interests.[73] The sorts of considerations that informed debates in the CTE and deliberation in AB were similar, mixing principled and prudential considerations in a balancing test. When the CTE reached political deadlock, the AB, in effect, picked up where it left off. All the disputants and three of the third-party participants in *Shrimp-Turtle* cited the 1996 CTE report in support of their claims; the panel and

---

[68] Weiler, *supra* note 6 at 344.
[69] Steinberg, *supra* note 17, at 256.
[70] Shaffer, *supra* note 6.
[71] Steinberg, *supra* note 17, at 252.
[72] Trachtman, *supra* note 16 at 362.
[73] Amy Gutmann and Dennis Thompson, *Democracy and Disagreement* 46 (1996).

the AB both referred to it; and after the case was decided, the CTE returned the favor by noting that many countries had expressed satisfaction with the *Shrimp-Turtle* decision. Even more, Canada stated that the report would be useful in the formulation of a statement on the interaction between MEAs and WTO rules, which the CTE then asked the Secretariat to prepare. As Trachtman observes, "the CTE sees itself in a cooperative project with the dispute settlement process to elaborate the application of Article XX of GATT."[74] In other words, the CTE and dispute settlement bodies are in a sort of dialogue, sending and receiving signals, not unlike the relationship between the SC and ICJ over *Lockerbie* and the SC and ECJ over the Taliban/Al Qaeda sanctions regime, discussed in Chapter 5.

V. CONCLUSION

More than most IOs, the WTO has been criticized for its "democratic deficit." That it has been the target of such criticism does not mean it is one of the least democratic institutions. The EU, after all, gets more heat than any other international organization, and yet it is hardly the least "democratic." Rather, the EU comes under fire because its members are all democracies and because it purports to uphold democratic principles, so expectations are highest there. As a "member-driven" organization that operates on the basis of consensus, with a small and not very autonomous Secretariat (compared to that of the World Bank, IMF, and UN for example), democratic expectations of the WTO are lower. The main reason it has been the brunt of criticism is because of the powerful impact of trade law on other areas of social, economic, and political life. The "trade and environment" debate is part of a larger debate about how and where to reconcile competing values in a pluralistic international community.

In this chapter, I outlined a number of developments in the WTO that bear on the larger argument of this book, namely, that the legitimacy of an IO depends in part on the quality of deliberations within it and the nature of the interpretive community that frames those deliberations. The WTO developments are largely positive from the point of view of bringing down the deliberative deficit, though their overall significance should not be exaggerated. The WTO continues to be dominated by powerful states and is driven by forces that do not lend themselves to "reasoned deliberation" in the Habermasian sense. Within that context, the following points are noteworthy.

First, *Shrimp-Turtle* and other contemporary cases (like *Beef Hormones*) represent a shift from legal formalism to an "interpretive struggle" over how to balance competing

---

[74] Trachtman, *supra* note 16, at 365.

values.[75] This interpretive struggle has taken place in the dispute settlement panels and AB. It has also taken place in a back and forth between those bodies, other WTO institutions, and member states. The interpretation of international law, like constitutional interpretation, occurs not only in tribunals but in other institutions. The *Shrimp-Turtle* case did not resolve the trade-environment dilemma; if anything, it set the stage for many more disputes on how to reconcile or balance the competing values. This is not necessarily a bad thing. Gerstenberg has argued that WTO law functions as a "catalyst for deliberative processes" in transnational settings.[76] The effect of the *Shrimp-Turtle* decision was to foster a process of reasoned deliberation about trade and the environment in multiple settings, national and international, judicial and nonjudicial.

Second, the WTO is neither a closed technocracy nor is it wide open to civil society. NGOs can submit amicus curiae briefs but not as a matter of right. There is more transparency in WTO proceedings than in the past, and the WTO does allow for consultation with NGOs, but access to meetings is severely restricted.[77] The "club model," in which trade governance is managed by a narrow group of trade cognoscenti, may have broken down,[78] but the organization is still intergovernmental at its core.

Third, the "interpretive community" has been penetrated by outsiders. While there may be differences of opinion on how dominant the "insider network" ever was, it seems clear that a narrow circle of trade specialists are no longer the only voices heard in interpretive disputes over WTO law. Howse observed in 2002 that the Secretariat was "sprinkled" with young staff whose backgrounds in public international law or sustainable development facilitate their seeing beyond the narrow economic outlook of traditional insiders.[79] These "new insiders" interact with national delegations, both formally in committees like the CTE and informally. They contribute to studies and reports that are often prepared in coordination with other IOs.[80] Symposia are held, bringing WTO officials into contact with civil society actors. The Secretariat consults with NGOs, including environmental ones, giving the latter a channel for influence that did not exist before. Whether they are now part of the "interpretive community" around the WTO or

---

[75] Patricia Nanz borrows the term "interpretive struggle" from Frank Michelman, an American constitutional law scholar. Nanz, supra note 2, at 78. Franck Michelman, "Morality, Identity and 'Constitutional Patriotism'" 76 *Denver University Law Review* 1010 (2000).

[76] O. Gerstenberger, "Expanding the Constitution Beyond the Court: The Case of Euro-Constitutionalism" 8 *European Law Journal* 173, 185 (2002).

[77] Jens Steffeck and Claudia Kissling, "Why Cooperate? Civil Society Participation at the WTO," *Constitutionalism, Multilevel Trade Governance and Social Regulation* 136, 150–51 (in C. Joerges and E. Petersmann eds., 2006).

[78] Howse, *supra* note 6; Jeffrey Dunoff, "The Politics of International Constitutionalism: The Curious Case of the WTO", in *Ruling the World?: Constitutionalism, International Law and Global Governance* 196 (J. Dunoff and J. Trachtman eds., 2009).

[79] Howse, *id.* at 117.

[80] Shaffer, *supra* note 6, at 57.

outsiders who have penetrated it, their influence suggests that the wall of "expertise" around interpretive communities is not impermeable.

Finally, one must hesitate before declaring that these developments have made the WTO more "democratic." From the perspective of the global South, it depends on whether opening the trade doors to nontrade specialists and civil society reinforces the dominance of the North or undermines it. That empirical question is beyond the scope of this chapter. But it does raise the question of whether the conditions exist for a "transnational public sphere" to emerge around the WTO.[81] To the extent that there is wider participation in the discourse about trade, more openness to public scrutiny, and more reason-giving that accounts for the concerns of all stakeholders, then the grounds for a more deliberatively democratic form of trade governance is being laid.

---

[81] Patricia Nanz asks whether the growing role of civil society in trade governance is heading in that direction. Nanz *supra* note 2, at 81.

10

CONCLUSION

LEGAL ARGUMENTATION AND deliberative politics influence world politics through a diffuse but consequential discursive process. To understand how and why, this book has focused on legal discourse as a distinctly powerful form of argumentation. I argued that the discourse occurs within and is constrained by interpretive communities, which tend to coalesce around international organizations (IOs). The power of interpretive communities depends on their ability to render cohesive judgment. This cannot be measured precisely of course, but decision-makers are conscious of the reputational costs that interpretive communities can extract. I have also argued that the legitimacy of IOs depends in part on the quality of deliberations in and around them and, by extension, on the legitimacy of interpretive communities.

In this conclusion, I synthesize the principal findings from the various cases discussed in earlier chapters and elaborate on their theoretical and policy implications. The policy implications include institutional reform. I do not offer specific reform proposals, which would need to be reconciled with or balanced against considerations other than deliberation, such as the need to keep great powers engaged in international institutions and the need for efficient decision making. However, my focus on deliberation does suggest an agenda for politically achievable reform of institutions that would enhance both their legitimacy and effectiveness.

A. Arguments Matter

The fact that argumentation occurs at all in world politics is circumstantial evidence that it serves a purpose. There is nothing compelling states to "argue," that is, to engage in the exchange of impartial reasons for acting or not acting. Neither the structure of the international system nor the procedural rules of any organization require it; government representatives can opt to remain silent, cast votes without explanation, or stomp their shoes on the table—there is no obligation to deliberate. Yet arguing is ubiquitous.

Why states argue—what purpose it serves—is a difficult question. The motive could be a genuine desire to persuade others of the rightness or wisdom of a position, perhaps even to be persuaded otherwise. But an important finding is that sincerity is not a precondition for meaningful discourse. Arguments may be deployed strategically, to rationalize positions in order to gain international and domestic support, regardless of whether the speaker genuinely hopes to persuade or the listener is open to persuasion. The United States sought to make the best legal case it could for war in Iraq in 2003 not because the Bush Administration believed in the importance of international law or the SC (some officials saw both as inimical to U.S. interests), but because potential allies would find it easier to support the United States. The allies may not have believed in the wisdom of going to war with Iraq, but they had an interest in preserving good relations with the United States. It would have been easier to persuade their own constituencies to back the United States if the legal basis for military action had been sounder ("this is not to serve U.S. interests but to enforce SC resolutions"). Conversely, the weak legal case made it easier for allies who had doubts about the wisdom of the policy to deny support to the United States. ("I wish we could help but I can't sign on to a war that my public sees as illegal.")

In addition to strategic reasons for arguing (the logic of consequences), there are constructivist reasons (the logic of appropriateness). Justificatory discourse can lead to the creation of new norms, shore up fragile norms, or undermine norms that one finds unappealing. The discourse around the responsibility to protect (R2P) is a case in point. The ICISS, UN Secretary-General, and other "norm entrepreneurs" originally sought to create a new norm, building on a body of existing human rights and humanitarian law. When challenges to the norm mounted, the discourse shifted to saving it from irrelevance. The disputation occurred in thematic debates, such as the World Summit, and in connection with particular crises, like Darfur and Myanmar. As striking as the substance of the debates, which have been inconclusive, is the extent to which they are being taken seriously by all concerned. The United States would not have worked hard to craft language at the World Summit that precluded any inference of a positive duty to act if it did not think the words of summit declarations were relevant. The NAM would not be pushing for a broad, noncoercive conception of R2P, if it was not worried about reviving the doctrine of unilateral humanitarian intervention. Influential supporters of R2P would not have engaged in a public debate over whether it applied to Myanmar's response to Cyclone Nargis if words did not matter.

B. Legal Arguments are Distinctly Powerful

Legal discourse is a powerful form of argumentation, not because the style of reasoning is distinctive, but because it is based on shared norms. International legal interpretation is, at its core, a search for inter-subjective meaning: what the relevant legal norms mean to the parties collectively as opposed to each individually or in the abstract. In a consent-based legal system, the principles and values embodied in the law are, by definition, shared by the subjects of the law. Thus, debate about the legality of the doctrine of preemption after the terrorist attacks of September 11, 2001 was within the framework of broadly shared understandings about the law of self-defense. The meaning and application of the law was up for discussion, but few of the participants in the debate claimed Article 51 of the UN Charter and associated elements like "imminence" were irrelevant.

This highlights the validity of Risse's notion of "argumentative self-entrapment." Once a state (a speaker) has committed to a norm, it feels compelled to justify its actions on the basis of that norm. The state can revoke its commitment to the norm (North Korea withdrew from the Nuclear Non-Proliferation Treaty), but that happens rarely and never casually. Hard law is especially "sticky" in this way because the discourse about compliance with it tends to be more demanding than for soft law. It is easier for a critic to say, "this is the law, these are the facts, your behavior is a manifest violation," and harder for the defendant to reply, "we read the law differently, it does not apply to this situation," or "it leaves room for exceptions." Legal discourse is a way of holding states accountable to the commitments they have made. Incremental changes in the law can occur through the discursive interaction, as was the case with Afghanistan, but even the most powerful states cannot unilaterally rewrite the law by dint of creative reinterpretation, as the fate of the doctrine of preemption demonstrates.

Finally, it is important not to be too quick to dismiss the significance of quibbles over "legal technicalities." While the challenges of nuclear non-proliferation do not boil down to winning arguments over the interpretation of precise articles in the NPT, those quibbles affect the context in which the political dynamics play out. Whether the DPRK is still a member of the NPT, what Iran's "inalienable right" to develop peaceful nuclear energy means, whether assistance to India's civilian nuclear program sets a precedent for Pakistan—these are elements of the diplomacy and political debates. They are especially important when it comes to the SC's management and signaling as opposed to enforcement functions. The SC, led by the P5, is operating within a non-proliferation regime that is affected by the fine print of the NPT. How the P5 operate, in turn, has an effect on the integrity of that regime. While the non-proliferation policies of the Obama

Administration are not all that different from those of the Bush Administration, the attitude toward international law and institutions is.

C. *International Legal Discourse and Political Deliberation are Not Categorically Different*

Though legal argumentation has its own structure, it is not categorically different from the sort of deliberation one hears in well-functioning legislatures. Both entail principled exchange on the basis of impartial values and reasons that all stakeholders understand as valid. Both *presuppose* that material power (the power to coerce) does not completely negate the power of the better argument. Material power counts for a great deal, but in engaging in deliberation and argumentation, one must assume it does not count for everything.[1] The "ideal speech situation" does not exist in the real world; it is a counterfactual presupposition that helps to make sense of the act of arguing.[2] If we assume the power to coerce always wins, then there would be no point in arguing, indeed not much point in trying to communicate at all. A courtroom looks more conducive to arguing than a legislature or intergovernmental negotiating forum, but the difference is one of degree, not kind. The "better argument" may get a better hearing in judicial tribunals than intergovernmental assemblies, but neither is ideal in the Habermasian sense, nor is either completely dominated by hegemonic voices. The WTO dispute settlement panels and Appellate Body are not pristine venues where the logic of arguing and principles of justice always prevail. Conversely, the UN Security Council is not a place where the great powers always get their way, as the compromises on the sanctions and counter-terrorism regimes embodied in resolutions 1267 and 1373 indicate.

D. *International Organizations are Nascent Public Spheres*

IOs are places where discursive interaction between states tends to be most intense. They operate on the basis of norms embodied in their constitutive acts and subsidiary instruments: states feel impelled to justify their actions on the basis of those norms, and other states tend to criticize those actions on the same grounds. Government representatives are the principals in this discursive interaction, but they are not the only players. To the extent that IOs are places where multiple actors are able to participate in the deliberations and that are open to public scrutiny, they are nascent public spheres. Habermas uses the term "public sphere" to mean sites for deliberation that are separate from political institutions. I use it differently, to mean places where policy makers engage with a wide range of stakeholders: governmental agents who are not at the table, secretariat officials,

---

[1] For a sophisticated study of the different types of power that impact international affairs, see Michael Barnett and Robert Duvall, "Power in Global Governance", in *Power in Global Governance* 1 (M. Barnett and R. Duvall eds., 2005).

[2] Thomas Risse, "Global Governance and Communicative Action," in *Global Governance and Public Accountability* 164, 172 (Held, D. and Koenig-Archibugi, M. eds., 2005).

parliamentarians, experts, transnational business, nongovernmental actors, and other voices of global civil society.[3] The UN Security Council is not an arena for inclusive exchange with all those affected by its decisions, but the description of it in Chapter 4 as a four-tier deliberative setting gives a sense of what this more modest conception of "public sphere" means.

The form and degree of engagement varies across organizations. The power of the executive head of IOs and secretariat staff is one area of variance. The constitutive acts of international organizations tend not to be precise about the degree of autonomy the secretariat has, leaving it open to interpretation. The Article 97–99 powers of the UN Secretary-General have been interpreted broadly, giving the office considerable margin for maneuver either independently or in carrying out mandated tasks. Chapter 4 described the role of the Secretary-General as norm entrepreneur with respect to R2P. Chapters 7 and 8 considered the "discursive power" of IO officials in operational activities. The impact of the OSCE High Commissioner for National Minorities on minority rights in Eastern and Central Europe, discussed in Chapter 8, is a good example.

As for nongovernmental actors, direct participation is not practical in most intergovernmental organizations (although there are exceptions, like the International Labour Organization). The question is whether the right balance between efficient decision making and deliberative inclusiveness has been struck in the functional areas where each IO operates. Channels for participation are not always formal and need not be. The UN Security Council will not give NGOs a seat at the table nor will the WTO. That does not mean that civil society is not heard in and around them. The negotiations on SC resolution 1540, aimed at preventing weapons of mass destruction from falling into the hands of non-state actors, were formally closed but "intentionally porous," giving experts and NGOs a chance to weigh in on what was a deeply contested act by the SC. This is precisely what the concept of a public sphere means—not an institutionalized public debate with rules of procedure and points of order, but a more free-wheeling exchange where voices other than those sitting at the table find a way of making themselves heard. Those at the table ultimately decide, but what they decide and how effective their decisions are is determined in part by the inclusiveness of the deliberations that led to them.

E. Interpretive Communities are Not Closed Technocracies

Interpretive communities set the parameters of debate, in effect judging what counts as a good argument. They frame the inter-subjective search for meaning and extract reputational costs from those who deviate too far from the conventions of the enterprise. Moreover, socialization to and internalization of norms occurs through this discursive

---

[3] I use the term in the way that Patricia Nanz and Jens Steffeck do. See P. Nanz and J. Steffeck, "Global Governance, Participation and the Public Sphere," in Held and Koenig-Archibugi, *id.*, at 197.

interaction.[4] Because interpretive communities occupy the halls of governmental, intergovernmental, and nongovernmental institutions, they cause norms to harden and become embedded in those institutions.

If interpretive communities are influential, then who they are matters. As noted in the introduction and Chapter 3, the concept is a way of describing how authoritative interpretations of the law are rendered, not a listing of card-carrying members of a club. But in some of the cases discussed in this book, actual individuals were identified, for example, those involved in the debates over Cyclone Nargis and the drone strikes in Pakistan. Who is recognized as a credible voice turns in part on expertise, based on immersion in the relevant area of law and practice. Indeed, the power of interpretive communities depends on that. An interpretive community extracts costs and confers benefits precisely because its collective judgment (to the extent that the judgment is cohesive) is regarded as a credible interpretation of the law.

A central question, to which there is no simple answer, is whether reliance on expertise legitimizes or delegitimizes decision making. Complex health and environmental issues benefit from expertise; we would not want those decisions to be made by popular vote.[5] Nor would we want judgments about the legality of state behavior to be made by popular vote. The problem is that self-selected experts have ways of defining what constitutes true mastery of a discipline and thereby shutting out dissenting voices. This study has found that this phenomenon, though real, should not be exaggerated. Technocracy—rule by experts—is probably impossible at the transnational level. There are too many channels of influence; the system of global governance is too pluralistic, too cacophonous to seal off decision making in this way. The story of trade and environment at the WTO illustrates the point. If the interpretive community associated with trade law was ever an insular, impermeable trade elite, that is no longer the case. Whether they are a third circle of the interpretive community or outsiders looking in, other stakeholders have penetrated the discursive interaction.

A final point about interpretive communities that emerges from the cases is that they encompass international tribunals. This may seem odd if interpretive communities are conceived as the functional equivalent of judicial bodies when the latter are not available to render authoritative judgment. Yet the *Kadi* case on the sanctioning of individuals associated with Al Qaeda and the Taliban demonstrates that the relationship between

---

[4] On socialization and internalization, see Ryan Goodman and Derek Jinks, "International Law and State Socialization: Conceptual, Empirical and Normative Challenges," 54 *Duke Law Journal* 983 (2005); Ryan Goodman and Derek Jinks, "Incomplete Internalization and Compliance with Human Rights Law," 19 *European Journal of International Law* 725 (2008). On internalization of norms through transnational legal process, see Harold Koh. "Why do Nations Obey International Law?" 106 *The Yale Law Journal* 2599 (1997); Harold Koh, "Bringing International Law Back Home," 35 *Houston Law Review* 623 (1998).

[5] Andrew Moravcsik, "Is there a 'Democratic Deficit' in World Politics? A Framework for Analysis," in Held and Koenig-Archibugi eds., *supra* note 2, at 220.

courts and IOs can be "dialogic." The ECJ did not strike down resolution 1267, but it did send a strong signal that the SC ought to reform its procedures (like the signal the ICJ sent in the *Lockerbie* case). The SC responded to the signal (and similar signals from other courts and quasi-judicial bodies), indirectly, by making some of the procedural reforms that the ECJ judgment implied were necessary. The ICJ and ECJ are not the guardians of international law against this powerful political body but rather influential voices in the interpretive community that surrounds the SC.

F. The Practices of International Organizations are a Source of Law

It is no surprise that norms affect the programmatic activities of IOs. Choices about how the IAEA should engage with the government of Iran, and peacekeepers with the government of Sudan are deeply influenced by non-proliferation and peacekeeping norms respectively. What is less apparent is how the practices of IOs—and the argumentation that surrounds those practices—impacts the norms. Operational activities of IOs are implicit interpretations of the law. In engaging in those activities, the IO may cause the law to harden or to soften. The discretion exercised by the SG and his subordinates in carrying out electoral assistance and peacekeeping tasks has reinforced democracy norms; debates over when, how, or even whether to protect civilians may be causing humanitarian principles to soften.

The law-hardening process depends on the acquiescence of states and so is analogous to customary law formation. But because the initiative often comes from the secretariats of IOs and because state consent is often several steps removed from the actual practice (for example, the sanctioning of electoral assistance by the assemblies of various international organizations), the theoretical implications are important. It is evidence of the proposition that IOs are independent actors, not just collections of member states.[6] It is also evidence that the practices of IOs can be a source of law. The entrepreneurship of the Representative of the Secretary-General on Human Rights for Internally Displaced Persons is leading to a hardening of some of the Guiding Principles on Internal Displacement. Moreover, to the extent that IO officials are interacting with nongovernmental experts and advocacy groups as well as state representatives—as is the case with the Guiding Principles—it indicates a more pluralistic and fluid form of lawmaking than treaties or customary law.

G. The Logic of Arguing is an Accountability Mechanism

Accountability is a problem for global governance. A fundamental principle of democratic societies is that decision makers ought to be accountable for decisions they make.

---

[6] Michael Barnett and Martha Finnemore, *Rules for the World: International Organizations in Global Politics* (2004).

That means being held to a set of standards and paying a price when those standards are not met.[7] In electoral democracies, politicians are held accountable to the citizenry through periodic elections and, on occasion, judicial processes. At the international level, it is less clear to whom decision makers are accountable and what the mechanisms for holding them accountable are.[8]

The logic of arguing sheds some light. "Reason-giving" is a form of accountability, as any student of administrative law knows. The requirement to explain one's decisions to those affected impels (though does not compel) decision makers to act on the basis of good reasons. Not surprisingly, one of the main criticisms of the 1267 sanctions regime was the lack of information provided to substantiate the case for listing an individual and the lack of reasons for not delisting. Demands for "independent review" are driven by a similar logic. It is doubtful that SC members will ever accept binding review of their decisions by another body. But even nonbinding independent review can enhance accountability, as the dialogic form of review by the ECJ in *Kadi* demonstrates. The new Ombudsperson established to help the work of the 1267 Committee does not have the authority to delist individuals, but the compilation of data and other functions the office performs could result in implicit recommendations to that effect. The member states will decide, but a respected independent agent providing the information and analysis on which to base their decision, makes it harder for the Committee to act arbitrarily. The situation is not unlike the role of the IAEA, UNSCOM, and UNMOVIC in Iraq. The SC retained the authority to decide whether sanctions should be lifted, or stronger action should be taken, but independent assessments of Iraq's WMD programs by these agencies were the foundation for Council deliberations. That those assessments proved to be relatively accurate suggests that, to avoid another Iraq debacle, they ought to be taken seriously.

Reputation is an important part of this. States, and by extension the organizations through which they operate, have an interest in preserving a reputation for playing by the rules.[9] It is one of the ways states hold each other to account in their direct dealings. It is

---

[7] See Ruth Grant and Robert Keohane, "Accountability and Abuses of Power in World Politics," 99 *American Political Science Review* 1 (2005); Robert Keohane and Joseph Nye, "Redefining Accountability for Global Governance," in *Governance in a Global Economy: Political Authority in Transition* (M. Kahler and D. Lake eds., 2003); David Held and Mathias Koenig-Archibugi, "Introduction," in Held and Koenig-Archibugi eds., *supra* note 2, at 1, 3.

[8] Grant and Keohane identify seven accountability mechanisms in world politics: hierarchical, supervisory, fiscal, legal, market, peer, and reputation. *Id.*, Table 2 at 36.

[9] On the impact of reputation, see Andrew Guzman, *How International Law Works* (2008); Joel Trachtman, *The Economic Structure of International Law* 91–98 (2008); Rachel Brewster, "Unpacking the State's Reputation," 50 *Harvard International Law Journal* 232 (2009). On whether international organizations have reputations, see Ian Johnstone, "Do International Organizations Have Reputations?" 7 *International Organizations Law Review* 235 (2010).

also what drives the felt need to engage in public justification. A point that is often underestimated in considering the impact of reputation on behavior is the "audience effect." Scrutiny of these justifications by an interpretive community (and broader audience of stakeholders) combined with the "civilizing force of hypocrisy" is a form of accountability. It is an indirect way of pressuring decision makers to practice what they preach. The pressure may bump up against other considerations, such as the felt need to act forcefully in a national security crisis regardless of how the justification is received. Those other considerations may be overriding, especially for powerful countries. Moreover, the price for failing in the exercise of public justification will usually be paid after the fact, but that is true of most accountability mechanisms, including elections. It is the *anticipation* of negative judgment and its associated costs that causes decision makers to think twice before embarking on a course of action that cannot be justified to attentive audiences. In ratcheting up the policy of drone strikes in Pakistan, the Obama Administration must have considered whether the strikes could be justified as a matter of law. It might well have gone ahead regardless, but the risk of being accused of targeted assassinations and extrajudicial killings was surely a factor in weighing the costs and benefits of the policy.

H. Bringing Down the Deliberative Deficit

The effectiveness of IOs depends in part on their perceived legitimacy. Legitimacy can be measured in various ways. "Input" legitimacy looks at the nature of the decision-making process; "output" legitimacy looks at the results of that process. Legality is an element of legitimacy, as is functional expertise. Increasingly, democracy is the principal measure of the legitimacy of national governments and supranational organizations.

Argumentation and disputation are not inherently democratic, deliberation is. Some disputes can be settled behind closed doors, with limited participation or public scrutiny. Indeed, this is often necessary. The SC would not be an effective crisis manager if all its meetings were in public, let alone open to participation by the entire UN membership and interested NGOs. But deliberation (as opposed to hard bargaining) has an irreducible democratic quality in that – at least indirectly – it must account for the interests of all stakeholders. This is not only a matter of legitimacy but also effectiveness. The quasi-legislative measures of the SC (resolutions 1373 and 1540) require the leadership of the great powers, the expertise of those who understand the flow of people and money, and the buy-in of multiple stakeholders, from the regimes in unstable countries that can serve as safe havens, to regional organizations, banks and port authorities.

Vote and voice are ways of accounting for the interests of all stakeholders, as are the mechanisms described above: reason-giving, public justification, and public scrutiny. Institutional devices like criteria for humanitarian intervention would serve the purpose. Framed as considerations to be taken into account in deciding whether intervention would be warranted in a given case, they would induce SC members to deliberate on the basis of agreed standards and give other actors a normative basis for weighing in on the debate.

Some democracy theorists claim there is no way of "democratizing" IOs—the lines of delegation are too long, and the attentiveness of ordinary citizens is too scattered.[10] Other observers ask whether there really is a democratic deficit in IOs and wonder whether critics are expecting more of them than we expect of national governments.[11] If democracy is understood as participatory or representative governance, both may be right. If it is understood in terms of deliberation, then reducing the democratic deficit is both necessary and possible. Because legal argumentation and political deliberation are intertwined in IOs, better deliberation in and around them is a way of "democratizing" the organizations and of enhancing the legitimacy of the international legal system.

---

[10] Robert Dahl, "Can International Organizations be Democratic? A Skeptic's View," in Ian Shapiro and Casiano Hacker-Gordon eds., *Democracy's Edges* 19–36 (1999).

[11] Moravcsik, *supra* note 5 at 212–39.

Index

Acculturation, 23–24, 46
Aden v. Council of European Union, 109n124
Adler, Emanuel, 41
African Union (AU), 78, 137, 145, 176
   Constitutive Act of, 58, 58n7, 76, 76n72, 145, 152, 179
   Convention for the Protection and Assistance of Internally Displaced Persons in Africa (the Kampala Convention), 175–76, 177
   Peace and Security Council, 76, 76n73
Ahmed Ali Yusuf and Al Barakaat International Foundation v. Council and Commission, 109n124
Ahtissari plan, 59
Al-Qaeda, 10, 90, 106, 108, 126, 148. *See also* Taliban/Al Qaeda (resolution 1267)
   Saddam Hussein and, 86
   United States's self-defense arguments against, 84–85, 90, 92
Albright, Madeleine, 88n32
Alston, Philip, 91, 91n42, 92, 92n51
Alvarez, José, 67, 94n61, 112
American Society of International Law, 172
American University Washington College of Law, 91
Andean Community, 145
Anderson, Kenneth, 91–93, 91n43

Annan, Kofi, 50, 66, 69, 76, 78, 149
Anti-Ballistic Missile Treaty, 41
Anticipatory self-defense, 87
Arbour, Louise, 72
Argumentation
   Habermasian sense, 16
   ideal speech situation, 15
   legal. *See* Legal argumentation
   logic of, 4, 209–11
   moral, 6
   in politics, 4
   in public settings, 16–17
   reasoned exchange, 13
Argumentative self-entrapment, 27, 205
Armed attack, 62, 63, 81–83, 85, 87
Arria formula gatherings, 61
ASEAN, 145
Asia-Pacific Economic Cooperation (APEC) forum, 84
Axworthy, Lloyd, 74

Baker, Andrew, 186
Barakaat Foundation, 109, 110
Basel Committee on Banking Supervision, 186
Bashir, Omar Al, 143
Beef Hormones case, 198, 200
Bellinger, John, 92

Biological Weapons Convention, 114
Blix, Hans, 125, 126n37
Bohman, James, 5, 5n3, 19, 26–27n66
Bolton, John, 71n55, 72
Bosnia v. Serbia, 72
Bounded objectivity, 36n6
Boutros-Ghali, Boutros, 49, 144
Brahimi Report, 141, 158
Bretton Woods institutions, 48
Brookings Institute, 174
Brunnée, Jutta, 22n42, 23, 46, 77n76
Buergenthal, Judge, 85
Bush, George W., 86, 118, 124, 130
  drone policy and, 10, 90–91
  1540 Committee and, 100, 102
  Iraq invasion, 46, 204
  nuclear non-proliferation policies, 126–29, 131, 134, 205–6
  preemption doctrine, 88n32, 111

Capstone Doctrine. See *United Nations Peacekeeping Operations, Principles and Guidelines*
Carnegie Endowment for International Peace, 126n36
Caroline incident, 89
Cassese, Antonio, 84, 86
Charter of Paris, 168
Chavez, Hugo, 145
Chayes, Abram, 22
Chayes, Antonia Handler, 22
Chemical Weapons Convention, 114
Clark, Ian, 30
Cleveland, Sarah, 92
Cohen, Joshua, 5n2, 20, 30, 31n88
Cohen, Roberta, 173
Coherence, 163n9
Cold War era, 59, 62, 63, 93, 112, 137–39, 165, 168, 168n26
Commonwealth, 145
Communications network, 78
Communicative behavior, 4, 47. See also Deliberations
  Habermas's theory of, 14–17
Communicative function of law, 7, 23, 24
Community(ies)
  epistemic, 41, 193
  international, 71n55, 72, 73, 75
  interpretive. See Interpretive community
  of practice, 41, 53n75, 57n5

Compliance, 96, 100, 205
  inducing, power of interpretive communities, 45–48, 152
  with international law, 23, 28, 28n76, 134, 163, 169, 180–81
  of Iraq with resolution 687, 124–25
  with law, 46
  management model of, 22, 135
  monitoring, 114, 117, 131
  reciprocal, 34, 45
  as reputational concerns, 68
  socialization theory of, 46
Conference on Security and Cooperation in Europe (CSCE), 165, 168, 170
Consent-based international legal system, 31
Constitutional Loya Jirga of 502, 147
Constitutive Act of the African Union, 58, 58n7, 76, 76n72, 145, 152, 179. See also African Union
Convention for the Protection and Assistance of Internally Displaced Persons in Africa (the Kampala Convention), 175–76, 177
Convention on International Trade in Endangered Species of Wild Fauna and Flora (CITES), 197
Cophenhagen Document of 1990, 168
Council of Europe, 108, 175, 176
  1995 Framework Convention for the Protection of National Minorities, 169
Counter-terrorism, 10, 81
  controversial doctrine of preemption, 87–90
  drone policy in Pakistan, 90–93
  interventions in Afghanistan and Iraq, 81
  resolutions 1373 and 1540, 93–105
  self-defense argument, 82–86. See also Self-defense arguments
Counter-terrorism Committee (CTC), 95–100
  resolution 1373, 96–99
  resolution 1540, 104
Counter-Terrorism Executive Directorate (CTED), 96–97, 96n73, 99
Cyclone Nargis, 74, 77, 163, 205, 208

Darfur Peace Agreement, 155
Decentralized legal system, 7, 31
Declaration on Peace, Democracy and Development, 2005, 175

Declaration on the Rights of Persons Belonging to National or Ethnic, Religious and Linguistic Minorities, 169
Deliberations
 ideal, 17
 impact of peacekeeping operations on principles of, 149–51
 impartial, 5
 for international institutions, 5
 at national level, 5
 over weapons inspections and military action against Iraq, 128
 and resolution 1373, 97–99
 and resolution 1540, 103–5
 at transnational level, 5, 19
 value of, 25
 and voting, 15
 in world politics, 14–20
Deliberative democracy, 4, 9, 211–12
Deliberative democrats, 5–6, 15, 17–19
Deliberative exchange, 4–5
Deliberative legitimacy, 64–65
Democratic People's Republic of Korea (DPRK), 120–22, 131–32, 134, 205
Deng, Francis, 171–73, 177
Distributive justice, 23, 24, 28. *See also* Justice
Doyle, Michael, 143, 168*n*18
Draft Articles on State Responsibility, 82
Dryzek, John, 19, 27*n*66
Due process, 106, 107, 111
Dunant, Henri, 48
Dworkin, Ronald, 35, 37
 justice, concept of, 38
 theory of law, 37–38, 37*n*10

ECOSOC, 176
ECOWAS, 63, 145, 175, 176
Edelstein, David, 143
Ekeus, Rolf, 167
El-Baradei, Mohammed, 117–19, 125
Elster, Jon
 civilizing force of hypocrisy, 16–17, 17*n*19, 23, 151*n*53
Emergency Loya Jirga of 1051, 147
Epistemic community, 41, 193. *See also* Community(ies)
Ethnic minority rights, 11, 167–70. *See also* Right(s)
European Commission, 43

European Convention on Human Rights, 108, 169
European Court of First Instance (CFI), 109, 110
European Court of Human Rights, 169
European Court of Justice (ECJ), 19*n*30, 109, 110, 112–13, 200, 209, 210
European Economic Community, 48
European Union (EU), 5, 18, 19*n*30, 31, 98, 145, 175, 193
 Copenhagen criteria for accession to, 58
European Union Council, 43
Evans, Gareth, 74

Fairness in international law, 24–25, 28, 39*n*22, 40*n*28, 59*n*15
Fassbender, Bardo, 26, 107
Financial Stability Forum, 186
Finnemore, Martha, 48
First Protocol to the European Convention on Human Rights, 165, 165*n*15
Fish, Stanley
 critiques, 39*nn*23,24
 on interpretive communities, 35–36, 36*n*6
 theory of interpretation, 37–39
Fiss, Owen, 36*n*6
Fox, Gregory, 164–66, 164*n*34
Fox, Vincente, 176
Franck, Thomas, 22*n*45, 23, 26, 46
 legitimacy, concept of, 28, 28*n*76, 163*n*9
 fairness theory, 24–25, 28, 39*n*22, 40*n*28, 59*n*15
Friends World Committee for Consultation, 171*n*41
Friendship, 40

G-20, 186
GATT, 11, 185–86, 193–96
 Article I, 196
 Article XI, 195, 196
 Article XIII, 196
 Article XX, 188–89, 195, 196, 198, 200
 elite cohesion strategy, 186
 trade-environment link and, 192
Geneva Conventions, 57, 152, 157, 174
Genocide Convention of 1948, 57, 152
 Article I, 72
Glennon, Michael, 76*n*71, 86*n*23, 88*n*28
Global Centre for the Responsibility to Protect, 73
Global Initiative to Combat Nuclear Terrorism, 114–15
Global public policy, 20

Global public reason, 5n2, 20
Goldsmith, Lord, 88
Good governance, 164, 166
Goodman, Ryan
    theory of acculturation, 23, 46
Gramscian international relations theory, 51
Greenstock, Jeremy, 95, 129
Group of 77, 65n27
Guiding Principles (GP) for Internal
    Displacement, 50, 171–73, 176, 179
Gulf Cooperation Council, 83–84
Gulf War, 1993, 49
    resolutions 1373 and 1540, 93–94
Gutmann, Amy, 16

Habermas, Jurgen, 4, 9, 26, 39, 39n26, 59
    argumentation, 16
    communicative behavior, 14–17
    ideal deliberative setting, 64
    ideal of communicative action, 14, 17
    ideal speech situation, 15, 15n9
    public reason, 15
    theory of communicative action, 14
Hague Peace Conference, 70
Harris, Shane, 92–93
Hegemony, 51–52, 94
Helsinki Final Act of 1975, 58, 165, 168
Hercules, 38
High Commissioner for National Minorities
    (HCNM), 167, 168n22, 169–70, 178–79
High Level Panel (HLP) on Threats, Challenges
    and Change, 88, 107
Holmes, John, 74
Hoon, Geoffrey, 88
Howse, Robert, 185, 186, 187n14, 201
    insider network thesis, 198n64
Human Rights Commission, 90
Human Rights Committee (HRC), 165, 169, 180
Human Rights for Internally Displaced Persons
    (RSG), 171, 209
Human security, 78, 80, 112
Humanitarian interventions, 9–11, 27, 41. *See also*
    International organizations (IOs); Kosovo
    humanitarian intervention
    defense of necessity and, 89
    and interpretive community, 67–69
    Kosovo and the challenges of. *See* Kosovo
        humanitarian intervention
    responsibility to protect and, 70–72, 74

Hurd, Ian, 28–29
Hussein, Saddam, 86, 124, 129

ICESCR, 174
Ideal speech situation, 14, 15, 15n9, 206
Ikenberry, John, 58n6
IMF, 52, 183, 185, 186, 200
Imminent threat, 87, 88, 154, 155
Impartial deliberation, 5. *See also* Deliberations
Impartiality, 16, 17, 151, 190, 204, 206
Independent International Commission on
    Kosovo, 28n72, 71, 77
Inter-Agency Standing Committee, 153, 172
Inter-American Democratic Charter (2001),
    58, 145
Interdiction of cargo, resolutions on,
    131–34
Internally displaced persons, rights of, 163,
    171–77. *See also* Right(s)
International Atomic Energy Agency (IAEA),
    100n90, 101, 102n23, 116–17, 119–20,
    122–25, 126n36, 134, 209, 210
International Civil Aviation
    Organization, 43
International Commission on Intervention and
    State Sovereignty (ICISS), 58, 58n8,
    71, 77
International Committee of the Red Cross, 152.
    See also Red Cross
International Court of Justice (ICJ), 26, 49, 57,
    63, 139, 161, 179
    Advisory Opinion on *The legal consequences
        of the construction of a wall in the Occupied
        Palestinian Territory*, 85
    Bosnia v. Serbia, 72, 85
    DRC-Uganda case, 85
    Lockerbie case, 85, 200, 209
    Nicaragua case, 82, 82n3
International Covenant on Civil and Political
    Rights (ICCPR), 145n25, 164, 167n20, 168,
    169, 178
    Article 23, 165
    Article 25, 164–65
International Covenant on Economic Social and
    Cultural Rights, 168
International Criminal Court, 58, 148, 152
International Criminal Tribunal for former
    Yugoslavia, 57–58, 82
International environmental protection, 197

International Force in East Timor
  (INTERFET), 140
International Human Rights Group, 172
International Labor Organization (ILO), 43, 49
International law, 6–7
  fairness of, 24–25, 28, 39n22, 40n28, 59n15
  legal opinion on, 8
  stickiness of, 6, 6n6
International Law Commission (ILC), 82,
  83, 89
International organizations (IOs), 3–5, 8, 26,
  206–7
  interpretive communities and, 41–50
  law and politics in, 9–12
  legitimacy of, 8, 16, 27–31
  operating framework, 26–27
  operational activities. *See* Operational
    activities, of IOs
  role in cultivating fidelity to law, 45
  role in legal disputes, 44
International Security Assistance Force
  (ISAF), 84
International socialization, 49
International soft law campaign, 91, 92. *See also*
  Soft law
International Uranium Enrichment Centre
  (IUEC), 119
Interpretive communities, 6–7, 86, 112, 125,
  201–2, 207–9
  on Anti-Ballistic Missile Treaty, 41–42
  competency or expertise of, 42
  concept of, 33–41
  constraints on, 35–36, 36n6
  deliberative democracy and, 4–9
  discourse within, 10
  existence of, 7–8
  and extent of influence, 44
  functioning of, 45–50, 67–69
  goal of interpretation, 37
  hegemony, notion of, 51–52
  humanitarian intervention and, 67–69
  implicit interpretations, 50
  inducing compliance, 45–48
  and international organizations, 41–50
  inter-subjective interpretation, 40
  as invisible college of international
    lawyers, 42
  lawmaking and, 48–50
  legal adviser, 42

legal argumentation and, 4–9
legal interpretation, 40–41
legitimacy of, 50–54
NPT bargain, 118–19
parameters of, 8
power of, 8, 10, 11, 35, 184
professional interpreters, 36, 42
rationale for state participation, 33–34
representatives of, 44
responsibility to protect and, 75–79
stages of interpretive practice, 37–38
technocratic, 185–86, 207–9
Interstitial lawmaking, 48, 49

Jinks, Derek
  theory of acculturation, 23, 46
Justice, 38, 189, 199
  distributive, 23, 24, 28
  transitional, 148–49
Justificatory discourse, 7, 8, 22, 77, 82, 92,
  130, 204

Kadi case, 109–10
Kalin, Walter, 172, 173, 173n49
Kampala Convention. *See* Convention for the
  Protection and Assistance of Internally
  Displaced Persons in Africa
Kennedy, David, 24, 51–52, 187
Ki-Moon, SG Ban, 74, 78
Koh, Harold, 6n6, 47, 49, 90, 92
Koskenniemi, Martti, 24, 51, 52, 187
Kosovo humanitarian intervention, 9–10, 27, 59.
  See also Humanitarian intervention
  argument under Article 2(4), 62
  Belgrade's self-defense argument, 62
  Council deliberations in, 55–62
  counterarguments, 63
  interpretive community, functioning of,
    67–69
  legal justifications, 62–63
  NATO's intervention, 41, 55, 62–63
  as normative movement, 69–73
  responsibility to protect, 69–73
  Security Council deliberations and actions,
    64–67
  Serbs's argument under Chapter VII, 62
Kouchner, Bernard, 74
Kratochwil, Friederich, 38–39, 49
  legal reasoning, 47, 47n51

Index

Laden, Osama Bin, 105, 106
Law
  compliance with, 45–48
  fairness of, 24–25, 28, 39n22, 40n28, 59n15
  global administrative, 31–32
  hard, 44, 75
  internal morality of, 22n42
  in international organizations, 9–11
  language of, 25, 51
  soft, 26, 57, 161–66, 178–81
  theory of, 37–38
Law of the Sea Convention, 132
Law's empire, 37n12
League of Arab States (LAS), 84
Legal adviser, 42, 67
Legal argumentation, 3, 6. *See also* Argumentation
  accountability issues, 209–11
  compliance, notion of, 22–24
  difference with political deliberation, 21–22
  Habermas's ideal of, 53–54
  impact on behavior, 47–48
  international, 21–22, 24–25, 206
  as an interpretive enterprise, 37n15
  on Kosovo crisis, 67
  limits of, 25
  nature of, 20–27
  normative judgments, 39
  positivist legal theory, 21
  powerful form of, 205–6
  sites for, 26
  standard forms of, 26–27
  strategic reasons, 204
  subjective theory of, 35
Legal internalization, 47
Legitimacy, of international organizations (IOs), 8, 16, 27–31, 28n76, 211
  accountability, 30–31
  determinants, 30
  normative and sociological meanings of, 29n77
  purpose of, 30
  and shared beliefs, 29
Legitimacy, of interpretive communities, 50–54
Legitimacy, of WTO, 185–87
Logic of appropriateness, 4, 204
Logic of consequentialism, 4, 204
Luck, Edward, 74
Ludwig Boltzman Institute, 171

Maastricht Treaty, 18
Melzer, Nils, 91
Mercosur, 145
Michel, Nicolas, 107
Military Staff Committee, 138
Moral entrepreneurs, 48
Moscow Document of 1991, 168
Murphy, Sean, 91

Nation, the, 18
National Security Strategy, U.S. (NSS)
  of 2002, 87, 88n32, 111
  of 2010, 89
NATO's intervention, in Kosovo, 41, 48, 55
  GA support, 64
  Islamic world reaction, 65–66
  legality of, 62, 65–66, 68–69
  non-NATO states, position of, 65
  Russian interpretation, 63
Nitze, Paul, 42
Non-aligned Movement (NAM), 65, 68, 102–4
Non-nuclear weapon states (NNWS), 115, 116
Nongovernmental organizations (NGOs), 9, 10, 43, 49, 61, 73, 112, 168, 171
Norm entrepreneurship, 48
  and responsibility to protect, 69–73
Normative principles, 8, 11, 189
  compliance concerns, 29, 29n77
  functions of IOs, 160, 163, 171, 176–77
  Kosovo episode, 56
  hegemony and, 52
  in legal discourse, 39, 47–50
  and norm entrepreneurship, 78
  of peacekeeping operations, 144, 150, 152–58
  Security Council decisions and operational activities, 57–58, 67
  for UN Charter, 26
  value of deliberation, 25
Nuclear non-proliferation, 10
  Additional Protocol (AP), 116, 116n3
  Article I of, 116–18
  Article III of, 116
  Article IV of, 118–20
  Article X of, 120–22
  IAEA, 116–17, 119, 123–24
  interdiction of cargo, resolutions on, 131–34
  interpretive disputes, 115–22

moratorium on creation of facilities for uranium enrichment and plutonium separation, 118
North Korea's status, 118, 120–22, 131
safeguards agreement, 117–18, 117n6, 123
Security Council action on North Korea, 131
Security Council regulations, 125–30
voluntary multilateral mechanisms, 120
weapons inspections and military action against Iraq, 123–25
withdrawal clause, 120–22
Nuclear Non-Proliferation Treaty (NPT), 7, 10, 115–22, 205
Nuclear weapons states (NWS), 115, 116, 119, 135
Nunn, Sam, 42

Obama, Barack, 10, 89–90, 102
  approach to non-proliferation, 115
  drone policy and, 91–93
  intervention in Afghanistan, 111
Obasanjao, Olusegun, 50
O'Connell, Mary Ellen, 91
Operation Desert Fox, 124
Operation Enduring Freedom, 84
Operational activities, of IOs
  ethnic minority rights, 167–70
  legalization criteria, 178–81
  right to political participation, 164–67
  rights of internally displaced persons, 163, 171–77
  soft law and legal argumentation, 161–64
  as a source of law, 209
Organization for Security and Cooperation in Europe (OSCE), 18, 50, 145, 152, 161, 170
  on ethnic minority rights, 165–68, 178–79
  Maastricht Declaration of December 2003, 175
Organization of African Unity (OAU), 58, 145, 176
  Commission on Refugees, 175
  Council of Ministers, 175
  Report of the Panel of Eminent Persons on Rwanda, 69, 69n41
Organization of the Islamic Conference (OIC), 84

Packer, John, 168n22, 170
Partial Test Ban Treaty (PTBT), 120
Participatory governance, 136, 145, 166
Participatory rights, 165, 167. See also Right(s)
Party pluralism, 165–66, 178, 180
Paust, Jordan, 91

Peacekeeping operations, 10–11
  in Afghanistan, 147–48
  bargain, 143–44, 149
  Cold War era, 137
  consent-based multidimensional, 151
  consent vs coercion, 140–42
  and dealing with weak transitional governments, 143
  and democratic norms, 144–51
  governance arrangements, 146–47
  history of, 137–38
  impact on deliberative norms, 149–51
  open-ended consent in, 140
  peace agreements, 140–41
  protection of civilians, 151–58
  robust missions, 137
  security transition and political transition, 147–48
  as social compact, 158
  societal restoration, 149
  Special Committee on Peacekeeping (C-34), 156–57
  "tactical" and "strategic" consent, distinction between, 141
  in Timor, 148
  UN Charter framework, 138–40
  withdrawal of consent, 144
Political internalization, 47
Political participation, right to, 164–67. See also Right(s)
Posner, Michael, 92
Powell, Colin, 86, 88n32, 95
Precedent, 63–68, 122, 158, 205
Preemption, 50, 87–90, 129, 205
Procedural rationality, 31
Professional community of interpreters, 39
Proliferation Security Initiative (PSI), 114, 115, 131–32
"Promotion of the Right to Democracy," 145
Protection of civilians (POC), 11, 74, 76, 79, 151–58, 175, 178, 180
  legal obligations, 157–58
  non-UN missions, 154–55, 154n62
  normative impact of, 156–58
  normative roots of, 152–54
  resolution 1894, 156–57
  responsibility to protect and, 153–54
  UNMIL, 155
  UNMIS, 155

Protocol to the Convention on the Suppression of Unlawful Acts against the Safety of Maritime Navigation 2005, 132
Public reason, 15, 18
   global, 5n2, 20
Public spheres, 5, 5nn2,3, 12, 18, 206–7

Quasi-legislative action, 10

Rational choice, 4, 13
Rational discourse, 16, 36, 68
Rawls, John, 15, 59
Reciprocal reasons, 16
Red Cross, 48. *See also* International Committee of the Red Cross
Refugee Policy Group, 171n41
Relational contracts, 143, 149–50
Reputation, for fidelity to law, 45–46
Resolution 1267
   targeted sanctions regime, 10, 105–8, 189
Resolution 1373, 10
   CTC analysis, 96–97
   debate on reform of CTC, 98–99
   and deliberative legitimacy, 97–99
   early stages of implementation of, 95–96
   guidelines, 98
   negotiation and implementation of, 95–97
   post-9/11 climate, 95
   Russian Federation views, 99
Resolution 1540, 10, 102n99, 114
   1540 Committee, 100
   and deliberative legitimacy, 103–5
   negotiation and implementation of, 99–103
Responsibility to protect (R2P), 10, 153, 204
   and crackdown on Burmese monks in Myanmar, 73–74
   critic of, 74–75
   debate on, 76–77
   disappointment of advocates, 77
   and interpretive community, 75–79
   misapplication of, 77–78
   NATO intervention in Kosovo, 69–73
   nonconsent-based intervention, 79
   norm entrepreneurs and participants in deliberative process, 78
   norm entrepreneurship and, 69–73
   post World Summit, 2005, 73–75
   power and limitations of nonstate actors, 78–79
   in resolution 1706, 76
   rhetorical support, 75–76
   scope of, 76
   in U.S.-led invasion of Iraq, 2003, 74, 74n66
Rieff, David, 27
Right(s)
   ethnic minority, 11, 167–70
   of internally displaced persons, 163, 171–77
   to life, 174
   participatory, 165, 167
   to political participation, 164–67
Risse, Thomas, 4, 17, 27, 205

Sabel, Charles, 30, 31n88
Sambanis, Nicholas, 143, 168n18
Samore, Gary, 121
Sanctions Monitoring Team, 107
Santiago Commitment to Democracy and the Renewal of the Inter-American system (1991), 58
Schachter, Oscar, 24, 42, 83, 163
Security Council of the United Nations. *See* UN Security Council
Security sector reform (SSR), 139, 147, 148
Self-defense arguments, 59, 62, 63, 81, 86n23
   against Al-Qaeda and Taliban, 84–85, 92
   anticipatory, 87
   controversial doctrine of preemption, 87–90
   counter-terrorism, 82–86
   DRC-Uganda case, 85, 85n22
   drone policy in Pakistan, 90–93
   ICJ Advisory Opinion, 85
   justificatory process of strikes, 91
   Kosovo humanitarian intervention, 62
   for military action, 89
   Security Council resolutions 1368 and 1373, 85
   in targeting decisions, 92
   weapons inspections and military action against Iraq, 125–26
SG's High Level Panel on Threats, Challenges and Change (HLP), 58
Shrimp-Turtle case, 11, 184, 195–200
   deliberative legitimacy argument, 198–200
   GATT obligations, 196
Sikkink, Katherine, 48
Slaughter, Ann Marie, 92
Smith, Gerard, 42
Social behavior, 29
Social constructivism, 4

Social constructivist international relations
    theory, 46
Social internalization, 47
Sofaer, Abraham, 42
Soft law, 26, 57, 173. *See also* International soft
    law campaign; Law
  areas of peace agreement, 165–66
  forms of UN practice, 165
  hardening of, 178–81
  and legal argumentation, 161–64
  on party pluralism, 165
  redundancy of, 162
Solana, Javier, 70
Srebrenica report of 1999, 69
Stiglitz, Joseph, 53*n*74
Strategic Defense Initiative, 41
Sunstein, Cass, 36*n*5, 38, 38–39*n*21

Taliban/Al Qaeda (resolution 1267), 105–11
  1267 committee, 105–6
  due process, and deliberative legitimacy, 108–11
  "focal point" functions, 108
  notifications, 108
  Ombudsperson's Office, creation of, 108
  procedural changes, 106–7
Targeted sanctions regime, resolution 1267, 10,
    105–8, 189
Technocratic elites, 184
Terrorism, as threat to the peace, 63, 95, 139.
    See also Counter-terrorism
Thakur, Ramesh, 74, 78
Thomas Watson Institute, Brown University, 107
Thompson, Dennis, 16
Toope, Stephen, 22*n*42, 23, 28*n*76, 46
Trachtman, Joel, 193, 195*n*47, 196, 200
Trade law, 188, 208
  interpretive community in, 184
Transgovernmental networks, 5–6
Transitional justice, 148–49. *See also* Justice
Transnational advocacy networks, 43–44
Transnational civil society, 19, 30, 42
Transnational deliberation, 5, 19. *See also*
    Deliberations
Transnational legal process, 49
Tuna–Dolphin case, 195, 198

UN Charter, 26
  Article 1(3), 173
  Article 2(4), 62–63, 83

Article 2(7), 139
Article 17, 131
Article 21, 131
Article 23, 131
Article 24(2), 123
Article 25, 123
Article 26, 123
Article 29, 123
Article 43, 138
Article 51, 62, 82, 87
Article 103, 109–10
Chapter VI, 75, 137–40
Chapter VII, 62–63, 71–72, 75, 99, 101, 103,
    120, 123, 138–40
Chapter VIII, 138
normative principles, 26
UN General Assembly, 26, 43, 76, 100, 124, 126,
    145, 165, 169, 173*n*53, 175
UN High Commissioner for Human Rights,
    72–73, 152, 171, 174
UN High Commissioner for Refugees, 174
UN missions, 73
  in the Central African Republic and Chad
    (MINURCAT), 140
  civilian mission (UNAMA), 84
  in Darfur (UNAMID), 76, 143, 149
  in the DRC (MONUC), 139
  in Haiti (MINUSTAH), 139
  High Level, 73
  in Lebanon (UNIFIL), 140
  in Liberia (UNMIL), 139
  in Sudan (UNMIS), 139
UN Security Council (SC), 9–10
  Article 2(4), 72
  Article 24, 60
  Article 25, 145*n*25
  Côte d'Ivoire (resolution 1572), 105
  degree of interaction among
    members, 59
  as a deliberative setting, 64–67
  Democratic Republic of the Congo
    (resolution 1533), 105
  draft resolutions, 61
  first tier deliberative setting of, 60
  fourth tier deliberative setting of, 61
  Haiti (resolution 917), 105
  Iran (resolution 1737), 105
  Iraq (resolution 1518), 105
  jus cogens norms, 109

Index

UN Security Council (SC) (*continued*)
Lebanon/Syria (resolution 1636), 105
Liberia (resolution 1521), 105
members of, 57
North Korea (resolution 1718), 105
outcomes of deliberations, 57
pattern of practice, 58–59
Permanent Members of, 59, 72
as quasi-judicial body, 105–11
regional developments, 58
regulations on nuclear non-proliferation, 125–30
resolution 678, 49–50, 123, 125
resolution 687, 49–50
resolution 1244, 63, 68
resolution 1333, 105
resolution 1368, 83, 85
resolution 1373, 10, 83, 85, 95–99
resolution 1441, 124–25, 127, 133
resolution 1511, 130
resolution 1526, 106
resolution 1540, 10, 99–105
resolution 1617, 106
resolution 1735, 107
resolution 1822, 108
resolution 1874, 132–34
resolutions relating to terrorism, 59
role in NATO bombing campaign, 70
second tier deliberative setting of, 60
Sierra Leone (resolution 1132), 105
Sudan (resolution 1591), 105
Taliban/Al Qaeda (resolution 1267), 105–11
third tier deliberative setting of, 60–61
views about rules of international life, 59
UN Special Commission (UNSCOM), 123–24
UN Special Rapporteur, 90, 91
UNAMSIL, 153, 154
UNDP programs, 152, 164, 166
United Nations Emergency Force (UNEF I), 137
United Nations Environment Programme (UNEP), 43

United Nations Monitoring, Verification and Inspection Commission (UNMOVIC), 124–25
United Nations Peacekeeping Operations, Principles and Guidelines, 141–42, 152, 156
Uniting for Peace resolution, 64
Universal Declaration of Human Rights, 57, 152
U.S.-led invasion of Iraq, 2003, 46, 74, 90, 204
enforcement of SC resolutions, 86
India position, 129–30
U.S. National Security Strategy, 2002, 87, 88*n*32

van de Stoel, Max, 167
Vienna Concluding Document of 1989, 168
Vienna Conference on Human Rights of 1993, 57
Vollebaek, Knut, 167–68
Voting, 4, 15

Weapons Inspection Regime, 123–25
Weapons of mass destruction (WMD), 88, 94
and resolution 1540, 101
Weiler, Joseph, 18, 189, 190
Wittes, Benjamin, 93
World Bank, 49, 52–53, 164, 166, 183, 185
World Council of Churches, 171*n*41
World Summit Draft Outcome document, 71–72
World Trade Organization (WTO), 43
Appellate Body (AB), 22, 184, 196–97
critique of GATT, 185–86
democratic deficit critique of, 185–87
and developing countries, 187, 187*n*14
in dispute resolution, 188–91
Dispute Settlement Body, 184, 195–96
legitimacy, 185–87
monitoring and surveillance functions, 191–94
Shrimp-Turtle case, 195–200

Yemeni government, 90

Zurn, Michael, 18